THE MEDIA
AND CONFLICTS
IN CENTRAL AFRICA

Marie-Soleil Frère

with a contribution by
Jean-Paul Marthoz

LYNNE
RIENNER
PUBLISHERS

BOULDER
LONDON

Published in the United States of America in 2007 by
Lynne Rienner Publishers, Inc.
1800 30th Street, Boulder, Colorado 80301
www.rienner.com

and in the United Kingdom by
Lynne Rienner Publishers, Inc.
3 Henrietta Street, Covent Garden, London WC2E 8LU

Library of Congress Cataloging-in-Publication Data
Frère, Marie-Soleil.
The media and conflicts in Central Africa / by Marie-Soleil Frère ;
    with a contribution from Jean-Paul Marthoz.
        p. cm.
    "A project of the Institut Panos Paris."
    Includes bibliographical references and index.
    ISBN 978-1-58826-489-3 (hbk. : alk. paper)
    ISBN 978-1-58826-465-7 (pbk. : alk. paper)
    1. War—Press coverage—Africa, Sub-Saharan. 2. Journalism—Africa, Sub-Saharan.
I. Marthoz, Jean Paul, 1950–   II. Institut Panos. III. Title.
PN5450.5.S63F74   2007
070.4'499670329—dc22

2006102907

British Cataloguing in Publication Data
A Cataloguing in Publication record for this book
is available from the British Library.

Printed and bound in the United States of America

The paper used in this publication meets the requirements
of the American National Standard for Permanence of
Paper for Printed Library Materials Z39.48-1992.

5 4 3 2 1

Contents

Acknowledgments

I WISH TO THANK the Institut Panos Paris for supporting the research for this book, as well as the UK Department for International Development, Irish Aid, and Cordaid for their support of Panos Paris projects in Central Africa in general and this book in particular. I am also grateful to the Belgian National Fund for Scientific Research and the Université Libre de Bruxelles for allowing me to devote time to this collaboration with the Institut Panos Paris. Thanks are also due to Ross Howard (Media and Democracy Group, Canada) and Pamphile Sebahara (Groupe de Recherche et d'Information sur la Paix, Belgium) for their contributions to the French version of the book and for the important details they provided about peace journalism and conflict issues for each country case study in the present volume.

Eva Palmans and Felix Nkundabangenzi helped to collect documentation in the early stages of the project. Victoria Ebin deserves thanks for her very useful proofread of the English translation of the French version. I also thank the reviewers of each country case study (their names appear at the beginning of the chapters they read), who made valuable comments and criticism from an "insider" point of view.

Many people contributed to the book, but they are not, of course, responsible for any mistakes or inaccuracies that may have slipped by. I take full responsibility for the content of the book with all its imperfections.

Central Africa

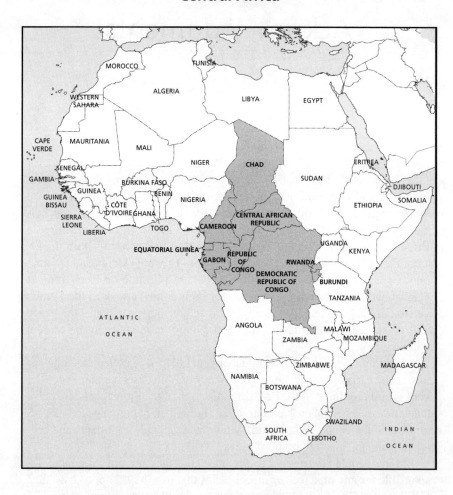

1

Introduction

NFORMATION—THROUGH ITS dissemination, withholding, and manipulation—has always been a powerful weapon in times of conflict. The appearance of the mass media has multiplied this potential by making possible vast propaganda and indoctrination operations.[1] But the media can also be used to strengthen democratic processes by awakening the consciences of citizens, developing a population's ability to exert pressure on its leaders, facilitating control over public affairs, and allowing for the international circulation of information.

The media constitute a two-edged sword. They can be the instruments of both destructive and constructive strategies, especially in societies undergoing change, destabilized by conflicts, or in the throes of political liberalization. History provides us with a multitude of examples that show the ability of journalists, from behind the shelter of their microphones or pens, to incite hatred, provoke violent mass movements, voluntarily manipulate information in the service of war-mongering strategies, promote antidemocratic reflexes, and, more or less consciously or perversely, create the roots of deep divisions within society.[2] Media professionals have also often contributed to taking the first step toward democracy, restoring peace in troubled regions, establishing respect and political dialogue between powers, and transforming the warriors of yesterday into negotiators in the process of conciliation. It is undeniable that the media have the capacity to both increase and decrease tensions within countries in crisis.

Central Africa is an area where these media dynamics can best be observed. On the one hand, this part of the world had until 2004 the greatest number of major conflicts (with "conflict" being defined as a situation that causes the deaths of more than 1,000 people a year).[3] On the other hand, the media are experiencing an unparalleled growth in this region, with thousands of newspapers and hundreds of radio stations having emerged since 1990 in countries where the media had always been a state monopoly. For these reasons, Central Africa is a rich field of study for those interested in the media's role in conflict and crisis situations. It is also one of the principal focus points, practically a laboratory, for regional and international nongovernmental organizations (NGOs),[4] public institutions, and civil society leaders looking for durable solutions to allow local populations to live in peace and to take up the challenge of development, solutions to which the media can contribute significantly.

The objective of this book is to look at practical cases taken from recent experience in nine Central African countries: Burundi, the Democratic Republic of Congo, Rwanda, the Republic of Congo, the Central African Republic, Chad, Cameroon, Gabon, and Equatorial Guinea. This research has two aims: to improve our understanding of the dynamics of the media in those states, and to identify strategies that can contribute to strengthening or weakening them, since the aim of documentation and reflection is to prepare us for action.

The vast geographical area referred to as Central Africa in this book is not a historical unit, a political-institutional entity, or a concept used by researchers who work there. Though the nine countries grouped together here share the same landmass, they are not part of a specific association. Their past histories, populations, and political situations, as well as their current economic situations, are very different. But they are all of particular interest for anyone who wants to examine the various facets of contemporary conflicts and the actual or potential role of the media in latent or violent crises.

These nine countries have been through dramatic changes since 1990, changes linked to the liberalization of both the media landscape and the political field. New political parties, new institutions, and new electoral processes have been established alongside private news media. Though these changes have led to freedom of expression and the merging of civil society organizations, the new political framework has not been consolidated. Major conflicts have erupted in some of these countries, leading them into extreme violence: the genocide of the Tutsi people in Rwanda; two wars that resulted, directly and indirectly, in the death of more than 3.5 million Congolese people in the Democratic Republic of Congo (DRC); huge civil massacres in Burundi; and civil wars in the Republic of Congo, the Central African Republic, and Chad. What role did the newly freed media play in those conflicts? How did they behave within those difficult contexts, and relate to those violent wars tearing the countries apart? What are the elements in the media environment that can help us understand the way journalists reported on the conflicts? Is it possible to analyze why the media remained neutral or chose one side? These are the issues this book seeks to address.

Since 1989 the Institut Panos Paris (IPP) has been conducting vast regional programs that aim to support media pluralism. The IPP's aim is to strengthen the abilities and skills of the main actors in the media as a way to support and consolidate emerging democracies. After ten years of experience in West Africa, the Institut Panos Paris turned its attention to the problematic area of Central Africa, where the political openings in the early 1990s resulted in what can be called "illiberal democracies."[5] Because the IPP is aware of the fundamental role played by the media in these processes, one of its Central African programs was called Media for Peace and was specifically devoted to helping local media face crises in a professional manner. The IPP's experience in the field revealed a lack of sufficient information and analysis, especially in French,[6] on the role of the media in conflict in Central Africa.

Chapters 2–10 describe the position of the local media in the troubled history of nine Central African states. Though there are important differences among these countries, they also share common features. The first is the nature of the recent crises in the region, which have generally been marked by competition to acquire power over resources, and by an accumulation of wealth that leads to control over the machinery of the state. Hence the recurrent appearance of predatory and kleptocratic governments and, in turn, rebel movements who challenge them for access to resources.[7] Both parties often use community, ethnic, and regional identities to secure a power base among the population. A second shared characteristic lies in the low level of institutionalization of state machinery, or the weakness of institutionally organized methods for the population to participate in the management and sharing of the benefits of public property. A common feature of fragile, unstructured states and authoritarian regimes with strong control over the state machinery is a failure to consider the will of populations who are dispossessed of their right to express themselves and their ability to act.

The media play a fundamental role in these contexts. First, they can provide space for encounters and dialogue between protagonists (who do not always have other common forums for discussion). Second, they are able to voice the preoccupations of populations who are generally neglected and condemned to silence. In the past few years, however, Central African journalists have not lived up to this ideal perspective.

They have often transmitted one-sided information from either the officially recognized government or the opposition. But positive initiatives are becoming more common, and some media have shown that they can resist pressure from the political world, demonstrating that their primary affiliation is with the public.[8]

To better examine the recent evolution of the media in Central Africa, the nine countries under study here are presented in three topical groups:

• The first group comprises the three so-called Great Lakes countries: Burundi, the Democratic Republic of Congo, and Rwanda. All have experienced violent civil war involving the death of hundreds of thousands of citizens, with important regional backgrounds and consequences.

• The second group comprises three countries that have also experienced violent civil war, but with less regional impact: the Republic of Congo (Congo-Brazzaville), the Central African Republic, and Chad. Even though these countries have been affected by the Great Lakes crisis, their civil wars have not expanded into international wars.

• The third group comprises three countries that have not experienced war since 1990, but in which the democratic process certainly faces major problems and important social tensions: Cameroon, Gabon, and Equatorial Guinea. Conflicts might thus occur very easily in these countries in the near future.

The analysis is based mainly in the years 1993–2004, which have been the most conflictual in the region. Except for the Rwanda case, the more recent transition processes and postconflict issues are not included in this study. Each of these case studies, based on concrete facts and examples, can help us better understand the way media can influence, positively or negatively, the emergence, development, and resolution of conflicts. Each also shows the challenges and constraints faced by journalists in a country that is experiencing an unstable political transition.

Chapter 11 focuses on another aspect of the role of the media in conflicts in Africa. Journalist Jean-Paul Marthoz, former international director of information at Human Rights Watch, looks at how the Northern media cover crises on the continent. As shall be seen, the circulation of "information without frontiers" proves to be an illusion in our globalized world. Under pressure from the major powers, the selection and handling of information can obscure some conflicts, occasionally turning a brief and momentary spotlight on them that serves only to implant a few additional stereotypes into the confused memory of the public. But conversely, during a particularly tragic or telegenic episode, some international media can use their prominence to modify the local or neighboring players' perception of their own situation, if only for a while.

Chapter 12 outlines the factors that influence how the media positions itself in times of conflict. It shows the many factors that influence journalists' behavior: the internal organization of the media companies, the relationship among journalists and poltical players, and the structure of the media environment, including professional solidarity. These factors can sometimes push the media into war-mongering attitudes or, on the contrary, help them to resist the pressure to spread propaganda.

Reporting on violent conflicts and wars has already become a research subject for many specialists of international politics, global journalism, and peacebuilding.[9] But their approaches, mainly developed in the Anglo-Saxon world, often remain very theoretical and are seldom applied to the francophone countries of Africa.[10] Over the past few years, interpretation and intervention tools have multiplied, giving rise to a current of media-oriented peacebuilding that spans "peace journalism" (Jake Lynch),[11] "conflict-sensitive journalism" (Ross Howard),[12] "proactive journalism" (Loretta Hieber),[13] and "mediation journalism" (Robert Karl Manoff, Johannes Botes).[14] These theoretical and practical concepts have been developed to guide the work of media professionals toward greater awareness of their potential impact on the search for peace.

Though professional journalism, if it respects the rules of balanced information and requires the checking and cross-checking of sources, can help defuse the tensions that often arise because of misunderstanding and lack of information (or disinformation) between players, one crucial question remains: Can or even must the journalist go further, by directing his or her professional practice toward supporting peace initiatives? If so, does such a commitment mean that the journalist has renounced his or her role as neutral and impartial informer?

This book does not aim to answer definitively the question of what a journalist's role should be in African countries in crisis, nor does it aim to propose a set of "recipes" for guaranteeing that the media become mediators for peace. Rather it aims to provide material for reflection and analysis—for Southern and Northern media professionals who want to take stock of their own practices, as well as for institutional, political, and development actors who want to identify the means to build peace in troubled regions. The book is also a tribute to the courageous men and women of Central Africa who, having chosen to become journalists, exercise their profession under dangerous, financially insecure conditions, subject to multiple threats and constraints. On a daily basis, they try to ensure that dialogue and the expression of contradictory views are still possible in a language other than that of weapons.

Notes

1. G. Chaliand points out that "in the 20th century, manipulation of the masses is not only a means of political action, it is politics itself and has the objective of winning over the hearts and minds through media-based persuasion." Gérard Chaliand (ed.), *La persuasion de masse* (Paris: Robert Laffont, 1992), p. 17.

2. Most of these mechanisms are illustrated in M. Mathien (ed.), *L'information dans les conflits armés: du Golfe au Kosovo* (Paris: L'Harmattan, 2001).

3. Swedish International Peace Research Institute, *Armaments, Disarmament, and International Security* (Oxford: Oxford University Press/Stockholm International Peace Research Institute, 2004).

4. English acronyms have been used when commonly cited in anglophone newspapers and scientific works. Otherwise, French acronyms have been maintained; English translations can be found in the comprehensive list of acronyms included at the back of the book.

5. These are states that try to put on a show of democracy by adopting mechanisms such as multiparty elections and the liberalization of the media sector, adopting a constitution, and establishing representative institutions, but they have retained their authoritarian reflexes. See F. Zakaria, "The Rise of Illiberal Democracy," *Foreign Affairs* (November–December 1997).

6. A reflection on the place and role of information in armed conflicts undeniably emerged in the French-speaking world following the Gulf War, leading to numerous publications in France, Canada, and Belgium. See, for example, Mathien, *L'information dans les conflits armés;* C. Beauregard and C. Saouter (eds.), *Conflits contemporains et médias* (Montreal: XYZ, 1997); A. Woodrow, *Information Manipulation* (Paris: Editions du Félin, 1991); Les Rencontres Internationales Média-Défense, *Les manipulations de l'image et du son* (Paris: Hachette, 1996). But this reflection is mainly concentrated on the vagaries of the coverage by Northern media (US and European) of wars in which the Western world was directly involved. Research on the role played by Southern media in the crises that affect them is practically nonexistent in French.

7. On predatory and kleptocratic governments, see J. F. Bayart, S. Ellis, and B. Hibou, "De l'état kleptocrate à l'état malfaiteur," in *La criminalisation de l'état en Afrique* (Brussels: Editions Complexe, 1997). Also see the key work by J. F. Bayart, *L'état en Afrique: la politique du ventre* (Paris: Fayard, 1991).

8. See the accounts in Institut Panos Paris and Collectif d'Échanges pour la Technologie Appropriés (COTA) (eds.), *Briser les silences: paroles d'Afrique centrale* (Paris: Karthala, 2003).

9. Most of the structures that address the role of the media in conflicts are presented in R. Howard, H. van de Veen, and J. Verhoeven (eds.), *The Power of the Media: A Handbook for Peacebuilders* (Utrecht: European Center for Conflict Prevention, European Center for Common Ground, and Institute for Media, Policy, and Civil Society, 2003).

10. The NGO Search for Common Ground (United States) implements projects in Burundi and the DRC, and the Hirondelle Foundation (Switzerland) in the Central African Republic and the DRC.

11. J. Lynch and A. McGoldrick, "Peace Journalism: How to Do It," *Transcend* nos. 1–2 (October 2000).

12. R. Howard, *Conflict Sensitive Journalism: A Handbook* (Copenhagen: International Media Support and IMPACS, 2003).

13. L. Hieber, *Lifeline Media: Reaching Population in Crisis—A Guide to Developing Media Projects in Conflict Situations* (Geneva: Media Action International, 2001).

14. R. K. Manoff, "The Media's Role in Preventing and Moderating Conflict," *Crossroad Global Report* (March–April 1997); J. F. Botes, F. Dukes, R. Rubenstein, and J. Stephens (eds.), *Frameworks for Interpreting Conflict: A Handbook for Journalists* (Fairfax, Va.: Institute for Conflict Analysis and Resolution, George Mason University, 1994).

2

BURUNDI

The Media During War, the Media for Peace

POLITICAL AND MEDIA pluralism emerged in Burundi in 1992, after decades of a one-party state with a monopoly on information that had accustomed people to hearing only "their master's voice." Article 6 of the press laws of June 25, 1976, stipulated that "Burundian journalists must always operate as committed patriots who are conscious of the party's ideals, in its role as the only body responsible for the life of the nation." The new constitution of 1992 departed from this viewpoint, stipulating that "everybody has the right to freedom of opinion and expression, so long as they respect public order and the law." Also in 1992, a government decree enlarged this freedom by officially suppressing the state monopoly over audiovisual media, though the press was the first medium to flourish. Yet these changes also marked the beginning of more than ten years of violence and political unrest in the country, leading to more than 300,000 dead and a total economic collapse.

A Decade of Media Pluralism and War

Until the political liberalization of 1992, the Burundian media landscape consisted of a state monopoly on the media sector, which comprised a national radio and television station, Radio Télévision Nationale du Burundi (RTNB); a state French-language daily, *Le Renouveau* (created in 1978); and an official weekly in Kirundi, *Ubumwe* (Unity). *Ndongozi* (The Guide), the Catholic Church's bimonthly publication, founded in 1940 (and suspended from 1987 to 1988), was the only privately owned publication. From 1992 onward, the new Burundian press, born in the heady days of the beginning of a multiparty state, polarized around

BURUNDI

Size	27,830 sq. km.
Population	7.5 million
Capital	Bujumbura
Ethnic groups	Hutu, Tutsi, Twa
Official languages	French, Kirundi
Human Development	
Index ranking (2005)	169 (out of 177 countries)
Life expectancy	42 years
Literacy rate	58.9 percent

Chronology

1885–1916: German colonization.

1924: League of Nations, then Belgian Mandate.

1959: Creation of the Union pour le Progrès National (UPRONA), a multiethnic party led by hereditary prince Louis Rwagasore.

1961: Assassination of Prince Louis Rwagasore.

1962: Independence. Burundi becomes a constitutional monarchy led by King Mwambutsa IV.

July 1966: Prince Ntare V seizes power after a coup.

November 1966: Captain Michel Micombero seizes power after a military coup. Monarchy is abolished and UPRONA is established as the single party.

1972: Hutu rebellion attacks in the south of the country. Heavy repression follows, with elimination of most of the Hutu elite.

1976: Colonel Jean-Baptiste Bagaza seizes power.

1987: Military coup by Major Pierre Buyoya. The constitution is suspended and a military committee for national salvation is established.

1988: Violent crisis. Tutsi are massacred by Hutu, and in reprisal the mainly Tutsi military kills thousands of Hutu.

1992: Democratization process under international pressure. A new constitution is adopted recognizing the multiparty state, and granting civil and political freedom.

June 1993: Melchior Ndadaye, supported by the Front Démocratique du Burundi (FRODEBU), becomes the first Hutu president, winning the election over Pierre Buyoya.

October 1993: Melchior Ndadaye is killed by a Tutsi faction of the armed forces. Beginning of the civil war.

(continues)

February 1994: Cyprien Ntaryamira, a Hutu from FRODEBU, is appointed president.

April 1994: President Ntaryamira dies in a plane crash (in which Rwandese president Juvénal Habyarimana also dies) in Kigali, plunging the country into violence.

June 1994: Creation, by a Hutu minister, of the Conseil National pour la Défense de la Démocratie (CNDD) and its armed wing, the Forces pour la Défense de la Démocratie (FDD). The Parti pour la Liberation du Peuple Hutu (PALIPEHUTU) creates the Front National de Liberation (FNL), another rebel movement.

October 1994: Sylvestre Ntibantunganya (of FRODEBU) is appointed president. Civil war expands.

July 1996: Major Pierre Buyoya seizes power through a military coup. Burundi is placed under total embargo by neighboring countries.

August 2000: Arusha Accords are signed by the main Hutu and Tutsi political parties (representing the Group of Seven and Group of Ten, respectively). Armed factions refuse to join, and the war continues.

November 2001: A transition government is established, led by Pierre Buyoya representing the Group of Ten.

May 2003: Domitien Ndayizeye, a Hutu representing the Group of Seven, takes over the presidency, in accordance with Arusha.

November 2003: Rebels from the CNDD-FDD (Pierre Nkurunziza branch) sign a separate peace agreement and enter the government.

February 2005: A new constitution is adopted by referendum.

July 2005: Legislative election. The CNDD-FDD wins with 58 percent, beating FRODEBU (22 percent) and UPRONA (7 percent).

August 2005: Pierre Nkurunziza becomes president, elected by parliament.

sentiments of ethnic identity, which were also the ideological backdrop for the new political parties. As the French NGO Reporters sans Frontières[1] noted, "Though it may seem shocking and paradoxical, the extremist papers with their inflammatory editorials, were born as the one-party state lost its grip."[2]

The first privately owned newspapers created at this time were openly partisan, but still, at the start, moderate. The former single party, the Union pour le Progrès National (UPRONA), comprising mainly Tutsi, was supported by the newspapers *L'Indépendant-Intahe* and *Le*

Carrefour des Idées. The newspaper *L'Aube de la Démocratie-Kanura Burakeye,* which had previously been circulated clandestinely, was on the side of the Front Démocratique du Burundi (FRODEBU). These papers did not hide their allegiances. They were created by political militants who were known to have roles in the parties' hierarchies.[3] Alongside these politicized newspapers, a handful of other periodicals that declared their "neutrality" appeared, such as *Le Citoyen, PanAfrika, La Semaine,* and *Le Phare,* but they often had a greater penchant for opinions than for information.[4] Most of the newspapers had very low print runs, about 2,000 copies, because of their relatively high price, a circulation limited to the capital, and a small number of potential francophone readers in a country with a high level of illiteracy.

At the time of the 1993 presidential election, the partisan nature of the Burundian press became even more apparent, with each paper openly supporting its candidate (Pierre Buyoya for UPRONA and Melchior Ndadaye for FRODEBU). Each party and each paper accused the other side of inciting ethnic tensions for its own advantage.[5]

FRODEBU's stunning victory (unexpected by large numbers of Burundian and international journalists) pushed the press to become more radical. The staunchly Tutsi newspapers reported on the fears of the minority, who had lost both power and government posts as they witnessed the triumphant return of vindictive Hutu refugees proclaiming their right to certain lands. President Ndadaye addressed the press several times, accusing some papers of "vulgar tribalism" and of reviving "divisions all the time by giving the impression that the Hutus are taking over all the posts, and that Frodebu is emptying the coffers."[6]

After Ndadaye's assassination on October 21, 1993, and the massacres that followed, newspapers continued to proliferate,[7] and gave birth to genuine hate media,[8] characterized by the demonization of the opposite community. On UPRONA's side were *Burundi Times, Le Patriote, La Balance,* and *Le Républicain;* on FRODEBU's side were *L'Eclaireur, Le Témoin-Nyabusorongo,* and *Le Miroir-Nturenganywe.* Finally, a few newspapers, such as *L'Etoile* and *La Nation,* defended the positions of the Parti pour le Redressement National (PARENA), former president Jean-Baptiste Bagaza's party, which was now seen as Tutsi extremist. Reporters sans Frontières noted, "The style is aggressive and defamatory, openly inciting racial hatred and murder and playing on each side's ancestral fears and resentments."[9] The media that were close to the pro-Hutu movements portrayed the Hutu as eternal victims, a majority badly treated by an ethnic minority who still monopolized the army and the civil service and who had always sought to reinforce its domination. Those who supported UPRONA fed the Tutsi minority's fear of becoming victims of violent revenge by the Hutu, who had long been excluded from power.[10] This sentiment became even stronger after the genocide perpetrated in the neighboring state of Rwanda, from April to July 1994.

When Burundi's president, Cyprien Ntaryamira, was killed in an aircraft accident that took the life of Rwanda's Juvénal Habyarimana, on April 6, 1994, the country was plunged into a period of chaos and insecurity, marked by continuous intercommunal violence. Political confusion, manifest in numerous internal splits and the creation of armed movements within certain parties, was reflected in the press. The country slid into civil war. The town of Bujumbura was deeply scarred by the conflict, and some districts were ethnically cleansed between 1995 and 1996. The papers became weapons of war. The press, however, already weakened by numerous social and economic constraints, was having a hard time surviving, as often happens in times of conflict, when obtaining supplies is difficult, potential readers are dispersed (and the few who remain have little money to spend), and the control of territories and towns is split among rival groups.

The war also led to a deterioration of security for journalists. In 1995, three journalists were killed on the road; the assassins were never found. The offices of politicized papers, such as *L'Aube de la Démocratie*[11] and *Le Témoin,* were ransacked; and journalists whose neutrality made them more vulnerable, such as Jean-Marie Gasana of *La Semaine,* were forced into exile.

Indeed, the neutral press faced even more challenges than did the partisan papers. As Antoine Kaburahe pointed out, "All Burundian journalists who were active during this period, or at least those who occupied the territory between the two extremist positions, were deeply afraid of popular reaction as each issue appeared. Conversely, for the journalist who had chosen sides, things were clear. He knew who his friends and enemies were, in which bar he could drink in peace."[12] For both factions, the search for neutrality was obviously suspect.

In the middle of this chaos, the first two privately owned radio stations appeared: the radio station of the Chambre de Commerce et d'Industrie du Burundi (CCIB FM) in 1995 (first authorized in 1993), and Radio Bonesha (The Scout) in 1996 (first created under the name Radio Umwizero [Hope]). Also, the Conseil National pour la Défense de la Démocratie (CNDD) launched Radio Démocratie-Rutoromangingo, which transmitted from Uvira, in neighboring Zaire.[13] At the same time, UPRONA obtained the frequency rights to create Radio Tanganyika (which never broadcast). After the emergence of the hate press, the phantom of "hate radios" loomed on the horizon, but never became a reality. On the contrary, Studio Ijambo (The Wise Words), supported by the US nongovernmental organization Search for Common Ground (SFCG), was created in Bujumbura, with the explicit aim of producing radio programs promoting dialogue, peace, and reconciliation by working toward better understanding between the communities.[14]

When Major Buyoya seized power again in July 1996, ending the power-sharing experiment, he suspended the political parties, the papers' usual sponsors, and a very restrictive government decree on the press was adopted. But he did not halt the development of radio pluralism; this continued with the creation of Radio Culture in 1999; the religious station Radio Vyizigiro (Hope) as well as Radio Publique Africaine (RPA) in 2001; Radio Isanganiro (Meeting Place) in 2002; and Radio Renaissance and Radio Mariya in 2004.

These radio stations tried to distinguish themselves from the official tone of the RTNB, and aimed to give a voice to all members of Burundi's population. Contrary to the majority of newspapers, they were not linked to political parties or factions.

The success of the radio stations[15] undoubtedly helped to marginalize the Burundian press, which has gradually been reduced to a few papers that appeared sporadically, barely more than once a month, and circulated furtively with print runs rarely exceeding 500 copies. Deprived of their political sponsors and suffering from an embargo that cut off their supplies of imported products, such as paper and ink,[16] the newspapers folded one after another. Yet a suspension of six extremist papers in 1996 was followed by the founding of a few new publications, among them *La Lumière,* which succeeded *L'Aube de la Démocratie,* and *La Vérité,* which was a PARENA supporter. However, they did not survive.

In 2005, on the eve of the pluralist election that ended the transition period, two weeklies attempted to appear regularly, *Arc-en-Ciel* and *Umuntu-Lumière.* A few other papers were publishing when they could, hardly more than once every two months: *Le Cénacle, Infop, Nouvel Horizon, Le Pélican,* and *Notre Terre.* Their content remained very political, even if they did not have the inflammatory tone of 1993–1994. Print runs fell from 2,000 copies in 1994 to less than 400 copies in 2005, with an increasing interval between print runs. Their owners survive by working in other sectors, including the public media. The state publications, *Le Renouveau* and *Ubumwe,* continue to appear, as does *Ndongozi.*

Several privately owned press agencies have found an original response to an unfavorable economic context.[17] Relying mainly on the Internet, the agencies Net Press, Aginfo, Zoomnet, Kirimba (The Court), and Azania (named for a South African bird) send their dispatches daily by fax and by e-mail, and manage to survive on subscriptions from the Burundian diaspora. Though their tone is moderate, they occasionally lapse, which the public authorities regularly reproach. These press agencies compete with the Agence Burundaise de Presse (ABP), which, though it has a network of correspondents in all the provinces, only publishes about four pages a day, sent electronically to about a hundred subscribers.[18]

In another recent phenomenon, about a dozen Internet sites have been created, broadcasting generally very partisan information about Burundi from outside the country. In 2003 the Conseil National de la Communication (CNC) took action against Net Press, whose website offered a link to a politicized foreign platform.[19] This decision has given rise to an intense debate that has revealed, even more than the government's residual desire to control freedom of expression, the difficulty of imposing quality criteria on information circulating on the Internet. Though electronic information still has only very low penetration within the country, this incident also reveals the persistence of hate and divisiveness.[20]

The Media During the Torment

Since 1993 the Burundian media have been operating in a context of chronic instability and violence, which makes it difficult to conduct professional, high-quality work. And yet the recent journalistic history of the country shows great diversity in the behavior of media professionals and their reactions to constraints.

Hate Media: 1993–1996

It is undeniable that in Burundi, between 1993 and 1996, certain papers contributed to the development of a political discourse of division and hate through the use of a rhetoric that reinforced stereotypes, fear of the "Other," and a sense of imminent threat. Their partisan tendency was no doubt reinforced by the fact that these initiatives in the press were personally linked to individuals. In practice, most of the newspapers were almost completely written by a single journalist who was simultaneously director, editor in chief, and main columnist.[21] Since each individual identifies with either the Hutu or the Tutsi, he or she has a personal and collective history linked to the country's traumatic events. As Jean-Pierre Chrétien wrote, "Being Hutu or Tutsi in Burundi, means that you remember who killed one of your relatives 15 years ago, or that you ask yourself who will kill your child in 10 years time, and each time you have a different answer. This fear is neither inert nor neutral."[22]

Fear was the main tool used by the extremist press. For example, the media that were close to FRODEBU played on the threat hanging over the Hutu people and justified the massacres of the Tutsi in the name of self-defense. For *L'Aube de la Démocratie,* the Hutu, who, with the election of Ndadaye, "glimpsed the dawning of their liberation" and "would finally recover their rights that had been usurped for centuries," felt "their lives directly threatened" when he was assassinated and were caught in the dilemma of "kill or be killed, kill or be enslaved once again and for ever."[23]

The media went out of their way to emphasize the radically different character of the "Other" as a way to incite fear and a general sense of insecurity. *Le Carrefour des Idées,* close to UPRONA, questioned Ndadaye's personality: "National hero or chief of a tribe of head-hunters?"[24] Outrageous assertions, humiliating cartoons, and insults all contributed to dehumanizing the adversary. Furthermore, the same paper did not hesitate to put a price on the heads of the leaders of the Hutu movements by offering "one million FBu [Burundian francs] to the person who brings them in on the end of his spear."[25] The Tutsi extremist press even indulged in mocking the physical characteristics of some Hutu personalities, thus reinforcing the morphological stereotypes that proved so dramatically murderous in neighboring Rwanda.[26] On the other hand, the Hutu extremist press expounded on the theme of the Tutsi's legendary cruelty, representing some political personalities of UPRONA gorging themselves by drinking "Hutu blood"[27] or in suggestive positions with pornographic overtones.[28] In their desire to portray the "Other" as barbaric or animalistic, some papers even went so far as to make accusations of cannibalism. The Tutsi extremist media accused Hutu militias of hiding their victims by eating them. "They will kebab us," ran a headline of *Le Carrefour des Idées:* "The Tutsi are threatened with cannibalism. The Hutu are totally capable of putting this plan into practice, if they can."[29] The dehumanizing of the adversary reached its paroxysm when the same paper asked: "Does the Hutu have a soul? That soul which, so they say, makes us superior to animals and closer to God."[30]

Another technique used by the papers to stir up anxiety was the use of analogies of current events, with simplified facts, as repetitions of past violence. The specific features of events, and the nuances necessary to understand them, were ignored. Thus, when *L'Eclaireur* wrote, "No one can deny that in 1965, in 1969, in 1972, in 1988, in 1991, in 1993, and in 1994, many innocent Hutu were killed by Tutsi extremists who promoted regionalism, cliquishness, tribalism, Machiavellianism, nepotism, interventionism, patronage, banditry, impunity, chaos, vendettas and many other evils that were very damaging to the good of the people,"[31] it would seem, then, that history demonstrates the absolute inevitability of the Tutsi inheriting such inhuman violence aimed at tyrannizing the Hutu.

Analogies were also used to generate fear by comparing current events with traumatic episodes that had taken place in other contexts. For instance, on February 11, 1994, *Le Patriote* claimed, "Before October 21, 1993, Frodebu was the embodiment of constitutional legality, in the same way that Adolf Hitler embodied German constitutional legality. This Burundian political party, like the Nazi party, gained power by elections. But after the Jewish Holocaust, did the Nazi regime's constitutional legality still have any meaning?"[32] Therefore, according to the paper, the threat of the "final solution" was hanging over the Tutsi.

Finally, another constant factor in the extremist press was the large amount of space afforded to the most threatening rumors, which incited an instinctive, self-defensive reaction, by violence if necessary. "The Tutsi army is determined to exterminate the Hutu," ran a headline of *Le Témoin*,[33] which could not support this assertion with any verifiable facts. Reports from the field were rare in a press dominated by editorials and commentaries. Over and above the material problems that journalists might encounter trying to get to sites where events had taken place, they quite obviously wanted to put their writing in the service of opinion, or even propaganda, and not information. In times of conflict, membership in one group or another, as well as ties of ethnicity, family, and professional patronage can become very constricting. Even the intellectual elite might end up with little room to maneuver.[34]

Rumors were as frequent as manipulation in the eminently strategic field of counting the numbers of victims after military offensives or massacres. During conflicts, those who are present often issue contradictory press releases, so that even the best-intentioned journalists have a hard time pinning down accurate and verifiable information. Manipulating these reports is a way of lessening one's own guilt and placing responsibility on the "Other," of damaging the morale of the opponent's partisans and boosting that of one's own troops.

The hate media also benefited from the climate of impunity. They set themselves up as dispensers of justice, defending members of their own threatened communities and raising their voices against "the exterminators" or "the perpetrators of genocide."[35] They could deploy their hate-filled discourse without limits and with no fear of reprisal.[36] The Burundian courts did not punish press offenses at the height of the crisis. From April 1993 to April 1996, fifty-six complaints concerning press offenses were recorded by the Bujumbura prosecutor's department, which did not immediately start to investigate them. As the Burundian media professionals themselves pointed out, "Thanks to impunity, a growing number of papers saw the light and joined their predecessors in an open season for press offences."[37]

However, the extremist press can be credited with one positive contribution. It lifted the veil on the taboo subject of intercommunal violence in rural areas, which the public press preferred to pass over in silence. Even if the information reported was partial and partisan, at least the public learned some previously hidden facts.[38] This violence, together with the tragic events that had taken place in Burundi over the preceding forty years, whose dates were in everyone's memory, finally found expression.

In the final analysis, it must be recognized that the hate media had limited influence because their main instrument was the press. Because they were written in French, in a country where literacy levels were low, and because they circulated mainly in the capital, the papers' discourses of hatred and exclusion were restricted to a circle of city-dwelling intellectuals and did not touch the countryside. Conversely, when the national radio stations echoed some of these abuses, they reached a larger audience, and no doubt had a greater impact.

The Slow Opening of the Public Media

An important aspect that explains the deployment of the hate media, apart from the "laissez-faire" attitude, is the absence of an alternative. It was difficult for any other discourse to make itself heard. The only competitors of the partisan press were the totally controlled public media and a few neutral papers that survived with difficulty.

For years, Radio Télévision Nationale du Burundi was used exclusively as a tool for publicizing the activities of officials of the single party, UPRONA.[39] In 1992, at the time of the constitutional referendum, the human rights organization Ligue Iteka noted, "It leaves little space for expression, other than that totally occupied by government propaganda."[40] Worse still, the public media opened the way for the extremist press before the 1993 election by using excessive and stereotyped terms when referring to the FRODEBU opposition, whose members were all characterized as "terrorists and saboteurs."[41]

When FRODEBU came to power in 1993, it exercised the same control over the RTNB as had the previous regime, which FRODEBU had once criticized for its monopoly on public media. Censorship, dismissals,[42] and intimidation multiplied, while divisions among journalists became deeper; some supported change that was seen as democratic progress, while others resisted a process that was considered dangerous for part of the population. The majority of RTNB journalists were Tutsi who complained about censorship, challenging the controlling authority each time a Hutu minister was in charge of the editorial body.[43] When people close to UPRONA acquired total control of the RTNB again in 1996, it was the turn of Hutu journalists to complain of the pressure they were under, so much so that some left the editorial body or went abroad to seminars from which they never returned.

The appearance of the armed rebel movements, and Major Pierre Buyoya's return to power, led to an increase in pressure on the RTNB by the army. In 1999, a morning slot on the national radio station that was given to the Burundian armed forces allowed them, among other things, to present deserters from the Forces pour la Défense de la Démocratie (FDD). These men explained on the air why they had fled the rebellion, and encouraged their former comrades to do the same.[44]

The public media did not hesitate to adopt certain strategies of the extremist media, such as inciting fear of the "enemy." Furthermore, their discourse was different in programs broadcast in French and Kirundi. For example, to designate the "armed bands"[45] (the terminology used for the rebel movements) in Kirundi, the RTNB used the expression *imirwi y'abicanyi,* literally, "the bands of killers."[46] Comparing the way certain events were treated in French and Kirundi is instructive. For example, Melchior Ndadaye spoke of "democracy" in French, and "liberation of a people for too long oppressed" in Kirundi, in the 1993 election campaign.[47]

Nevertheless, in the second half of the 1990s, no doubt due to the influence of the privately owned radios stations, the RTNB openly progressed toward more diverse views. Surprisingly, in May 2001 it allowed itself to criticize both the government and the opposition for having failed to restore peace.[48] During conflicts between professionals and the government, it gradually allowed all concerned parties to express themselves, even if one of them opposed the government.[49] Studio Ijambo's productions, some of which were broadcast by the public radio station as early as 1996,[50] no doubt helped change the national channel's image, even if these programs were often partly or entirely censored.[51] Censorship became lighter, and pluralistic programs open to diverse political opinions appeared. But self-censorship continued to such an extent that, in 2000, a report remarked that it was "second nature to professionals in the Burundian public media."[52]

Since it was always considered as a symbol of power, the RTNB was one of the first targets of the putschists in all the coups in Burundi.[53] So once again, in April 2001, when a group of Tutsi extremist soldiers turned against President Buyoya, they seized the national radio station, and only that station, to announce the overthrow of the regime. The authorities then had to turn to the privately owned radio stations to broadcast their own message, reassuring the population and coordinating the counteroffensive by loyalist troops. For once, President Buyoya praised the privately owned radio stations for allowing all parties to express themselves.

Today the RTNB is continuing its process of gradual opening as information gains precedence over state propaganda. The journalistic commentary genre has practically disappeared from the airwaves, as journalists now prefer to offer up their microphones without having to produce an analysis that might commit them to one side or the other. Suffering from lack of equipment, the public station started receiving regular aid from Belgian and US agencies, which helped it transition to digital equipment in 2005. Before this, the RTNB found itself technically outclassed by the privately owned radio stations, which had lighter and better-performing equipment.

Privately Owned Radio Stations: A Progressive Mobilization for Peace

Radio Télévision Nationale du Burundi has been forced to change in the past few years, because its competitors have begun to find favor with listeners. The Burundian privately owned radio stations have played an important role in promoting a pluralism of ideas, bringing to the forefront the impact of the Tutsi-Hutu conflict on the population and restoring some mutual understanding (if not confidence) among the communities. The impact of Studio Ijambo and its programs on all the privately owned radio stations' programming and production strategies is undeniable.[54]

Studio Ijambo's first concern was to work toward better mutual understanding. It developed a range of programs (magazines, radio plays, and game shows) that promoted discussion and dialogue. It created a radio soap opera titled *Ababanyi Ni Twebwe/Umubanyi Niwe Muryango* (We

Are the Neighbors/The Neighbor Is Part of the Family), about the daily life of two families, one Hutu and the other Tutsi, showing that understanding between the communities was still possible, even in a situation of extreme polarization. Another program, *Inkingi Y'Ubuntu* (A Pillar of Dignity), turned the spotlight on the experiences of anonymous "righteous people" who risked their own lives during the crisis to save people who belonged to the other ethnic group. While at the end of the 1990s the RTNB broadcast lengthy songs of praise to certain political leaders, Studio Ijambo produced *Sangwe* (Welcome), a musical program for young people from different social classes and ethnic groups that promoted artists whose songs could help achieve peace and help youth communicate.

The new privately owned radio stations committed themselves straightaway to this movement toward pluralism and openness, all the more so because several founders and presenters of the stations (including RPA and Radio Isanganiro) were former journalists of Studio Ijambo. This experience was probably also the inspiration for the founding of Studio Tubane (Studio Let's Cohabit),[55] which produces programs that promote reconciliation and provides them to various local stations.[56]

The Burundian privately owned radio stations have worked in many ways to prepare people for peace and promote good citizenship in this fractured country. From the day it was created, Bonesha FM has tried to emphasize reconciliation initiatives. In 2000, when the Arusha Accords were signed, the radio station dedicated many broadcasting hours to popularizing and explaining the agreement, which was very controversial at the time.

Next, the privately owned radio stations were a great help in giving the public a voice, thus distinguishing themselves from the institutional mouthpiece, the RTNB. The RPA took its name, Radio Publique Africaine, from this mission. It explicitly set out to be the voice of the voiceless. According to its director, Alexis Sinduhije, the idea of creating this radio station sprang from "a long reflection on the fact that the Burundian people have nowhere to express their suffering, aspirations and vision of the social and political life of their country and take a part in re-building it."[57] Radio stations have set up practical mechanisms to ensure that people can call them directly to explain problems in their districts or denounce unjust situations.

Radio Isanganiro, which is very interactive, has set up a system of local correspondents, equipped with mobile phones, that it uses for certain programs, such as *Aho Iwanyu Havugwa Amaki?* (What's the News in Your Area?). Ordinary citizens who have become radio correspondents lead discussions in the provinces. Radio also tries to support the peace process by bringing together Burundians inside the country and Burundians abroad (exiles and refugees) and asking them to share their views on the national situation.[58]

The radio stations have also played an essential role in helping the various belligerent forces express themselves, in order to dispel the rumors and disinformation generated by the refusal to communicate. The radio stations have paid for this on more than one occasion. In November 2003 the government closed Radio Isanganiro and the RPA for a week, accusing them of having allowed Pasteur Habimana, the spokesman of the Front National de Libération (FNL), to speak. The Burundian authorities had asked the privately owned radio stations on several occasions to no longer give air time to the armed rebel movements. The other radio stations (Bonesha FM and CCIB FM, along with Studio Ijambo) then decided to boycott the government's activities and not talk about them until the measures were lifted. The pressure generated by this solidarity and the ensuing popular discontent forced the authorities to lift the ban after several days.

The Burundian radio stations also contributed to making the authorities accountable to the population. In January 2003, following the theft of a soldier's weapon in a Hutu district of Bujumbura, a battalion took violent reprisals that resulted in approximately ten deaths and the pillaging of several houses. The radio stations' coverage of the event forced the army to publicly present its excuses for this excess and, in an event unique in the history of Burundi, restore the pillaged goods to their rightful owners.[59]

Investigations conducted by the radio stations have also led the public authorities to end certain forms of impunity. After the murder of a World Health Organization (WHO) representative, Kassy Manlan, in Bujumbura, the RPA launched an investigation, keeping in regular contact with the victim's family and lawyers, and often broadcasting the conversations. As a result of the RPA's reports on the subject, five new suspects were arrested in October 2003, two of whom were officers in the Burundian security services and members of the first commission of inquiry responsible for investigating the assassination.[60]

Finally, the radio stations have played an important role in helping the population reappropriate a transparent historical memory in a country marked by decades of silence and contested official versions of past events. The RPA turned many Burundians' perception of recent history upside down with its investigations into the assassination of King Ntare V. In April 2004, Radio Isanganiro also reopened discussions of the painful events of 1972, which until then had been impossible to report in a consensual manner.

International Media on the Lookout

In some countries, the foreign media play an important role in the perception of internal conflicts. This does not seem to have been the case in Burundi, even if international radio stations like Radio France Internationale (RFI), and above all the British Broadcasting Corporation (BBC) and Voice of America (VOA), both of which now transmit in Kirundi, were for a long time an important counterbalance to the far too official information of the RTNB.

At the start of the process of democratization, the international media were accused of blindness, because they did not perceive the reigning tension in the country on the eve of the 1993 elections.[61] Foreign journalists gave an image of an electoral campaign animated by the joy of rediscovered pluralism. They reported on the songs and dances that punctuated electoral meetings, but missed the explosive character of certain inflammatory political speeches made in Kirundi. Their naive and stereotyped analyses also contributed to representing the central issue of the election as strictly "ethnic." The minister of communications at the time, Alphonse Kadege (UPRONA), accused the foreign press of "making the election tribal."[62]

After the traumatization caused by the Rwandan genocide, the Western media's attitude toward Burundi changed. As Jean-Pierre Chrétien pointed out, the foreign media had started to delight in broadcasting "at first-hand the views of the worst extremists," thus trying to make up for their delay in appreciating the extent of the genocide in Rwanda.[63] But did this "unhealthy anticipation" in the case of Burundi lay the groundwork for an outbreak of violence that those who try too hard to witness can end up provoking? Colette Braeckman, a journalist at the Belgian daily *Le Soir* and a specialist in the region, noted: "A good number of those who 'missed' the genocide in Rwanda inadvertently or because they were not available did not intend to 'miss out' on the imminent tragedy in the other country of a thousand hills." Bujumbura had become "the capital of preventive diplomacy where many observers were practicing self-fulfilling prophecy."[64]

In considering the foreign media and their influence in Burundi, the key role was played, several times, by Radio Rwanda. In 1993 it was the first to announce Melchior Ndadaye's assassination, and it also reported that several Burundian ministers, in response, called for resistance and civil disobedience, leading to a popular mobilization aimed at avenging the death of the head of state.[65]

Foreign radio stations that were only accessible on shortwave before 1998, gradually installed FM transmitters in Bujumbura (the RFI in 1998, the BBC in 2000, and the VOA in 2003). With the appearance of the privately owned local radio stations, the Burundian public mainly turned to stations from Bujumbura. A survey conducted by a special commission set up by the Ministry of Communications in 2000 estimated that the most frequently listened-to stations, excluding the RTNB, were the BBC (54.5 percent), Bonesha FM (41.5 percent), the VOA (33.7 percent), the RFI (29.3 percent), and Radio Rwanda (19.6 percent).[66] However, the creation of the RPA and Radio Isanganiro contributed significantly to modifying these figures, leading to a craze among listeners, especially young people, and sparking off evident interest in foreign radio stations. Today, Burundians are sophisticated consumers who switch from one station to another, depending on the times of their favorite programs.[67]

Public Authorities and the Media

During periods of conflict, relationships between public authorities and the media (privately owned and public) often become more complicated, at one moment marked by confrontation, and at the next by manipulation and the need for mutual concessions. The need to inform and ensure citizens' security comes from a different set of logic, which can sometimes diverge from and even become incompatible with itself.

Institutional and Regulatory Framework

Several changes have been made to the press laws in Burundi, reflecting key political changes such as the opening to pluralism and the outbreak of internal armed conflict. After the new constitution, recognizing pluralism, was adopted in 1992, a new press law was promulgated on November 26 of the same year. It stated that "every journalist is free to express his or her opinions in the press and to look for, receive and communicate information of any type whatsoever" (Article 4). Nevertheless, this law still protected certain sensitive sectors (the economy, the army, and state security) and maintained a triple prior deposit (legal, administrative, and judicial), whose duration (four hours before distribution for dailies and twenty-four hours for periodicals) imposed a heavy constraint on the media directors. It explicitly provided for punishment for the dissemination of statements "tending to incite racial or ethnic hatred" (Article 52).[68]

A new government decree adopted in 1997 maintained this triple deposit constraint that journalists had been campaigning against; another target of their complaints was the all-inclusive interpretation of the notion of "national unity," which had been invoked several times when journalists were detained. But the minister of communications at the time, Pierre-Claver Ndyicariye, reckons that it was "too early to revise the press law, which was sufficiently liberal." He added that, "everywhere in the world, war creates a climate that favours the suppression of certain freedoms, including that of the press."[69]

And yet the transitional constitution of October 28, 2001, reaffirmed, in Article 34, that "everybody has the right to freedom of opinion and expression, providing they respect public order and the law." A new more liberal press law that met some of the profession's demands was finally adopted in November 2003. Among other things, it provided for the protection of sources; ended prior authorization; abolished triple deposit before publication, replacing it with a single legal deposit; and guaranteed the conscience clause. But there was still room for certain tendentious interpretations of the law, and it provided for heavy fines and prison sentences for press offenses (Articles 50 to 57).[70]

The move toward pluralism also included establishing a regulatory body, with a somewhat ambiguous position. Sometimes it was subject to the executive, and at other times it took a clearly different stance. The government decree of 1992 had already provided for the establishment of the Conseil National de la Communication, which was responsible for overseeing freedom of the press and promoting audio-visual and written communication on respect of the law, public order, and good behavior. Although the CNC had decisionmaking powers on press freedom, its role vis-à-vis the government on communication issues was only consultative. It was composed of seventeen members,[71] named by presidential decree, but was almost completely paralyzed from the time of its creation by a complete lack of operating resources. It was not until 1998 that it was allocated premises and received a minimum of equipment.

However, the CNC's lack of equipment did not stop it from trying to operate. On March 18, 1996, it suspended the extremist papers *Le Carrefour des Idées, La Nation, L'Etoile, L'Aube de la Démocratie, Le Témoin, L'Eclaireur,* and *Le Miroir* (four of these had already ceased publishing for financial reasons). The CNC has often been seen as a censor. On May 17, 2002, it demanded that the Burundian media stop disseminating interviews with dissidents and rebel groups.[72] A few months later it banned the privately owned monthly *PanAfrika* for having copied extremist statements and not checking its information against the CNDD's site.[73]

Nevertheless, in June 2001, the CNC demanded that authorities put an end to the harassment and intimidation of journalists who were investigating the disappearance of WHO's representative in Burundi. In September 2003, it was the CNC that, using its power to confirm or annul any suspension measures ordered by the minister of communications, authorized Radio Isanganiro and the RPA, which had been suspended by the government for having given airtime to the FNL, to start transmitting again.

Attacks on Freedom of the Press

Whatever legal and institutional mechanisms exist to guarantee freedom of the press in countries where there is open conflict, journalists often work in conditions of great uncertainty where access to information is hindered by administrative red tape and frequent retention of data.

Journalists must also deal with the army's eruption into public life; their definition of appropriate information sometimes differs from that of political authorities. In Burundi, confronting the army was an extremely difficult task, because its composition and history was an issue in the conflict and the subject of demands by the rebels. An observer pointed out that in Burundi, journalists knew they could defy politicians but not the military, and no one really dared to take on the latter.[74] A veil of silence was systematically drawn over the results of military operations, and the death of a soldier in combat could not be communicated on the radio. In the national context, even the title of the obituary column could be political information.

If journalists wished to travel in the troubled areas, they needed good contacts with military authorities. Journalists from privately owned radio stations or studios were frequently harassed, arrested, or illegally detained for having recorded the testimony of local people about the insecurity in their district.

In the past few years, attacks on journalists' freedom in Burundi have changed. In 1995, during the period of massive and generalized violence, some press offices were attacked, such as those of *L'Aube de la Démocratie* (a FRODEBU paper) and *Le Témoin-Nyabusorongo* (directed by an active FRODEBU militant), which were burned down. Journalists were also killed, including two from the RTNB and a South African colleague from the Worldwide Television News, yet it is not certain whether their deaths were related to exercising their profession or to the general insecurity on the roads caused by armed bands. At the time, many journalists wrote under pseudonyms in order to protect themselves.[75]

Subsequently, attacks on journalists' rights have been less extreme, in part because of the government's control and also because journalists have learned to self-censor; in addition, many media have disappeared. Nevertheless, in 1998 and 1999, the director of the online press agency Net Press, Jean-Claude Kavumbagu, had a run-in with the authorities, who tried to close his agency and arrested and imprisoned him. He was arrested again in 2001 and 2003, when new privately owned radio stations that proclaimed and practiced real pluralism probably aroused the mistrust of the government, which at the time was "in transition" and weakened by the upsurge of violence orchestrated by the two rebel movements who had not signed the Arusha Accords.

Furthermore, the public authorities and police have regularly reproached the media for either giving airtime to the opposition and covering its activities, or disseminating its statements, which the government deems a threat to national unity and defamation. The question of the rebel forces' access to the media is very sensitive. Already in 2001, Abbas Mbazumutima and Gabriel Nikundana of Radio Bonesha had been arrested following the broadcast of an interview with the FNL's spokesman. They were accused of "inciting civil violence," proscribed by Article 44 of the press law. On July 8, 2003, the minister of communications, Albert Mbonerane, called a meeting of managers of the privately owned media and threatened them with closure if they continued to broadcast press releases concerning FNL and FDD rebels. The minister added, "The rebels should use their own means of communication."[76] Two months later, because of this injunction, Radio Isanganiro and the RPA were suspended for a week. The public authorities sent the RPA a letter accusing it of "violating Article 44 of the press law by defaming the government and disseminating propaganda favourable to the country's enemy."[77]

In conflict situations, journalists' dissemination of information always clashes with the authorities' strategy to restrict the flow of information for security reasons. Thus, in 2002, Minister Mbonerane declared: "We are in the context of civil war in Burundi and no one, including journalists, is authorized to sabotage the government's action, whose prime objective is to return the country to peace and security."[78]

The methods used by the police to intimidate journalists range from physical aggression to arrests and seizure of equipment. In 2002, while covering opposition demonstrations, journalists from Bonesha FM and

Studio Ijambo were manhandled, beaten, and arrested. In 2001, Alexis Sinduhije was arrested, detained, and beaten by Special Investigations Bureau personnel for broadcasting an interview with South African soldiers, whose arrival at Bujumbura was supposed to be secret. Nor were the rebel forces always kind to journalists.[79]

Anonymous threats, usually by telephone, are another technique for applying pressure. The RPA's managers were threatened repeatedly while investigating the assassination of Kassy Manlan, the WHO representative in Bujumbura, in which several Burundian officials were possibly implicated. Jamming the airwaves is another method that authorities can use to restrict the freedom of the media. In August 2003 the RPA protested that the Agence de Régulation et de Contrôle des Télécommunications (ARCT) was jamming its information programs. The ARCT replied that it was a retaliatory measure against stations that had not paid their annual fee. Radio Bonesha and CCIB FM also complained that its signals were being jammed.

That self-censorship persists in such a context is understandable. When the media are silent to repression, "some uninformed observers tend to interpret that silence as indulgence towards one or other party in the conflict. Though this may be true for some papers, others are well aware of the extreme and imminent dangers they face if they do not compromise somewhat their professional ethics."[80]

On several occasions, the Burundian media have chosen to remain silent in order to protect individuals. For instance, in 2000, when the minister of defense, Alfred Nkurunziza, publicly expressed his wish that the army could open fire on foreign journalists reporting from Bujumbura Rural, the media chose not to report these excessive statements, which could have led to their recrimination. Between 1996 and 1999, when the country was embargoed, clandestine networks brought food and industrial products through the border areas, but the media chose not to denounce this almost fraudulent traffic because it helped the population survive.[81]

As Innocent Muhozi, former director general of the RTNB, pointed out, "African journalists are confronted with dilemmas like this every day and end up becoming more hardened than their colleagues from the North, who rarely need to question their own professional practices. When journalists from the North cover conflicts, they occur far from their own countries and the consequences of their reports do not directly affect their audience or those close to them."[82]

The Burundian public press has been confronted with such dilemmas many times since 1990. In August 1993, there was an entry competition at the Higher Institute for Military Officers in which Hutu refugees from Zaire took part for the first time. The RTNB filmed a report, but any allusion to these returning refugees' participation was banned on the pretext that members of the mainly Tutsi army might then escape from their officers' control and harm these potential young recruits, who were suspected of sympathizing with the armed branch of the Parti pour la Libération du Peuple Hutu (PALIPEHUTU). Jean-Marie Ngendahayo, the minister of communications at the time, concluded, "We may hide some information when, firstly, the essential part of the information is not hidden and, secondly, that information may be harmful to peace. And for the sake of peace, we are ready to hide a lot of things."[83]

State Aid to the Privately Owned Media

The public authorities, however, wish to show goodwill toward privately owned media. The November 2003 press law exempted public and privately owned press and communication enterprises from the value-added tax (VAT) and provided for the creation of a public fund for aiding press enterprises, just like those in many other countries on the continent. However, the methods by which it was to be implemented were vague. Some analysts noted that the Burundian authorities had done little to train or help journalists during the move toward democracy. They concluded that the authorities realized they had much to fear from a professional press and therefore encouraged the status quo rather than risk being confronted by journalists doing their job correctly.[84] In such a context, the existence of the lowest-quality extremist press is an ideal argument for justifying the state's lack of support for privately owned media. For this reason, the few serious publications that were above reproach and could be seen as real counterbalances, were stifled.

Characteristics of the Professional Environment

Journalistic Identity vs. Ethnic Identity

If a journalist wants to be professional, his or her vocation and commitment to the profession must take precedence over any other considerations of membership or loyalty to a group. One way to acquire this journalistic identity is through training. Yet in Burundi, there have been no initial training opportunities since 1991, when, on the eve of the liberalization of the media scene, the School of Journalism, created in 1981, closed.[85] Since the school's objective was to provide personnel for the state media and the press services of public institutions, its training "never established the dividing line between propaganda and information."[86]

Although the first promoters of privately owned media, until October 1993, were always professional journalists and well-educated leading figures of the political parties, the subsequent period of proliferation of the media opened the doors to "a whole category of people without professional experience, inspired by feelings of hatred and devoted to a form of violent political activism strongly tainted with ethnicity."[87]

This meant that access to information was strongly dependent on the political or ethnic "brand" of the medium or journalist. In a period of intense crisis, as the districts of Bujumbura were progressively and sometimes violently "ethnically cleansed," the locations of the newspapers' offices reflected their allegiances. *Le Carrefour des Idées* was in a Tutsi district, while *L'Eclaireur* and *Le Témoin* had offices in some of the most virulent Hutu districts.[88] Naturally, newspaper journalists were careful to avoid entering the "opposing" district.

Once again, it was the emergence of the privately owned radio stations that helped rehabilitate not only professional standards but also the need to go beyond "ethnic" membership. Studio Ijambo, RPA, and Radio Isanganiro all had teams composed of equal numbers of Hutu and Tutsi. And yet, even today, not just any journalist can obtain an interview with prominent political personalities. "Community relationships" continue to exert their influence.

Professional Associations: Weak but United

"How can we understand the passivity of journalists when they see colleagues indulging in excesses?" asked an observer in 1999.[89] Yet Burundian journalists had several organizations that could have defended professional principles. The Association Burundaise des Journalistes (ABJ) was created in 1990 by professionals who, at the time, all came from the public media. It sometimes attempted to react to abuses, but without success. When the number of privately owned presses increased and the profession became open, the ABJ was very quickly "overtaken by the arrival of another category of journalists who were not members of the association and who respected nothing about the profession."[90]

With support from the United Nations Educational, Scientific, and Cultural Organization (UNESCO), the ABJ created a code of ethics and professional practice, which 240 Burundian media professionals adopted in 1995. It was revived in 2004 and now includes the rights of journalists to information, personal safety, and equipment, among other things, as well as a conscience clause. But "committed journalists" are not always concerned by professional ethics. They see themselves as "combat" journalists or militants whose cause is of a higher order than professional principles, which they often completely ignore.

It is also thanks to UNESCO that the Maison de la Presse (Press Center) was opened in May 1997. Its aim is to support the emergence of responsible media that would help pacify people rather than exacerbate tensions or provoke violence. The center was inaugurated in May 1997 and today is open to all press and audiovisual media professionals, from both private and public sectors. It offers training and awareness-raising courses. It also has a small rudimentary printing press, which is used to publish a few privately owned newspapers. With the support of the Institut Panos Paris, it has also created an Internet café where journalists and the public can read e-mail and do research.

Other initiatives have demonstrated that professionals and civil society want to defend high-quality journalistic practices. In December 1992, the Association pour la Promotion et la Protection de la Liberté d'Expression (APPLE) was formed. It was dedicated to defending freedom of the press and promoting the rights and duties of journalists. At present, it is in limbo.[91] The Centre d'Alerte et de Prévention des Conflits (CENAP) was formed in 2002. The mission of this mixed organization, made up of journalists and representatives of civil society, is to monitor events and discourses that may generate conflicts, to warn of situations of serious abuses, and to collect information on conflicts and peace processes. Finally, in 2004, the Observatoire de la Presse Burundaise (OPB), a self-regulatory body, was created. Its role is to monitor violations by professional journalists in order to ensure that they respect the professional code of ethics. It has the authority to form a "jury of peers" to judge colleagues charged with violations of the code and, if they are found guilty, to publish a moral condemnation.[92]

Emergence of a New Public

The media do not exist in their own right; they are at the service of the public over which they can exercise considerable influence. Traditionally, the Burundian population did not have a high regard for journalists, whom they long considered to be mercenaries at the service of whoever was in power. As political power shifted, journalists were capable of crucifying the person they had praised the day before. The public's contempt was strengthened by the fact that most journalists in the new privately owned press had taken up the profession in order to make a living rather than to exercise a vocation. Moreover, journalists' paltry salaries contributed to their vulnerability to corruption.

The media, used as propaganda and recruiting tools in conflict situations, generally have a very good idea of their audience and structure their discourses according to their potential public. In 1994 and 1995, at the height of the crisis, the Tutsi extremist papers were published in French, because they targeted a readership of city-dwelling civil servants who were concerned about maintaining their privileges in the state apparatus. At the same time, the pro-Hutu press published a Kirundi version, aimed at local populations, and a French version for the international community.[93]

However, the Burundian experience proves wrong the thesis that the public turns away from "neutral" media in times of crisis in favor of those that are more engaged. In practice, readers ended up rejecting the extremist press. A survey conducted by the Ministry of Communications showed that even in 2000, listeners who remained faithful to the national radio station, the RTNB (which maintained a penetration rate of 96 percent), considered it unappealing because it was subject to censorship.[94] A survey conducted in May 2001 by a US university estimated a penetration rate of 67 percent for Bonesha FM, 40 percent for the RTNB. At the same time, Search for Common Ground, which conducts impact studies, estimated that 90 percent of Burundians listened to the twice-weekly radio drama series on reconciliation. An independent evaluation conducted in 2001 concluded that 95 percent of listeners thought that Studio Ijambo told the truth, and that 91 percent thought that the studio's work contributed to reestablishing peace in the country.[95]

Burundi's privately owned radio stations have certainly contributed to reassuring the silent majority that reasonable and balanced voices from the middle ground exist, though they have been stifled by the extremist discourses of a handful of individuals.

The Cost of Quality Information

The Burundian example clearly demonstrates that high-quality, pluralist, and balanced programming and information come at a high cost, especially in conflict areas where political and security issues hinder the accessibility of information. Coverage outside the capital is absolutely crucial, because the rural regions are the site of chronic violence, massacres of civilian populations, and fighting between armed forces and rebels.[96] Ensuring coverage of these regions requires a large investment (vehicles, means of communication, etc.); minimum salaries are also essential for guaranteeing professional commitment.[97]

Burundian radio stations have benefited from funding, mainly from foreign donors, to put their policies into practice. With the support of the European Union (for Radio Bonesha),[98] Search for Common Ground (mainly for Radio Isanganiro), and the Ford Foundation (for the RPA), they have obtained the resources to operate in a context in which traditional funds (commercial advertising, contributions from local partners) are not available. Even the few newspapers that tried to maintain a neutral and moderate tone in the mid-1990s survived thanks only to financial support and equipment from Reporters sans Frontières.

In addition to financing the media directly, international funding agencies and financial partners regularly provide funds to support initiatives aimed at strengthening the Burundian media and making them more professional.[99] They present seminars on the role of the media in establishing peace, publish studies on the behavior of the media, offer training courses on professional practices, and award prizes for the best journalism. However, it is always difficult to measure the real impact of these types of interventions, because they do not bring about immediate and visible changes.

Conclusion

In 2005, Burundi experienced its most recent electoral period, which is always a time of significant tension. During the 1993 elections, the RTNB was wholly subservient to the party in power, while the privately owned press initiated hate-filled discourses.[100] The difference compared to media coverage of the 2005 election is striking: all political parties were able to obtain access to the media, and ethnic appeals during "door-to-door" campaigning were never reported.

Yet the situation of the media today is very different from that of 1993. One could even say that the media are in advance of the politicians, whose rigid and unilateral discourses were described by the Burundian League for Human Rights in 1999 as follows: "The discourses on both sides are still mired in the repetition of the crimes committed by the other side and the danger that it represents, in emphasizing the violence and injustices suffered . . . but each side excuses and even justifies the wrongs, violence and atrocities committed by its own partisans. Each group reproduces the faults it denounces in the opponent."[101]

Of course, political discourse and ambition are still dominant. Radio stations have certainly not alone put an end to the Burundian conflict. As Francis Rolt, former director of Studio Ijambo, said, "In spite of the impact that radio can have in conflict situations, its work may be limited in depth and the time it can be maintained because there is an essential part of the work of resolving conflicts that cannot be done by the radio."[102] And yet, as an observer remarked, "The Burundian radio stations have changed the face of the country and strengthened the democratic process."[103]

In 2005, radio stations were an important asset in the success of the electoral process and the search for a transition toward peace in Burundi. During the constitutional referendum, on January 28, 2005, seven media outlets (including five radio stations) joined forces for four days in an operation called Media Synergy, initiated by Studio Ijambo. Sixty-five journalists worked together to provide transparent, extended, and high-quality coverage of the polling process. Bringing together a vast pool of shared correspondents spread throughout the territory, the media produced sixteen joint special programs, broadcast simultaneously on different partner stations, systematically describing the voting and vote-counting operations. This experience was repeated and extended for the legislative polls that took place on July 4. Eleven media outlets, represented by 140 journalists, jointly covered the process, ensuring transparency and discouraging fraud.

Have the Burundian media definitively turned their back on their old demons? They certainly now constitute a positive force for establishing peace and a constitutional state in their country. But they are still in a very fragile position. Today, their main concern is their sustainability in a country where donors might withdraw now that peace and democracy have been achieved. Private radio stations have received foreign support for years, which helped them to remain independent from key political players. With less funding and a new political balance (the question is no longer one of Tutsi parties vs. Hutu parties, but of tension among Hutu parties themselves [FRODEBU vs. the CNDD] and among Tutsi parties themselves [UPRONA vs. PARENA]), the Burundian media face new challenges. May professionalism remain the main path out.

Notes

I thank Cyprien Ndikumana, Christine Deslaurier, and Francis Rolt for their meticulous proofreading and comments.

1. Reporters sans Frontières (Reporters Without Borders) is based in Paris and defends freedom of the press throughout the world (see http://www.rsf.org).

2. Reporters sans Frontières (ed.), *Burundi: le venin de l'intolérance—etude sur les médias extrémistes* (Paris, July 1995), p. 7.

3. Immediately after FRODEBU's victory in the 1993 presidential election, a number of editors and lead writers from *L'Aube de la Démocratie* took up

political posts in the government or in the state media. For instance, Sylvestre Ntibantunganye, the paper's editor in chief, became minister of cooperation in the Ndadaye government.

4. See Reporters sans Frontières, *Burundi: le venin de l'intolérance,* pp. 10–12.

5. See A. Kaburahe, *Burundi: la mémoire blessée* (Brussels: La Longue Vue, 2003).

6. Speech by Melchior Ndadaye, August 23, 1993, cited in Reporters sans Frontières, *Burundi: le venin de l'intolérance,* p. 44.

7. Eva Palmans notes: "Out of 22 papers, appearing regularly in Burundi, at the end of 1994, 15 were created after the coup of October 1993 and have most often taken up positions in favour of extreme solutions." E. Palmans, "La liberté de la presse au Rwanda et au Burundi," in *L'Afrique des Grands Lacs, Annuaire 2002–2003* (Paris: L'Harmattan, 2003), p. 61.

8. This expression was popularized by Reporters sans Frontières, which published two books in 1995 based on this concept: *Les médias de la haine* (edited by Renaud de la Brosse [Paris: Editions La Découverte]) and *Rwanda: Les médias du génocide* (edited by Jean-Pierre Chrétien [Paris: Karthala]).

9. Reporters sans Frontières, *Rapport annuel,* 1995.

10. As Jean-Pierre Chrétien stresses, in Hutu circles the "majority" principle was always invoked, and in Tutsi circles that of "security." Reporters sans Frontières, *Burundi: le venin de l'intolérance,* p. 2.

11. As the paper's office was also FRODEBU's office, it is impossible to say whether the publication or the political group was targeted.

12. A. Kaburahe, *Burundi.* See also A. Kaburahe, "Le Burundi entre 1990 et 2003: espoir et inquiétude," unpublished.

13. With many listeners in Bujumbura and the countryside, it broadcast news bulletins and very virulent editorials against the 1993 putschists. On the way to being classed a "hate medium," it stopped transmitting in 1996 during the offensive by Laurent-Désiré Kabila's forces in eastern DRC. See J. Mzima, "L'état actuel de la presse au Burundi," unpublished (Brussels, May 1999), p. 16.

14. The SFCG has launched similar projects in Liberia, Macedonia, Russia, and other countries. See S. Bailly, "Burundi, Studio Ijambo: les mots sages contre les radios de la haine," in *Media résistance* (Paris: Karthala, 2000), pp. 120–132.

15. In 2002, about 85 percent of the population had access to a radio receiver, a marked contrast with the small proportion of the population reached by the written press. See M. Philippart, *L'état des médias au Burundi* (Paris: GRET-PARMA, October 2002), p. 6.

16. From June 1995 to June 1996, the cost of printing papers increased by 150 percent, forcing most of the publications to change printers, the cheapest of them definitely being the UPRONA print shop, though it demanded to inspect the contents of the newspapers it printed.

17. As analyzed in M. Phillipart, *L'état des médias au Burundi,* p. 6.

18. For a long time, the ABP's correspondents were totally subservient to local authorities (governors of provinces, administrators), on whom they depended for travel and access to telecommunication.

19. In July 2003, Jean-Claude Kavumbagu, director of the Net Press agency and considered close to radical Tutsi circles, was imprisoned for five

days for having established a link between his site and that of Agora (linked to the Burundian opposition and based in Denmark), which virulently attacked President Domitien Ndayizeye and other government dignitaries. In 2001, Kavumbagu had already been arrested for his connection to items published by an anonymous electronic press agency, Le Témoin, whose initiators are nevertheless unknown.

20. L. M. Nindorera, *Médias burundais, gestion et prévention des conflits: perspectives* (Bujumbura: International Human Rights Law Group, September 5, 2002).

21. On the other hand, the radio stations were generally more collectively run, and were therefore less identifiable with a single individual; they thus may be easier to transform into forums for pluralistic expression.

22. Reporters sans Frontières, *Burundi: le venin de l'intolérance*, p. 2.

23. *L'Aube de la Démocratie*, cited in J. F. Barnabé, "Les médias assassins au Burundi," in Reporters sans Frontières, *Les médias de la haine*, p. 70.

24. *Le Carrefour des Idées*, December 15, 1993, cited in Reporters sans Frontières, *Burundi: le venin de l'intolérance*, p. 61.

25. *Le Carrefour des Idées*, October 28, 1994, cited in Reporters sans Frontières, *Burundi: le venin de l'intolérance*, p. 61.

26. The Hutu were characterized, following the old clichés of the colonial administrations, as being small, having a flat nose, and corresponding to the "Bantu type"; the Tutsi were characterized as tall and slender, having a straight nose, and corresponding to the "Nilotic type." On those ethnic stereotypes, see Chapter 4.

27. *Le Témoin* no. 6 (September 1994), cited in J. F. Barnabé, "Les médias assassins au Burundi," p. 66.

28. *Le Miroir*, September 17, 1994, cited in J. F. Barnabé, "Les médias assassins au Burundi," p. 67.

29. *Le Carrefour des Idées*, October 22, 1993, cited in J. F. Barnabé, "Les médias assassins au Burundi," p. 58.

30. *Le Carrefour des Idées*, May 27, 1994, cited in J. F. Barnabé, "Les médias assassins au Burundi," p. 66.

31. *L'Eclaireur*, October 19, 1994, cited in J. C. Manirakiza, "L'ethnicisation de la presse au Burundi" (1997), p. 7.

32. Cited in Barnabé, "Les médias assassins au Burundi," p. 59.

33. *Le Témoin* no. 6 (September 1994), cited in J. F. Barnabé, "Les médias assassins au Burundi," p. 69.

34. In practice, journalists were not alone: many other members of the intellectual elite (academics, magistrates, medical practitioners, etc.) contributed to the radicalizing of political discourse.

35. On both sides, there was the fear of a "plot," a certainty that there was a "plan" involving the total extermination of members of the other group. As the UN's International Commission on Burundi stated in 1966 (S/1996/682): "The members of each of the 'ethnic' groups feel themselves collectively engaged in a fight to the death in order not to be exterminated or enslaved."

36. Marked by the Rwandan experience and wishing to put an end to this situation of impunity, in 1995 Reporters sans Frontières officially drew President Ntibantunganya's attention to abuses of *La Nation* and the *Carrefour des Idées*, asking him to suspend these two newspapers.

37. APPLE, *Guide de la presse burundaise, 1996* (Bujumbura: APPLE, 1996), p. 9.

38. S. Ndayishimiye, "La presse burundaise de la naissance à nos jours," communication dated November 22, 1997, to the Association pour la Défense et la Promotion de la Presse (Brussels), p. 10.

39. The decree "Concerning the Organization of the Burundi National Radio-Television," of April 11, 1989, defines the RTNB as "a public establishment of an administrative nature with its own legal status and independent management" (Article 1), but specifies that it is "placed under the administrative control of the Minister of Information. This control may be exercised by means of suspensive veto, approval, special authorization, cancellation or substitution" (Article 28).

40. Cited in Reporters sans Frontières, *Burundi: le choix de la censure* (Paris, August 2003), p. 21.

41. As Gérard Mfuranzima, the radio director, recognized. Cited in Reporters sans Frontières, *Burundi: le choix de la censure,* p. 24.

42. The director of the RTNB, Louis-Marie Nindorera, former adviser to President Buyoya, was sacked on September 25, 1993, for having tried to protect his journalists from the pressure applied by the government.

43. As the RTNB was mainly made up of partisans of UPRONA when FRODEBU came to power, Melchior Ndadaye declared to the journalists: "We have not come to power with Frodebu journalists, we do not have any. You are here, you are state employees. Do your work, but do not continue to work in the same way you did before. Do not consider yourself to be the beaten party's journalists. If you still see yourselves in that way, it will not work." Cited in Reporters sans Frontières, *Burundi: le choix de la censure,* p. 34.

44. Mzima, "L'état actuel de la presse au Burundi," p. 7.

45. The BANG (nongovernmental armed bands) and the BAG (government armed bands).

46. Mzima, "L'état actuel de la presse au Burundi," p. 7.

47. C. Braeckman, *Terreur africaine: Burundi, Rwanda, Zaïre—les racines de la violence* (Paris: Fayard, 1996), p. 152.

48. Committee to Protect Journalists, *Africa Report, 2001.*

49. Ligue Iteka (Ligue Burundaise des droits de l'homme), *Rapport 1999 sur les droits de l'homme,* Bujumbura, 1999.

50. Francis Rolt, former director of Studio Ijambo, insists that without the collaboration of the RTNB and the open-mindedness of its director at the time, Innocent Muhozi, Studio Ijambo would have never seen the light of day, because there would have been no space for its programs on the airwaves.

51. In 1999, six Studio Ijambo programs supplied to the RTNB were completely or partially censored. Censorship often consisted of removing the one-sided interventions of the opposition's representatives. Search for Common Ground strongly and rightly insisted that these programs were broadcast as they were in order to guarantee a balance. Since then, the proliferation of privately owned radio stations that are willing to broadcast Studio Ijambo's productions has led to reduced censorship by the RTNB.

52. International Crisis Group, "Burundi: les enjeux du débat," *Africa Report* no. 23 (July 12, 2000), p. 24.

53. Mzima, "L'état actuel de la presse au Burundi," p. 3.

54. See L. Slachmuijlder, "Media as a Tool for Dialogue and Reconciliation: The Experience of Search for Common Ground in the Great Lakes Region," unpublished, p. 2.

55. First installed in Brussels when it was created in 1996, Studio Tubane moved to Bujumbura in 2000.

56. There was also a third studio, Trans World Radio, a Protestant religious project.

57. Cited in A. Kaburahe, "Le Burundi entree 1990 et 2003: espoir et inquiétude," unpublished article, Brussels, 2004, p. 11.

58. F. Munezero, presentation at the Organisation des Médias d'Afrique Centrale Festival, Bujumbura, May 3–5, 2004.

59. Slachmuijlder, "Media as a Tool for Dialogue and Reconciliation," p. 3.

60. Committee to Protect Journalists, *Attacks Against the Press, 2003*, p. 11. The station's work in this area has not always been appreciated. A few months earlier, the CNC had condemned Radio Publique Africaine for "usurping the function of judicial authority." Cited in Institut Panos Paris, *Africentr @lemédias* no. 12 (June 2003).

61. Cited in A. Kaburahe, "Le Burundi entree 1990 et 2003: la démocratie impossible?" unpublished article, Brussels, 2004, p. 5.

62. Cited in Reporters sans Frontières, *Burundi: le choix de la censure,* p. 23.

63. J. P. Chrétien, "La résistible ascension de la haine au Burundi," in Reporters sans Frontières, *Burundi: le venin de l'intolérance,* pp. 4–5.

64. Braeckman, *Terreur africaine,* pp. 127–128.

65. Ibid., p. 163.

66. Cited in C. Ndikumana, "L'évolution récente des radios au Burundi" (Bujumbura: Institut Panos Paris, 2000), p. 3. One should note that the BBC and the VOA broadcast an hour-long program in Kirundi every day. When they aired these programs after the genocide of the Tutsi people in Rwanda, they were called by the Burundians "Calamity radios," because the broadcasts always brought bad news (see A. Kaburahe, *Burundi,* p. 16).

67. Data on the audience are not very reliable, rare, and often contradictory. The most recent can be found in a 2002 SFCG study, a 2003 research project commissioned by the City Hall of Bujumbura, and a 2003 survey conducted by Voice of America, whose figures do not correlate at all.

68. For an in-depth analysis of the 1992 law, see Reporters sans Frontières, *Burundi: le choix de la censure.*

69. Cited in Reporters sans Frontières, *Rapport annuel, 2002* (Paris).

70. The fines could be as large as 1 million Burundian francs (about US$1,000), and the prison sentences as long as five years, for cases of insulting or defaming the head of state or public personalities. The publishing director, the editor in chief, the editorial secretary, as well as the journalist who wrote the article, could all be charged.

71. This number was reduced to eleven by the 2003 press law.

72. For an analysis of the way communication regulatory bodies handle the question of political media content in Burundi, the DRC, and Rwanda, see M. S. Frère, "Après les médias de la haine: la régulation en RDC, au Burundi

et au Rwanda," in F. Reyntjens and S. Marysse (eds.), *L'Afrique des Grands Lacs, Annuaire 2005–2006* (Paris: L'Harmattan, 2006).

73. See http://www.burundi-info.com.

74. Mzima, "L'état actuel de la presse au Burundi," p. 5.

75. APPLE, *Guide de la presse burundaise, 1996*, p. 8.

76. Institut Panos Paris, *Africentr@lemédias* no. 13 (July 2003), p. 7.

77. Committee to Protect Journalists, *Attacks Against the Press, 2003*, p. 11.

78. Reporters sans Frontières, *Rapport annuel, 2003*, p. 2.

79. Bonesha FM's director of programs, Ali Bizimana, was killed on August 5, 2002, in a rebel ambush in the northern district of Bujumbura, but no one can determine if this act was linked to his professional activities.

80. APPLE, *Guide de la presse burundaise, 1996*, p. 9.

81. These examples were put forward by Burundian journalists during a workshop organized in January 2004 by the Institut Panos Paris, the SFCG, and the Agence de la Francophonie. See Institut Panos Paris, SFCG, and AIF, "Rapport de l'atelier de Bujumbura sur les médias et la construction de la paix" (Bujumbura, January 19–28, 2004).

82. See Institut Panos Paris, SFCG, and AIF, "Rapport de l'atelier de Bujumbura."

83. Cited in Reporters sans Frontières, "Burundi: le choix de la censure," August 1993, p. 28.

84. APPLE, *Guide de la presse burundaise, 1996*, p. 16.

85. In the 1970s and 1980s, some Burundian journalists were also trained in Kinshasa (at the IFASIC). See Chapter 3.

86. International Crisis Group, "Burundi: les enjeux du débat," *Africa Report* no. 23 (July 12, 2000), p. 26.

87. APPLE, *Guide de la presse burundaise, 1996*, p. 8.

88. Barnabé, "Les médias assassins au Burundi," p. 59.

89. Mzima, "L'état actuel de la presse au Burundi," p. 21.

90. A. Ntamikevyo, "Evolution de la presse au Burundi," unpublished paper (Bujumbura, 1996), p. 3.

91. The association was established by Innocent Muhozi, a journalist with the RTNB (who later became the director-general). It paid particular attention to the situation of journalists working in the public audiovisual service.

92. See Institut Panos Paris, *Africentr@lemédias* no. 22 (May 2004).

93. Barnabé, "Les médias assassins au Burundi," p. 58.

94. G. Mfuranzima, "Modes d'accès aux médias et la communication des différents acteurs de la société burundaise," Actes du Forum des États Généraux de la Communication, Bujumbura, December 13–15, 2001, pp. 27–28.

95. Slachmuijlder, "Media as a Tool for Dialogue and Reconciliation," p. 3.

96. APPLE had already pointed out this constraint in its *Guide de la presse burundaise, 1996*, p. 7.

97. This was demonstrated once again in 2004 when ONUB (Opération des Nations Unies au Burundi) established a studio aimed at producing radio programs. The studio hired all the best journalists from local radio stations, attracting them with higher salaries.

98. The radio station was created by the Association pour l'Action Humanitaire, a French NGO supported by the ECHO program (of the European Commission's Department of Humanitarian Aid).

99. UNESCO and the Institut Panos Paris have been particularly active in supporting the initiatives of the Maison de la Presse, but also those of CENAP and the OPB.

100. Reporters sans Frontières, *Burundi: le choix de la censure*, pp. 21–27.

101. Ligue Iteka, "Open Letter to the Leaders and Members of the Burundian Political Classes" (Bujumbura, 1999), p. 4.

102. Cited in Bailly, "Burundi, Studio Ijambo," p. 124.

103. E. Palmans, "Les médias audiovisuels au Burundi," in *Annuaire de L'Afrique des Grands Lacs*.

3

DEMOCRATIC REPUBLIC OF CONGO

Providing Information in a War-Torn Country

A GLOBAL, INCLUSIVE agreement on the management of political power in the Democratic Republic of Congo, signed on December 17, 2002, was the founding act of the country's peace process. It provided for the establishment of five transitional civic institutions, including the Haute Autorité des Médias (HAM), charged with organizing the media for elections. The establishment of HAM was tangible proof that, along with concerns for human rights during elections or practical matters related to organizing elections, the media could help determine the political future of the country. The stakes are significant in this vast territory, where everything has been bled dry and dismembered, and needs rebuilding, beginning with the civic conscience of a citizenry who have been living hand-to-mouth for years. In 2004, there were an estimated 231 publications in the country (most of them appearing irregularly), 126 radio stations, and 52 television channels.[1] These media can provide a valuable contribution to communicating political choices and mobilizing the population for peace and reconstruction.

Liberalizing the Media, Unleashing the Word

The recent history of the media in the DRC can be divided into four periods. The first, which preceded Joseph Désiré Mobutu's speech of October 20, 1990, was completely monotone. Apart from the Office Zaïrois de Radio Télévision (OZRT), there were a few privately owned publications, but their owners, in fact, were close to Mobutu, and wholly at the regime's service. In Kinshasa, the newspapers *Salongo* and *Elima,* created in 1972, passed on the government's propaganda,

41

DEMOCRATIC REPUBLIC OF CONGO

Size	2,344,860 sq. km.
Population	58 million
Capital	Kinshasa
Ethnic groups	250, including Luba, Mongo, Kongo, Lunda, Tchokwé, Téléla
Official language	French
Main local languages	Lingala, Swahili, Kikongo, Tshiluba
Human Development Index ranking (2005)	167 (out of 177 countries)
Life expectancy	45 years
Literacy rate	65.3 percent

Chronology

1885: The Territory of Congo, explored by Morton Stanley, is recognized as the personal property of King Leopold II of Belgium.

1908: The territory becomes the "Colony of Congo," under rule of the Belgian government.

June 1960: The Democratic Republic of Congo (DRC) becomes independent, with Patrice Lumumba as prime minister and Joseph Kasa-Vubu as president.

January 1961: Lumumba is assassinated.

November 1965: Colonel Joseph Désiré Mobutu, minister of defense, overthrows Kasa-Vubu and declares himself president.

1967: Mobutu establishes a single party, the Mouvement Populaire de la Révolution (MPR).

1971: Mobutu launches an "authenticity policy." The country is renamed "Zaire," and foreign companies, including mining enterprises, become state property.

October 1990: Mobutu, under international pressure, proclaims multipartyism and freedom of the press.

1991: Mutinies by soldiers in Kinshasa deteriorate into pillaging.

1992: A national conference is held, under the direction of Archbishop Laurent Monsengwo. Etienne Tshisekedi, leader of the Union pour la Démocratie et le Progrès Social (UDPS), the main opposition party, becomes prime minister.

1993: Tshisekedi leaves the government.

1994: Nearly 2 million Rwandan Hutu cross the Zairian border. Huge camps are established for these refugees, including Interahamwe militias and former members of the Rwandan Armed Forces (RAF) responsible for the genocide.

(continues)

1996: Laurent-Désiré Kabila leads a rebellion supported by the Rwandan government. The Rwandan Patriotic Army (RPA) dismantles refugee camps, and tens of thousands of refugees as well as Zairian civilians die in the east of Zaire.

May 1997: The Alliance des Forces Démocratiques de Libération du Congo (AFDL) reaches Kinshasa with military support from Rwanda, Uganda, and Angola. Mobutu flees Zaire, and the name of the country is changed back to "Democratic Republic of Congo."

July 1998: A new rebellion breaks out in the east, with Rwandan and Ugandan support. Kabila's regime is backed by Angola, Zimbabwe, and Namibia.

1999: The front line is stabilized. The country is divided into three parts: one under the rule of Kabila's government, one under the Rassemblement Congolais pour la Démocratie (RCD) and backed by Rwanda, and one under the Mouvement de Libération du Congo (MLC) and backed by Uganda.

July 1999: A cease-fire is signed in Lusaka. The United Nations Mission in the Democratic Republic of Congo (MONUC) is implemented. The cease-fire is not respected.

January 2001: Laurent-Désiré Kabila is assassinated. His son, Joseph Kabila, becomes president.

October 2001: Peace talks, known as the Dialogue Inter-Congolais (DIC), start in Addis Ababa.

February 2002: Peace talks continue in Sun City, South Africa.

July 2002: The DRC and Rwanda sign a peace agreement in Pretoria. The Rwandese army (now called Rwandan Defense Forces [RDF]) withdraws.

September 2002: The DRC and Uganda sign a peace agreement. Angolan and Zimbabwean troops also withdraw.

December 2002: A global, inclusive agreement is adopted in Pretoria by all participants of the peace talks (government, rebel groups, opposition political parties, civil society, Mai Mai militia).

April 2003: A transitional constitution is adopted, and transition institutions are established.

December 2005: The new constitution of the Third Republic is adopted through referendum.

April 2006: Elections for the presidency and legislature are approved, with 32 candidates for the former and 8,000 for the latter.

July 2006: First round of presidential elections. Joseph Kabila receives 44.81 percent of the votes, and Jean-Pierre Bemba is second with 20.03 percent.

October 2006: Joseph Kabila is elected president with 58.05 percent of the votes.

and a single newspaper was authorized in each province: *Jua* in Bukavu, *Mjumbe* in Lubumbashi, and *Boyoma* in Kisangani. The Catholic Church also had its own written media, but kept its distance from political questions. A few other privately owned initiatives were theoretically authorized, but the publications never appeared regularly.[2] Even if some titles took the risk of denouncing the country's economic and political situation, "the journalists had to take care that their criticisms avoided explicitly or implicitly, directly, or indirectly, implicating the head of state."[3]

During the second period, from 1990 onward, the liberalization of political life led to the appearance of a multitude of new titles; the former progovernment papers switched over to the opposition en masse. A year later, more than 120 papers were created,[4] and the National Conference period saw the startup of some 200 additional titles. These publications had two main characteristics. On the one hand, they dealt mainly in denunciations, aiming to expose "the scandals and collusions of the Second Republic."[5] Most of the press constantly attacked, with great virulence, all the organs of government, including the president. On the other hand, these papers appeared in the wake of certain politicians, at a time when parties were developing exponentially and the major figures who were supposed to represent an alternative to Mobutu (Etienne Tshisekedi, Nguza Karl I Bond) were jockeying for position.

From 1990 to 1995, 638 press titles were authorized to appear, and more than 400 political parties were formed. The papers can easily be classed as being partisans of the "radical opposition" (*Le Potentiel, Le Phare, Elima, Umoja, La Référence Plus*) and as being close to the "presidential sphere of influence" (*Le Soft de Finance, Salongo, L'Avenir*). The opposition did not hesitate to criticize the behavior of those who were expected to have leading roles in the long-awaited change.[6] Nevertheless, in spite of authorizing the frenetic pluralism, the government resisted real freedom of the press and journalists remained subject to threats and violence, since Mobutu always tried to take back with one hand what he had just given with the other.

Starting in 1992, the number of privately owned radio stations increased in the provinces, including Radio Maendeleo[7] in Bukavu (1993), Radio Zénith in Lubumbashi (1994), and Radio Amani in Kisangani (1995). In Kinshasa, most of the new radio stations that appeared were religious. Along with their two precursors, Radio Elikya (created in 1995 in Kinshasa by the Catholic Church) and Radio Sango Malamu (Protestant), the evangelical and messianic radio stations proliferated, including Radio Télévision Puissance, Radio Télévision Message de Vie, and Radio Télévision Armée de l'Eternel.

They jostled with privately owned commercial radio stations, such as Raga FM, Radio Télévision Kin-Malebo (RTKM), and the Malebo Broadcast Channel (MBC), and community radio stations, such as Réveil FM. In the provinces, where periodicals are nonexistent or appear irregularly, radio is still the most suitable medium, and a large number of private initiatives have developed in all the provinces.

Private television stations were quickly set up in Kinshasa. A businessman created Antenne A in 1991, then Canal Kin and Canal Z (the latter of which became Canal Kin 2) led the way for many privately owned commercial stations, such as Raga TV, Télé Kin Malébo, Tropicana TV, and the Channel Media Broadcasting (CMB), and religious stations, such as Télévision Sango Malamu, Amen Télévision, Radio Télévision Sentinelle, and Radio Télé Kintuadi. The television stations were often offshoots of radio stations, with which they shared personnel and infrastructures.

In this feverish climate, the media often paid scant respect to professional ethics and lapsed into many abuses. In August 1994 the minister of press and information, Massegabio Zansu, reproached journalists for transgressing "professional rules by writing, printing and distributing lies that could endanger peace, national harmony and public security."[8]

The third period began with Laurent-Désiré Kabila's seizure of power in May 1997, after which political parties' activities were suspended, depriving the press of its usual subject matter and sources of finance. The government was extremely suspicious of journalists and very hard on them. Many were intimidated, subjected to violence, arrested, and imprisoned; between May 1997 and January 2001, more than 160 journalists were jailed.[9]

Journalists' working conditions became more precarious when the war broke out in 1998. Since the price of raw materials had increased, the impoverished population had even less money than before for buying newspapers, and distribution in the occupied areas was impossible. Journalists in the west of the country, who were already politicized and susceptible to corruption because of their extreme poverty, indulged in virulent propaganda against the Rwandan "enemy" and encouraged "Tutsi hunting" in the areas controlled by President Kabila's government. In the east, journalists were subjected to violence by the various military forces, who wanted to use the local media for their own purposes. The audiovisual media were subjected to heavy pressure, both in the areas controlled by the government and in the areas controlled by the rebel movements. The government's nearly total control over information meant that journalists had no choice but to hazard guesses about national events, or to look to the international media for information on what was happening.

President Joseph Kabila, who succeeded his father, Laurent-Désiré, after the latter's assassination in January 2001, was easier on the press. His government adopted a few symbolic measures that gave the media more latitude. In February 2002, in agreement with Azarias Ruberwa's Rassemblement Congolais pour la Démocratie (RCD) and Jean-Pierre Bemba's Mouvement de Libération du Congo (MLC), Kabila authorized the installation of Radio Okapi. Working under the authority of the United Nations Mission in the Democratic Republic of Congo (MONUC), this "humanitarian" radio station gradually extended its production and broadcasting network to the whole of the territory. The peace process and withdrawal of Rwandan and Ugandan troops also eased the pressure on the media in the east of the country, and opened a fourth period for Congolese media.

In Kinshasa, a handful of dailies—*Le Potentiel, L'Observateur, Le Phare, La Référence Plus, Le Palmarès, L'Avenir, La Tempête des Tropiques,* and *Uhuru*—now appear regularly, representing the embryo of a business that survives with difficulty. Their contents are often highly politicized and of uncertain professional quality, in both form and substance. There are a few periodicals; those that stand out are *The Post,* for the quality of its layout; *Le Révélateur,* for the quality of its journalism; and *Le Manager Grognon,* for its caricatures.

The papers rarely have print runs of more than 1,000 copies,[10] and some do not exceed 300. The provincial press is mainly weekly and often irregular. It has immense problems obtaining raw materials and printing. Papers in neighboring provinces, for example, are printed in Kinshasa,[11] and papers in the east of the country are printed in Kampala.[12] They also suffer from an extreme lack of qualified personnel. The private radio and television stations survive with difficulty. They lack equipment and financial resources, and their staff are untrained, which means that their programs are generally poor.

The fourth period is marked by an obvious willingness among media professionals to overcome their political and personal differences and become better organized in order to help reconstruct their devastated country. In March 2004 they held the National Congolese Press Congress, described as a "reform" meeting, where new and more representative professional organizations were created, with the aim of fully engaging journalists in the transition process. While it is true that the country needs to be completely rebuilt, the same can be said for the

Congolese media, which need to restore (or establish) their credibility and professionalism. They also need to gain the public's confidence, the authorities' respect, and the esteem of their colleagues. The war in the DRC went past the battlefield; the media sector was torn apart by the conflicts and recurrent violence.

The Media During War: From Propaganda to Resistance

Giving a complete, precise, and balanced report on the evolution of the entire Congolese press since the beginning of the war in 1996 is an impossible task. In reality, the vastness of the country, the diversity of local situations, the multiplicity of media players, and the various developments in national and regional events generated extremely varied reactions from journalists, all the more so because some media had fluctuating editorial policies. The Kinshasa press's method of relaying anti-Tutsi propaganda; the seizure of Kivu radio stations by political players who invaded the studios, weapons in hand, and ordered their press releases to be read; and the positive reporting by the Katangan regional media when "local boy" Kabila took power: all these events require explanation and need to be seen in a specific context.

Politicized Media Playing on the Ethnic Theme

The new privately owned papers appeared in the effervescent period of political liberalization at the start of the 1990s and quickly became polarized between, on the one hand, newspapers in the "presidential sphere of influence," often linked to one of the many parties created by Marshal Mobutu's followers, and on the other hand, publications close to the "radical opposition." The latter, by far the most numerous, constituted a "denunciation" press, mainly guided by the wish to emphasize the government's failings. They also reported the positions and declarations of politicians who were trying to set themselves up in opposition to Mobutu, and who all had the same critical discourse. The papers battled each other through press releases that generally did not dispute the facts, but attributed responsibility for the country's catastrophic situation to the opposing party.[13] As they were progressively confronted with problems of financial survival, the papers became more dependent on political support, because, as a journalist remarked in 1996, "Only the politicians have the means to support the press. If we are neutral, we don't get any money and we die."[14]

In 1990, certain Congolese media had already demonstrated that this political subservience could lead to distorted information and hate-filled discourses as instruments of division. When students were massacred on the campus of the University of Lubumbashi in May 1990, the *Voix du Zaïre* (of the OZRT) played a significant role in dissimulating the extent of the killing, and relayed only partial information. A dispatch by Agence Zaïroise de Presse (AZAP) gave the official version and mentioned "a fight between students . . . for tribal causes."[15] This version, brandishing the threat of a repeat of the tribal wars that killed thousands at the start of independence and that had allowed Mobutu to claim his position as the guarantor of national unity, was essential in a state split among 250 different communities.[16] The opposition press, which had long been silent, due no doubt to lack of access to information,[17] later took pains to disprove the official version in order to demonstrate the eminently political nature of the events on the campus.

The following year, in 1991, ethnic feelings were once again manipulated during the violent and murderous expulsion of the Kasaian population from Katanga.[18] The Katangan outstation of the national television channel, and the local papers that supported the government (*Le Lushois, Le Libérateur-Ujamaa*),[19] carried messages filled with hate and xenophobia, inciting the people to expel their countrymen from the neighboring province.

Ujamaa, a paper in Lubumbashi, ran the headlines "The Kasaians must leave" and "These dogs without collars."[20] *La Cheminée* went one better in August 1992: "They are thieves, liars, sorcerers, braggarts, flatterers, profiteers. . . . They live in total and primitive promiscuity in very large families and share their house with sheep, chickens and dogs in insupportable hygienic conditions, they make too much noise because of their big mouths."[21] And the papers denounced "the Kasaian hegemony," which was "politically protected by the second Republic."[22] Two years later, after several hundred thousand Kasaians had fled to their home province, *Le Libérateur-Ujamaa* exclaimed triumphantly in December 1994: "Where is the Katangan who regrets having regained control of his living space? There's nothing better than being master in your own home."[23]

For its part, the opposition press in Kinshasa tried to report on the dramatic situation of the Kasaians in Shaba, but was then accused of being controlled by the Baluba and supporting Etienne Tshisekedi. Administrative and political measures were taken to prohibit the transport, distribution, and sale of Kinshasa periodicals in Shaba.[24] Meanwhile, Télézaïre, the national television station, contented itself throughout the crisis by asserting that "everywhere in the country is calm."[25]

Analyses of conflict in ethnic terms are common in unstable situations where those with political ambitions seek to mobilize the population and provoke violence. At the start of the war in Kivu, in 1996, the Congolese press initially presented the conflict as ethnically based. Then the hypothesis of foreign manipulation involving Rwanda became widespread. Later, perhaps following the foreign press's highlighting of Kabila,[26] the opposition press began to note that a possible alternative to Mobutu was emerging. The splits in the media reappeared in force. Those who favored the rebellion because they favored change were initially accused of being "collaborators" by the official, pro-Mobutu media. Others declared it a foreign occupation, identifying the Banyamulenge with Rwanda, and described it as Balkanization involving massive deportations and massacres of the Congolese population of Kivu. Presented as external aggression, the Kivu war was used to reinforce Congolese nationalism in the service of a moribund government.

As soon as Laurent-Désiré Kabila took power, the government media and certain private pro-Mobutu papers (*L'Avenir, Le Forum des As, La Cité Africaine,* and later *Le Palmarès*) declared their allegiance to the Alliance des Forces Démocratiques de Libération du Congo (AFDL). The opposition papers quickly resumed their distance from the new regime. The demarcation between the government press and the opposition press was again clearly drawn. It was then reinforced by the "Casprom" affair, a dispute over a donation of US$1 million made by the head of state to the private press in July 1998. Its selective distribution methods deeply divided media professionals.[27] The papers that refused to take this money (*Le Potentiel, Le Phare*) clearly thought that the others had been bought by Kabila, citing as proof subsequent modifications in editorial lines.

In the provinces, the media were confronted with the continuing violence in the east, while triumphant regionalist noises were being made in Katanga. Local papers (*Mukuba, Expansion Lubilanji*) rejoiced that their time had come after the former supremacy of the Ngbandi political players from Equateur and the Baluba players from Kasai. "Today, whether people like it or not," wrote a paper in May 1998, "power resides in Katanga because a local boy is in charge of the country's fate."[28]

The second war, which broke out in August 1998, involved a diverse range of movements and fronts, including the officially recognized presence of several foreign armies, sometimes rivals, on Congolese territory. This led to corresponding divisions in the press, with each media outlet putting itself at the service of one or sometimes more armed groups, when financial opportunities arose. Some Congolese papers clearly flaunted their "permanent ideological versatility," changing their editorial lines to suit the positions of the political families that courted them.[29]

Once again, the conflict gave rise to ethnic tensions. Already, at the start of 1998, *La Voix du Patriote,* a radio station in the east controlled by the Mai Mai, had broadcast appeals to hatred and preached the elimination of the "Tutsi." Violence against the Banyamulenge followed, inciting local populations to repel "the visitors" and help the "Bahutu brothers to reconquer Burundi and Rwanda." President Kabila, on a visit to Bukavu, tried to reassure the Congolese Tutsi and condemned that "much vaunted radio station that makes so much noise."[30] But after Rwanda joined the war, on August 2, 1998, President Kabila in turn called for the "murder of the Tutsi" on the Radio Télévision Nationale du Congo (RTNC),[31] leading to a wave of arbitrary arrests, violence against individuals from the east of the country, and even summary executions of people whose features were similar to those "Rwandans." Some Kinshasa media encouraged the hunting down of "infiltrators"—that is, anyone with "Nilotic" looks.[32] Following the attack by rebels in the Kinshasa suburbs a few weeks later, the director of Kabila's private office, Abdoulaye Yerodia Ndombasi,[33] called for the "eradication of the vermin," encouraging the capital's population to take part in a manhunt to eliminate members of that "race with pretensions to hegemony."[34]

Many Congolese media that disseminated these words claimed they were just doing their job of informing the population of the government's position. It is a difficult balance, and raises the question of the media going too far by offering a platform to politicians. As Donat M'Baya Tshimanga, president of Journalistes en Danger (JED), remarked, "The media, possibly without knowing it, are playing with fire when they give a platform to warlords who use the latent rivalries between different ethnic groups for their own purposes."[35] Again, in August 2003, *L'Avenir* raised the alarm, this time against Rwandan women invading the streets of Kinshasa as spies in the pay of the enemy.[36]

Media Passing on Rumors

The Congolese media not only relay the politicians' passionate and bellicose messages, but also regularly transmit information that has not been checked or has been obtained from doubtful sources. A remark by one of Joseph Kabila's ministers of information, Kikaya bin Karubi, on World Press Freedom Day (May 3, 2001), that "the Congolese journalist's ethics are sorely tried by the daily handling of information that is constantly distorted, unchecked or even deliberately false," cannot be rejected out of hand. He also noted that some papers were mainly used as "platforms for storytelling or settling accounts."[37]

The journalists retorted that the government's habit of withholding information, and the impossibility of traveling to the conflict zones, obviously prevented them from obtaining firsthand information. For instance, the president of the JED noted that when the conflict between the Hema and the Lendu, two ethnic groups in Ituri, broke out, "No Congolese paper sent a reporter to the area. The information published came from two main sources: the foreign media [RFI and VOA] and the declarations of different protagonists." Only Radio Okapi and the BBC immediately dispatched correspondents to the scene. And, continued Donat M'Baya, "In that part of the country, the radio stations are controlled by the warlords with all the consequences that implies in terms of journalistic independence."[38]

The withholding of information is always a common practice in periods of conflict and tension, but President Laurent-Désiré Kabila made it a principle of government.[39] In February 2002 the Congolese government banned the papers it considered antigovernment from covering the peace work of the Dialogue Inter-Congolais (DIC) in Sun City. The definitive list of accredited journalists for the Kinshasa region was drawn up by the presidential press department.[40] The satirical papers (*Le Manager Grognon, Pot Pourri*) were among those excluded.[41]

Journalists were also subjected to so much pressure that they became paralyzed with fear. As a JED report pointed out, "The Congolese press, which could have been a first-hand witness, was totally absent from the scene of war. It was contented with official press releases or second-hand information. It's true that the Congolese press does not have sufficient resources to get to the scene of operations but, above all, it has become fearful. It is banned from seeing what is happening and even from talking about it, often to the country's detriment. This is true in both the East and the West. When it dares to say something, it is accused of "'demoralising the fighters and the population' and of 'being in league with the enemy'— in short, of 'treason.'"[42] The director of Radio Télévision Matadi was accused of "collaborating" with the enemy for simply commenting on the air about the rebel forces' declarations that the town had been taken, and spent fourteen months in prison.

The number of taboo subjects in the DRC multiplied at the start of the war: the corruption of members of the government (on both sides of the front line), foreign support for the different fighting forces, and soon after, the reshaping of alliances within the transitional government, were all subjects better avoided.[43] In October 2002, in Uvira, *Le Messager du Peuple* was subjected to threats and intimidation after publishing an article on the supposed diversion of funds by the territory's administrator.

The paper's editor in chief was forced to take refuge in Bujumbura for having declared on the airwaves of an international radio station that Rwandan soldiers were actually present beside the RCD-Goma forces in the attack that retook the town of Uvira.

Reporting statements by Etienne Tshisekedi, the symbolic leader of the Union pour la Démocratie et le Progrès Social (UDPS), the opposition party, as well as covering his movements, could also be risky. In 2002 the local representative of the security service ANR prohibited three media outlets working in Tshisekedi's province (Radio Fraternité Buena Muntu, Radio Télévision Debout Kasaï, and Radio Inter Viens et Vois) from reporting on him in any way.

Giving airtime to anyone critical of the authorities could be dangerous. In April 2000, Raga TV and the RTKM gave Ambassador Kyungu wa Kumwanza, an associate of Laurent-Désiré Kabila, a chance to speak. He questioned the government's competence and credibility; the managers of these two channels were immediately called in for questioning and forbidden to leave the country.

The withholding of information, the difficulty of accessing conflict areas, fear, and the persistence of taboo subjects are major obstacles to collecting information, and make it impossible for journalists to check and sift through rumors.

Courageous Journalists Who Tried to Resist

Though some media were politically subservient or tended toward sensationalism and rumors, there were also courageous journalists who carried out acts of bravery in this war-ravaged scene. Despite all the obstacles, they tried to fulfill their duty to inform their countrymen as fully as possible.

In the east of the country, information even became an "outpost of resistance."[44] It circulated freely and abundantly within the provinces and toward the exterior. The violence to which the population fell victim was known to the whole world in a few hours, thanks to the Internet and mobile phones. Some community radio stations, like Radio Maendeleo in Sud-Kivu, tried to regularly report on the suffering of civilian populations caused by the war; it also gave them an opportunity to express themselves and make their voices heard. Because they took care to denounce the violations of human rights perpetrated in their sight, far from the capital, these radio stations were often harassed by the fighting forces who were carrying out the abuses. The director of Radio Maendeleo, Kizito Mushizi, bore witness: "Since the state decayed under Mobutu and the armed barbarism that has followed his departure, we have often been faced with difficult choices between self-censure and the survival of communities. The second choice has often prevailed."[45]

In a situation where there was no longer any justice or responsible government, people turned to the media to explain their problems, to denounce the intolerable situation in which they found themselves, and to attempt to obtain reparations. Thus the radio stations in the east broadcast testimonies of women who had been systematically raped in the villages, of people who had been tortured by soldiers and armed bands, and of peasants who had been subjected to arbitrary taxes imposed by authorities in need of money. In 2000 the newspaper *Les Coulisses,* published in Goma, criticized the confiscation by the RCD of land belonging to Congolese citizens, and denounced the occupying power's project of circulating its own currency in the areas under its control. The paper's editor, Nicaise Kibel'bel Oka, was threatened and subjected to violent attacks and arbitrary arrests on several occasions, and finally had to flee the town for Beni, after being blacklisted for language that did not conform to the spirit of the new authorities.

The media also played an important role in maintaining the idea of a unified Congolese territory and Congolese nation. As a well-known observer of the Congolese political scene commented, "It is remarkable that, in spite of all the attempts made and the centrifugal forces deployed, the idea of balkanization of their country has never taken root in the minds of the Congolese people."[46] Even certain religious radio stations, whose ways of exerting influence are not immune from criticism, took part in this struggle. Thus in 2003, Radio Télévision Message de Vie, owned by popular preacher Fernando Kutino, launched a political campaign on its airwaves titled "Save the Congo." It invited the Congolese population to become involved in the future of their country. The authorities were unhappy with the underlying criticisms of Joseph Kabila's government that were apparent in these programs. The police raided the radio station's premises and Pastor Kutino went into exile.

Radio Okapi, launched in February 2002, also played an essential role in maintaining national cohesion and a sense of community among geographically and ideologically divided peoples. This radio station was founded within the framework of MONUC and overseen by the Swiss Hirondelle Foundation, specialized in establishing "humanitarian" radio stations in countries in crisis.[47] Because it made a point of being present throughout the country and allowing all the protagonists in the conflict to speak, Radio Okapi was able to transmit nonpartisan information in an extremely tense situation involving an increasing appetite for information.

With ten local transmitters installed in each province, and thanks to an extension of the satellite telephone network, Radio Okapi had a national coverage that no other radio station could provide. The station tried to build bridges between the various communities and offered a platform for their various positions via a few flagship programs, such as the famous on-air magazine *Dialogue Between Congolese*.[48] These strategies allowed the Congolese to take back ownership of information about their own country. Today, Radio Okapi seems to have an increasing audience, though no comprehensive statistics are available.

However, for some Congolese observers, Radio Okapi also gave undue prominence to personalities who were involved in the conflict but who did not really represent anyone and had no legitimacy. They were allowed to speak in the name of interests that they claimed to defend. For example, Radio Okapi was said to be used by "warring parties for political marketing,"[49] a point of view demonstrating that, during a time of conflict, allowing all parties to speak is both a political and a professional act.

Control of the Public Media

The Congolese public media have a long tradition of "praise singing" and propaganda. For many years, there was direct censorship by the Ministry of Information and the Press, which had to be informed of the entire content of a program before it could be broadcast.

Liberalization of the media sector led to no real changes in the state media. Subsequently, the war meant that the RTNC came under total military control. The crisis in the audiovisual public media was glaringly obvious in Kinshasa and provincial stations, where obsolete equipment, poorly motivated, underpaid personnel, and technical difficulties interfered with broadcasts. The RTNC's systematic adoption of the government's position, not to mention its role as a propagandist during a period of conflict, lost it a large part of its audience, especially in the provinces, where its signal was often interrupted because the station could not cover retransmission costs charged by its satellite operator.

The arrival of Laurent-Désiré Kabila and the return of Dominique Sakombi Inongo, the former Mobutu propagandist, as minister of information, brought the personality cult back in full force to the airwaves of the audiovisual public media. In place of Mobutu's effigy descending from the clouds like a demigod, a portrait of Laurent-Désiré Kabila imprinted on a star-spangled banner invaded the small screen several times every day. Joseph Kabila, who has replaced Minister Sakombi, has been more discreet.

In the east, the rebellion also took total control of the RTNC's installations and staff from the very start of the war. In fact, the war had been "declared" in the traditional manner, by means of radio. On August 3,

1998, a "military commander" announced over the RTNC-Bukavu's air-waves that Sud-Kivu was "separating itself from Kabila's regime"; later in the day, the radio denounced "Kabila's incompetence, corruption and nepotism," and then declared that "the province was now autonomous."[50]

During the five years of occupation, the RTNC-Bukavu journalists became "simple propagandists, nothing more than mouthpieces who broadcast their master's voice all day long . . . praise singers, fanatics whose only freedom is to sing of the wonders—half-hearted at the start—of the one who controls them and does not even pay for services rendered,"[51] because, like all other civil servants, the journalists in the occupied provinces had not been paid since 1996. The rebel authorities exercised total control over the radio station's programs and personnel, dismissing the director of RTNC-Bukavu every six months. The local office of Agence Congolaise de Presse (ACP) was also taken over by the RCD's apparatchiks and forced to publish a bulletin praising the local authorities at Goma. The situation was the same in Kisangani, where the RTNC's local transmitter was used by the RCD. In August 2003, when the RTNC-Kisangani decided to cut the former rebel move-ment's propaganda programs from its schedule, now that it was a member of the transitional government, the public media coordinator in the territories under RCD control threatened and then suspended the station managers for "gross insubordination."

Influential International Media

The Congolese pay great attention to how they are seen by the interna-tional media. Didier Mumengi, Laurent-Désiré Kabila's first minister of information, prohibited the retransmission of radio or television news pro-grams from foreign channels by the private audiovisual media (as had been done under Mobutu's regime). The following were affected by this meas-ure: Radio Elikya (which retransmitted the Radio Vatican news programs), Raga FM (which retransmitted news from the VOA and the BBC), along with the RTKM (which retransmitted the RFI) and television station Antenne A (which rebroadcast France 2). The foreign radio stations were obliged to negotiate and install their own FM relays.[52]

Many Congolese think that the international media contributed to highlighting the personality of Laurent-Désiré Kabila at the start of the rebellion in 1996, and convincing the hope-starved population that he would be a credible alternative for the country. When he came to power, the "Mzee" ("wise old man" in Kiswahili) at first benefited from a de-gree of international popularity, especially with the Anglo-Saxon media, which indirectly led to enthusiasm among potential investors and funding agencies. But this success was short-lived. The Belgian press, which is influential in the Congolese political circles and with Congolese leadership—if only because the Kinshasa press often copies its articles or editorials—was either suspicious from the start (*La Libre Belgique*) or, after a period of enthusiasm, increasingly doubtful about the new leader and his circle (*Le Soir*).[53] The French media did not hide their lack of enthusiasm for someone who took such clear-cut positions in order to separate himself from the French-speaking world. Gradually, President Kabila became increasingly bitter with the outside world and ended up attacking the foreign press. In April 1998, Radio Amani of the archbishopric of Kisangani was closed by government order for having retransmitted the spoken news programs of the RFI and the BBC.

The foreign media are perhaps more feared now because the war increased the Congolese public's interest in international news. As Journalistes en Danger noted, in 1999, "Readers are returning in force with enthusiasm to the trans-African media, such as *Jeune Afrique,* and the Western press, particularly Belgian and French. Yet these media, which cost up to five times as much as our papers, had practically disappeared after the political opening on April 24, 1990, and during the long period of the National Sovereign Conference."[54]

This development has resulted in heavy pressure on local correspondents of international media. Kin Kiey Mulumba, former editor of *Le Soft,* who became the head of the RCD's Department of Information,[55] constantly monitored correspondents from the BBC and the VOA, making threats and reproaches after broadcasts on sensitive topics or even prohibiting the coverage of certain events, such as the general strikes that paralyzed Goma in 2000.

In June 2000, Caroline Pare, a BBC producer, and her Congolese assistant, were arrested while searching for documents on the assassination of Patrice Lumumba in 1961. Pare was expelled. In July 2002, another BBC journalist, Arnaud Zajtman, was refused permission to report from the east of the country by the RCD-Goma, which criticized the channel for noting the rebel movement's responsibility for the deaths of 200 people during the clashes at Kisangani in May.[56]

Freedom of the Press: Excessive and Threatened

An Open Regulatory and Institutional Framework

For a long time, the DRC media were governed by Decree 70/057, of October 28, 1970, and Decree 81/011, of April 2, 1981 (the latter modified the former), concerning freedom of the press in the Republic of Zaire. The latter text specified that the Congolese journalist was, above all, "an MPR [Mouvement Populaire de la Révolution] militant, responsible for spreading the party's ideals."

This ruling, which only covered the written press, had become obsolete with the liberalization of the sector. The National Conference then issued a series of recommendations aimed at reforming the texts and redefining the communication principles and structures to conform with the requirements of a democratic society. The National Conference's Information, Press, and Audiovisual Commission had, among other things, denounced the government's prohibition of freedom of expression, use of censorship, withholding of information entitled to the public, lying and falsification of the truth, and distortion, manipulation, and partiality.[57]

In 1995 the États Généraux de la Communication (Communications Convention) revised these texts.[58] The result was Law 96-002, of June 22, 1996, which applied to the entire media sector. In Article 8, the law stipulated that "Everyone has the right to freedom of opinion and expression. By 'freedom of expression,' this law means the right to inform, to be informed, to have opinions and feelings, and to communicate them without hindrance, whatever the medium used, on condition that the law, public order, other people's rights, and accepted standards of behavior are respected."

The 1996 law was very liberal. It ended the state monopoly over the information sector, which still existed on paper (if not in reality); it also proclaimed the neutrality of the public media, and officially instituted a declaration system rather than one of prior authorization.[59] However, it did not address the status of journalists, which was still governed by the decree of 1981, now obsolete because it had been drawn up in a context where pluralism and private initiatives did not exist.

Though it had already been established, the regulatory framework for the press has been inoperative since it was adopted, because of a flagrant disparity between the 1996 text and its application. A report by Roberto Garreton, a UN special reporter on human rights in the DRC, made public on February 1, 2001, clearly stated that "freedom of expression does not exist in the Democratic Republic of Congo and the Congolese people do not enjoy the right to information. . . . In those territories under government control, journalists are constantly harassed." In the east, "there are no opposition papers and the rare independent radio stations have been suspended, censored and stopped from broadcasting any other news than the official news."[60] Therefore, the very liberal 1996 law oversees a sector characterized by the breakdown of law and order and arbitrariness.

Attacks on Freedom of the Press

From the very start of liberalization of the media, in a context in which the Mobutu government was strongly resistant to real democratization, press enterprises were subjected to much violence: presses were bombed,[61] some editions were seized and burned,[62] and papers were suspended and banned, not to mention frequent kidnappings, imprisonments, and assassinations of journalists. In 1991 the printing shop of *Elima,* a private daily that had switched its support in favor of the opposition, was burned down, and the offices of *Umoja,* which had also become antiauthority, were ransacked. In 1994, Pierre Kabeya, a journalist for *Kin-Matin,* was kidnapped, tortured, and killed for his coverage of the trial of members of the commando squad involved in the massacre of students at Lubumbashi. Adolphe Kavula, editor in chief of *Nsemo,* died from the wounds he suffered during a kidnapping by another commando unit after he denounced the army's involvement in trafficking banknotes.[63]

Pressure was also applied in more indirect ways, by threatening directors of media companies in order to coerce them into firing journalists, or by indirectly intervening in their private lives. "When you upset the leaders," a journalist recounted in 1996, "they're not going to arrest you and throw you into prison. They're going to ask themselves, 'Where does that man work? Where does he live? How does he make a living?' It is on those levels that they will try and undermine you."[64] Because of this tactic, a number of journalists lost their nonjournalism jobs or were thrown out of their lodgings.

Under Laurent-Désiré Kabila's regime, journalists were subject to even harsher repression. Straightaway the new government denounced the "abusive use of the freedom of expression." According to the African Media Institute (AMI),[65] "Since 1999, journalists have become the main target of attack directed against public freedom by the security services."[66] Forty-three journalists were held for questioning, incarcerated, or detained in 1998, fifty-three in 1999, and forty-two in 2000. The first journalist imprisoned was Polydor Muboyayi Mubanga, one of the most prominent figures of the Congolese press and editor of the daily *Le Phare,* for having written about the formation of a Praetorian guard around the AFDL based on ethnic affiliation, similar to Mobutu's infamous Division Spéciale Présidentielle (DSP). Muboyayi was beaten and locked in solitary confinement for three months. The assistant editor in chief, Tshivis Tshivuadi, was forced into internal exile for six months. Freddy Loseke, editor of the newspaper *La Libre Afrique,* well-known for the liberties he took with the professional codes of practice, was the journalist most frequently imprisoned, often under appalling conditions, during this period.[67]

The outbreak of the second war, which led to the de facto partition of the country, caused an increase in repression at a time when journalists' work was hindered by more obstacles than ever before. Radio Maendeleo, in Bukavu, was closed by the rebels several times, first from October 1996 to April 1997, then from July 1999 to August 2001, and finally from December 2002 to July 2003.[68] In 1996, in the space of a few hours, the station lost two of its collaborators, who were killed in town, and it ceased transmitting. The second time, in 1999, it was closed after having covered a meeting where representatives of the rebellion were booed by the public. An adviser to the rebellion justified the closure by saying, "There is no democracy during war. You have not helped our movement to become accepted, we are going to suspend you for not respecting the terms and conditions."[69] The third time, in December 2002, the RCD spokesman, Lola Kisanga, canceled the radio station's operating license and announced its definitive closure, accusing it of "meddling in politics instead of sticking to its mission of popularising development messages." Two days earlier, the station had broadcast a program on residents' complaints about the RCD's introduction of new registration plates for vehicles, symbolizing the country's partition.[70]

In the context of war and anarchy, the Congolese media have been subject to violence, attacks, and repression from an increasingly diverse range of perpetrators, and the victims have not always been journalists. The perpetrators of violence against media professionals are not limited to the supposedly competent public authorities. In a country where judicial power has decayed, "anyone who has a little bit of power—political, administrative, economic or military—thinks they have the right to mete out justice. Friends or family members in the police, army, security services or even the judiciary are all called on to contribute to hunting down the 'undesirable' media or journalist."[71]

The Agence Nationale de Renseignement (ANR) was one of the first organizations involved in the repression of media professionals. For example, in 2001 it called in for questioning and then locked up Frédéric Kitengie, a correspondent of the sports editorial staff of the RFI, who was stationed in Johannesburg but reporting from Kinshasa.[72] The ANR is supposed to be a public service, but some of its agents seem more preoccupied with settling the private affairs of certain public figures.[73] In Kasai, after Radio Télévision Lumière (RTL), a religious channel, had broadcast a program criticizing the mercenary behavior of a pastor, one of the members of the church, who was also a member of the ANR, ordered that the RTL's director should be taken in for questioning. In 2003, Guy Kasongo Kilembwe, editor in chief of the satirical newspaper *Pot-Pourri,* was arrested by the police, apparently on the orders of Pius Muabilu, a parliamentarian but also, above all, managing director of the L'Avenir press group. Muabilu had resented an article in the satirical paper that accused him of diverting public funds in order to launch his private media group. These incidents show that public forces are frequently hijacked to settle private quarrels.

Military justice was the second major source of repression of the media. Several journalists have been judged and condemned by court-martial. Joseph Diana, a journalist with Radio Télévision Matadi, was charged with "treason in wartime." His case opened after thirteen months of preventive detention and was dismissed for lack of evidence. The same court condemned Thierry Kyalumba, director of publication for the newspaper *Vision,* to four years' imprisonment in March 1999 for "disclosing state secrets in wartime." Modeste Mutinga (*Le Potentiel*) and André Ipakala (*La Référence Plus*), two of the best-regarded editors in the DRC, were brought before the same military court after having been arrested for taking part in a meeting in South Africa organized by the South African NGO African Centre for the Constructive Resolution of Disputes, aimed at promoting reconciliation and dialogue, in which former dignitaries of the Mobutu regime and people close to the rebels took part.[74] The reasons for arresting or calling someone in for questioning are frequently never given, and the journalist, who often spends several days in prison, never knows exactly why he has been singled out.

Apart from these excessive interventions by the ANR and military courts, journalists were also regularly confronted by civilian justice, but descriptions of the offenses showed how "widely" the law could be interpreted. For instance, in September 2000, Aimé Kakese Vinalu, editor of the weekly *Le Carrousel,* who called for the unification of the opposition in an editorial, was condemned to two years in prison for "treason" and "inciting revolt against the established authority."[75] Many magistrates, especially in the provinces, may have heard talk of the 1996 law, but do not have a copy of the text and so cannot refer to it when judging a press offense.[76]

Journalists could also fall into the hands of the Détection Militaire des Activités Anti-Patriotiques (DEMIAP). At the end of 2002, in Kasai, a journalist working for Radio Kilimandjaro, Kadima Mukombe, was arrested and held by the service for "offending the army," because in his program he had criticized the local military commanders for putting more effort into the illegal trade in diamonds than into looking after their troops.[77]

Finally, in the east (Kivu, Maniéma, and Ituri), the media were faced with arbitrary violence from at least eighteen armed groups called "negative forces" in the UN reports.[78] Even if they did not attack journalists directly, they became angry when their abuses and massacres of local populations were publicly denounced. As Colette Braeckman pointed out, the region has lived for many years in an infernal cycle of triangular terror—occupation, resistance, and repression—and this trilogy also describes the relationship between the media and the authorities in the region.[79]

The media were also at risk from within. Until recently, obtaining a press card depended on paying for a subscription to the Union de la Presse Congolaise (UPC). This meant it was easy for members of the political police to obtain a card and infiltrate media circles in order to identify journalists critical of the authorities.[80] Several publications have unmasked government agents among the technicians in the computing services of their companies.[81] Radio Amani in Kisangani also ended up identifying informants among its young recruits in 1996.

Thus, there were many methods of repression. People have given up counting the number of times that journalists have been victims of arbitrary arrests, beatings, and injuries, to say nothing of the countless incidents of damage to equipment. Many media outlets have also been banned or suspended. For example, on September 14, 2000, Minister Sakombi Inongo suspended ten radio and television stations for not respecting the final provisions of the "Cahiers des Charges,"[82] a vaguely worded document adopted in haste, in 1996, by Mobutu's last minister of information.

But the people whom journalists have annoyed have devised even more "original" methods, including the nationalization of private audiovisual media. In 2000, Minister Sakombi Inongo announced that the RTKM, owned by Aubin Ngongo Luwowo, a former minister of Mobutu accused of being close to the rebellion, and Canal Kin 1 and Canal Kin 2, owned by Jean-Pierre Bemba, leader of the MLC, were being "put under state supervision." The first was suspected of having used public funds to set up his station and was therefore requisitioned by the Office des Biens Mal Acquis (OBMA); the station was renamed RTNC 4. The other two partner stations were renamed RTNC 3, and a new program schedule, based on promoting the Kabila regime, was imposed on them by the minister of communications. Minister Sakombi Inongo stated,

"Canal Kin and RTKM are the property of opponents who are in open rebellion against the government. As our country is at war, these radio and television channels should no longer operate. But because ex-Canal Kin and ex-RTKM employ our countrymen, in order to save their jobs, the government of national Salvation has taken measures to preserve them by placing them under the supervision of the Minister of Communication."[83]

In October 2001, Minister Kikaya bin Karubi returned the channels to their respective owners. As Journalistes en Danger noted, "By handing these channels back to their owners, the government led by Joseph Kabila, is signaling a break with the policies and methods of the government of his late father. It is drawing a line through the personality cult and monologue that the former president's sycophants imposed on the public and private media."[84]

Direct intervention in the radio stations' programming by the various authorities was also constant during the Congolese crisis. In June 2003 a new schedule of programs was imposed on Radio Sauti Ya Rehema by the RCD-Goma. It reserved an hour each day for military programs and forced the station to relay news bulletins from the RTNC, which was in the hands of the RCD.[85] Kilimandjaro, a community radio station that transmits from Tshikapa in Western Kasai, was banned by the provincial authorities from transmitting programs in vernacular languages, because the authorities had detected "a wish to intoxicate the population." In 2000, all political programs were banned for a short time.

Like the diverse and surprising range of perpetrators of violence, the penalties inflicted on the media were also often excessive. For instance, in 1999 a government dignitary did not think twice about locking up several journalists in his private residence for ten days and having them whipped with a sjambok (whip) twice a day. In 2000, over a dozen journalists were arrested and whipped with sjamboks, according to their age and weight, for having attended a press conference given by Arthur Zahidi Ngoma. In August 2000, Zimbabwean troops, supporting the DRC's regular army, seized a television team from the Kasai Horizon private station and forced them to roll in the dust while singing military songs.

Another strategy used by the government to stop the distribution of newspapers identified with the opposition has been to systematically seize them at N'Djili airport in Kinshasa, in order to stop them from leaving the country. Traveling in the opposite direction, issues of Le Soft International, published in Brussels, have been seized and burned at the airport several times.

As well, it was not always the journalist who became the victim. Sometimes it was other members of the editorial team, or visitors who found themselves in the newspaper's offices by chance, or members of the journalist's family who were taken hostage by those who wanted to mete out justice. The most dramatic case occurred in June 2004 in Bukavu, where rebel forces looking for the director of Radio Sauti Ya Rehema went to his home and executed the son of the building's owner, thinking that he was the journalist.

Grudges against a journalist can rapidly extend to his or her acquaintances. In 2000, Katako Okende, a lawyer retained by the editor of *Le Carrousel,* was arrested while he was defending his client. He was detained for "complicity" and accused of "high treason in wartime" for having been found in possession of newspapers that supported the political opposition.

Repression not only affected newspapers and radio stations, but also extended to associations that defend journalists' rights and, more generally, to human rights organizations that were in contact with the media.[86] Because Journalistes en Danger denounced the violence that the government perpetrates against the press, it had been accused several times of being a "pro-Rwandan" organization, and its president and secretary-general were even forced to live clandestinely for two weeks at the start of 2001.[87] In addition to journalists, those to whom journalists hold out their microphones were sometimes persecuted, leaving citizens in fear of expressing themselves publicly. For instance, in 1999 the president of the Association of Prison Officers spent many months in preventative detention without judgment, for having denounced on radio the detention conditions in the country's prisons.

Sometimes repression even affected the media associated with the government. For example, in 2000 the Congolese army raided *L'Avenir,* which was very close to Laurent-Désiré Kabila, and removed personnel and equipment, forcing the newspaper to shut down for several days.

Conditions have become less repressive since the start of the peace process. However, the formation of a transitional government, which has brought most of the former rebel leaders to Kinshasa, has led only to a slight improvement in journalists' working conditions in the formerly occupied areas. Though the peace agreements have increased security and stability, to the benefit of the general population and journalists, and have also made it easier to travel from one region to another, local authorities often continue to give orders to local media. The ongoing troubles in the east are also taking their toll of victims. In June 2003, in Ituri, Acquitté Kisembo, an interpreter for the special envoy of Agence

France Press (AFP), was kidnapped, along with six other people. It is still not known whether he was executed by the Lendu militia or by men from Thomas Lubanga's UPC.

Characteristics of the Professional Environment

Though punishment of journalists is often excessive and shocking because of its summary, violent, and informal nature (to say nothing of its lack of respect for human rights), it is true that the Congolese press has indulged in numerous abuses. Badly paid or unpaid journalists, who are more susceptible to corruption, often have little basic training and respect for professional principles. Who could then be surprised when *Pot-Pourri* was accused in December 2001 of "personally insulting the head of state" when it ran a headline saying that Joseph Kabila was an "operetta's major-general parachuted in as head of state"?

A Catastrophic Economic Situation

The DRC's ongoing economic crisis, worsened by the successive pillages (1991, 1993), and followed by the so-called wars of liberation (1996–1997) and then aggression (1998–2002), has plunged the country into a chaotic and desperate situation. Corruption and making-do are the general rules, even in press circles. "To make ends meet, journalists are forced to do odd jobs, to sell space in their columns to local politicians, who can write what they want, often with the help of the journalists themselves."[88]

This is why the practice of "coupage"—giving a fee to journalists who cover an event—has become general practice. "The sum is fixed by the organisers to motivate the journalists to write the article 'correctly,' that is to say favourably."[89] Other terms for designating this type of practice more accurately include "the transport," which is the sum paid to journalists, after the event, to cover their travel costs; "the compensation," which is the sum paid to editors for on-time publication; and "the motivation," which is the small additional sum slipped to each person working on the production line of a newspaper or program to ensure that they do their work and not hinder the process.[90]

In a context where there is virtually no advertising and the little that exists is given according to political sympathies, and where the population is too poor to buy a newspaper that costs as much as several meals, only those media that have a sponsor (political or funding agency) survive. Radio Okapi demonstrates that balance, neutrality, and presence throughout the country, which are all essential to true pluralist information, require such large financial resources that it is difficult to imagine them being mobilized at any time other than the present "emergency" period, with UN and financial partners ready to loosen the purse strings. This enormous machine costs US$8 million a year, a large sum, but it is essential to the correct operation of the radio project.[91] Radio Okapi's journalists do remarkable, rigorous, and balanced work for US$700–1,000 per month,[92] whereas their colleagues from the local press and audiovisual media are paid at most US$50 per month, when they are actually paid. Quality work certainly has a price, but for Radio Okapi in the DRC, the price is totally out of line with the realities of the local market.

Furthermore, there is a question mark hanging over the future of Radio Okapi. Will this station revert to the Congolese authorities at the end of the peacekeeping mission, so that its infrastructures can be reintegrated into the RTNC? Will it be privatized and run the risk of falling into the hands of businessmen who eventually become involved in politics? Will it be handed over to a consortium of local radio stations so that it can be managed in a cooperative way by noninstitutional partner? Will it simply shut its doors? This crucial question, which is closely linked with that concerning the scale of the resources necessary for its operation, has not yet been decided.

Finally, it should be noted that although the financing of the media is haphazard, the sector nevertheless attracts numerous "patrons." There is a proliferation of new media as each journalist strives to become a manager. "Everybody wants to be the boss, with the legitimate illusion of living a better life," noted the JED.[93] And this illusion is strengthened by the behavior of some bosses of media businesses who are not shy about showing off external signs of their well-being. "The editor—who considers the title is his private property—behaves like a potentate, who doesn't have to answer to anyone, not even the taxman. He uses the company's funds as he likes and generally has no known salary."[94]

Unsuitable Training Mechanisms

Certainly abuses by the Congolese media, and lapses in their coverage of the war, also owe a lot to journalists' lack of training. Yet currently, Kinshasa has three structures for journalist training: the Institut Facultaire des Sciences de l'Information et de la Communication (IFASIC),[95] the Facultés Catholiques de Kinshasa (FCK), and the University of Kinshasa's Department of Communications. There is also the Institut Congolais de l'Audiovisuel (ICA),[96] which trains mid-level radio and television technicians and producers. The IFASIC suffers from a lack of infrastructure, lack of motivation among the teaching staff, whose knowledge is obsolete, and overpopulation by students. Because the school supports itself through registration fees, it cannot refuse students and today has more than a thousand in buildings constructed to house 200 at most. The FCK's communication faculty, created in 1993, is better equipped and less overpopulated. Its main orientation is toward social communication research; it trains "social communicators" primarily for work in the religious media. The University of Kinshasa's Department of Communications was established in 1998, but is still relatively virtual, as it has no practical infrastructure for students. None of these training schools has a program that corresponds to the practical realities of working as a journalist in the DRC, and none has a specialized module on covering conflict. In the provinces, the Universities of Kisangani and Lubumbashi have also recently developed communication departments, but they both lack equipment and teaching staff.

In Bukavu, which has three main radio stations (Radio Maendeleo, Radio Maria, and Radio Kahuzi), "less than five journalists of the 15 employed by these three stations have received a haphazard training in a local institution with a poor reputation, the Higher Audiovisual Institute.[97] Given this background, the other 'professionals' in the stations have been recommended and introduced either by sponsors or other presenters . . . , or on the basis of friendship or family links with directors of press businesses."[98]

This means that most journalists working in the Congolese media are young recruits with various profiles and motivations who only have very rudimentary basic knowledge, even if they have formal qualifications. They are rarely driven by a professional vocation, but exercise the profession because it is a way of surviving while waiting for something better.

An Uninterested and Impoverished Public

At the time of the National Conference, the Congolese public was active and involved in the media sector. Newspapers sold well and readers sent in contributions for publication. From 1993 onward, as the economic crisis worsened, the papers' print runs declined. The privately owned press gradually sank into sensationalism, employing attention-grabbing headlines instead of accurate information. An observer remarked, "The newspaper sellers demand these front-page headlines even more strongly than the editorial boards," protesting each time that "the headline doesn't seem hard enough against Mobutu to us."[99]

Paradoxically, while the papers were relying on sensationalism to please readers, the latter were becoming less and less interested in this attention-grabbing but not very credible journalism, even though they still cast an eye over the headlines at the "standing parliament."[100] Today, with the impoverishment of the urban middle classes and their disillusion with the personal ambitions that guide political and media activism, readers have turned away from the press. The population, when it has the means, has turned to the radio (or television in Kinshasa) en masse, because the average Congolese now lives on less than a dollar a day. A university professor receives the equivalent of US$10 a month, and civil servants sometimes have salary arrears of over a year.

The public has also turned massively to the religious media and, more specifically, to the "messianic" radio and television stations, which, if they spread a message based on "manipulating the irrational" and "religious obscurantism,"[101] seem to provide the only source of hope. Religion has become the ultimate refuge of the Congolese, as sects spread throughout the country.

Professional Associations and Institutions

Added to the journalists' lack of training and the public's growing lack of interest, no doubt a factor weighing against responsible journalistic practice during the war was the breakup within the profession caused by opposing political alliances, geographic dispersion, and the absence of any established professional structure. There are currently more than 4,500 people employed by the Congolese media who describe themselves as "journalists." Among them, more than 500 belong to the public media (with the status of civil servants), nearly 2,000 belong to the private radio stations, and about 1,500 belong to the privately owned press.[102]

For years, the unique federated professional organization that was supposed to represent the whole of the profession and that was responsible for issuing press cards was the Union de la Presse Congolaise, founded in 1970 and formerly named the Union de la Presse Zaïroise (UPZA). Financed by the government during the years of the state monopoly, it lost its legitimacy with the de facto pluralism of media and fell into a state of lethargy as soon as government financing dried up.[103] On several occasions, during important periods in Congolese political life (the National Conference in 1991, the Communications Convention in May 1995, the adoption of the new press law in 1996), the need to reform the structure or dissolve it, and replace it with another that was more representative and consensual, was mooted. Moreover, nearly all the successive ministers of information since 1991, whatever the regime in power, either had a project for dissolution of the UPC in their desk drawers or explicitly stated their wish to, at the least, restructure it.

Faced with the UPC's lethargy, in contrast to the liveliness of the media sector, many professional associations and organizations emerged, either to meet obvious needs or to satisfy personal ambitions. The war gave rise to two types of organizational initiatives. It led to the creation of regional associations, as most of the provincial media felt abandoned by the Kinshasa-based professional associations, which were incapable of taking their specific realities into account.[104] Or NGOs were created to support, help, and defend the media, particularly in crisis situations (Médias pour la Paix,[105] Journalistes en Danger).

Large numbers of other structures were created, reflecting different sectors (the radio,[106] press, and television) and topics (sports journalists, health, the diplomatic press) or bringing together categories of staff (heads of companies, employees, women).[107] Sensing that any external partners would have been disoriented by the sheer number of these initiatives, the profession finally found it necessary to create a federation of all these structures, the Fédération des Organisations Professionnelles des Médias (FOPROMEDIA), to act as an intermediary with the outside world.

Within this context, a National Press Congress was finally held, from March 3 to March 5, 2004, bringing together more than 200 members of the profession as delegates from all of the country's provinces.[108] After five days of discussions, the participants adopted a series of important decisions to shape the future of the Congolese media. A new federal structure was established, the Union Nationale de la Presse Congolaise (UNPC), and was headed by a management committee in which the private press had a dominant role. The new president of the UNPC, Kabeya Pindi Pasi, is director of programs for a private television channel, Tropicana TV. A woman, Chantal Kanyimbo, a leading journalist for the RTNC, was elected vice president. The UNPC's mandate is to coordinate activities of member groups and associations; defend freedom of the press and the general rights and interests of the press and its members; organize the profession and represent it within and outside the country; promote the press on the moral, professional, and material levels; maintain and promote contact and exchange of views between the press and public and private institutions; and organize professional training and trade union activities on behalf of its members.[109]

The Observatoire des Médias Congolais (OMEC), a self-regulatory body, was also established. This independent professional organization, comprising members of the profession and the public, was given the role of ensuring that journalists respect the rules of ethics and professional practice as included in a code revised for the purpose.[110] Polydor Muboyayi, director of publication of *Le Phare* and president of FOPROMEDIA, was elected president. This reorganization of media professionals, who had been geographically and ideologically divided for many years, was made possible only by the end of the war and the tentatively renewed stability.

Another driving force in this restructuring was the establishment of the Haute Autorité des Médias, a civic transitional institution, with Modeste Mutinga, chairman of the *Le Potentiel* press group and founder of the NGO Médias pour la Paix, elected as its head. The HAM had a range of responsibilities: ensuring that the law on freedom of the press is respected, guaranteeing the public's right to pluralist information, checking the neutrality and balance of the public media, regulating the whole of the media field, and promoting access by the Congolese media to the Informational and Communication Technologies. The HAM has consultative powers (for the government) and coercive powers (vis-à-vis the media).

The HAM, which will be replaced by the Conseil Supérieur de l'Audiovisuel et de la Communication after the transition period, enjoys the support of several financial partners (Belgian, French, British, German, and European aid agencies, as well as the UNDP), which support its operations and provide technical assistance and expertise. Furthermore, the whole of the Congolese media sector receives substantial funds from the major donor agencies, whose monies are routed through specialized NGOs (Institut Panos Paris, the Groupe de Recherche et d'Echanges Technologiques [GRET], Internews, the Hirondelle Foundation and the SFCG). Numerous thematic workshops have been organized for journalists who are trying to raise awareness in the media of their responsibilities in reporting. Some partners support the restructuring of the media sector (supporting the OMEC, popularizing the code of professional practice, campaigning for the decriminalization of press offenses, etc.). They also provide support and training structures, or offer equipment to selected media. With the support of the UK Department for International Development, the Institut Panos Paris has also helped end the isolation of provincial radio by equipping approximately fifteen stations in Kivu and Katanga with World-Space receivers and computing equipment.

Aid to this fragile sector that has emerged from the informal economy must be carefully designed and targeted, and collaboratively planned, in order to contribute to the consolidation of professional and responsible media.

Conclusion

It cannot be denied that the media have been both a stakeholder and an instrument in the Congolese conflicts. Furthermore, the various protagonists in the peace negotiations have taken care to associate them with

the different stages in the process. In 2001, during the Sun City negotiations, many Congolese journalists from the public and private media,
including those close to Kabila and those from the most radical opposition, were invited and supported by the Congolese government or by the
services facilitating the negotiations, to cover the peace process taking
place in South Africa.

Today, the pressing question is whether the same media can become
agents in the process of peace and reconstruction. Since the 2001 negotiations, they have been developing and strengthening their reflexes as
propagandists, and, during the transition period, most journalists have
continued to act as spokespeople for a faction represented in the government. The government media relay the positions of the president of
the republic, while each of the four vice presidents had his own television channel for getting across his message. Arthur Zahidi Ngoma (un-
armed opposition) used Antenne A; Yerodia Ndombasi (presidential
movement) used the RTGA (L'Avenir Group) and Digital Congo (belonging to Kabila's twin sister); Azarias Ruberwa (RCD) used the RTP;
and Jean-Pierre Bemba (MLC) owns his own television channels (Canal
Kin and CCTV) and a radio station (Radio Liberté) with transmitters
throughout his province.

A premature election campaign was already under way months before the election, a worrying development given that elections are always
a source of tension and potential violence, which can easily erupt if the
media do not behave responsibly, or if their tendency to serve their
political faction gets the better of their stated aim to help citizens support democracy and the constitutional state.

On May 15, 2004, the public and private media signed a "code of
good behavior" with the political parties. The aim of this commitment
was to ensure that the political parties would have equitable access to the
media and ensured that "the various political players received impartial
treatment during preelectoral and electoral periods." For their part, the
political parties undertook to ensure that the journalists covering their
activities would be respected and protected, promising that they would
not use the media "to abuse the electorate by lying, buying consciences
or any other reprehensible behaviour."[111] But these commitments have
been widely violated. Since March 2006, the HAM has been fighting
against the political hate speeches flowering in the media, using all
means at its disposal—dialogue, visits to newsrooms, and open threats to
suspend talk shows that were too obviously biased and insulting for
some key players or communities—but with very little success.

Events in June 2004 in Bukavu, then in January 2005 in Kinshasa,
demonstrated how quickly the political situation could destabilize. And

the reflexes of withholding information and repressing journalists resurfaced with the slightest sign of instability. In June 2004 the minister of information's first reaction was to ban radio and television discussion of the events in Bukavu in order to prevent the broadcasting of "messages that might aggravate the situation. . . . The newsrooms that would say things tending to demoralize the Congolese army or undermine these sad events . . . will be hit by the law."[112]

During the electoral campaign, mobilizing ethnic and regional affinities was seen as a winning tactic by the various political forces in play. The crucial stage of the election eventually took place in relative peace and stability as the HAM displayed great vigilance. Most of the Congolese media actively backed "their" candidate and made as much money as they could by selling some spaces or minutes to other politicians. The HAM has paid a high price for its involvment in regulating the media; the institution was ransacked by Bembas's supporters two days before the first round of the presidential election on July 27, 2006. In spite of the aggressive tone of some media, the election was not wracked by explosions of violence. Therefore, there is hope that the situation in the DRC can be stabilized, regardless of the actions of some irresponsible journalists.

Notes

I would like to thank Steve Matenga for his critical proofreading and comments.

1. See the 2004 study Institut Panos Paris (ed.), *La situation des médias en République Démocratique du Congo* (Paris, 2004), carried out in collaboration with Aimé Kayembe.

2. For example, Léon Moukanda's *Umoja* and Polydor Muboyayi's *Le Phare,* which appeared irregularly and did not deal with politics. They only really existed after the liberalization in 1990.

3. G. de Villers, "Zaïre, années 90: faits et dits de la société d'après le regard de la presse," *Les Cahiers du CEDAF* nos. 1–2 (1992), p. 2.

4. The minister in charge of the press and information delivered more than 500 authorizations to publish at that time, but not all the titles saw the light of day. B. Kasonga N. M., "La répression de la presse au Zaïre pendant la transition," *Cahiers Africains* nos. 9–11 (1994), p. 283.

5. C. Braeckman, *Le dinosaure: le Zaïre de Mobutu* (Paris: Fayard, 1992), p. 346.

6. de Villers, "Zaïre, années 90," p. 2.

7. Until 2004, this radio station was an offshoot of a twelve-member regional NGO committee. Its creation, in Bukavu, was preceded by that of Radio Kahuzi, a religious station that was established in 1992 by a pair of American Protestants (nicknamed Radio CIA), but that is not listened to much and not well known by the local public.

8. A. Maja-Pearce (ed.), *Annuaire de la presse africaine* (Brussels: FIJ, 1996), p. 321.

9. According to Journalistes en Danger, a Congolese NGO created in 1999 and dedicated to defense of freedom of the press in the Congo. The JED was sponsored for a long time by Reporters sans Frontières. Since 2002 it has been a member of IFEX, which shows that its work has met with international recognition.

10. During the prosperous period (1990–1991), average print runs were about 7,000 copies.

11. This was the case of *Mbwetete* (in Matadi).

12. Like *Les Coulisses* (published in Beni) and *Le Souverain* (in Goma).

13. For example, coverage of the pillaging in 1991 and 1993, and coverage of the National Conference's setbacks.

14. Cited in M. S. Frère, *Voyage dans la presse zaïroise* (Brussels: FIJ, 1996), p. 8.

15. For Colette Braeckman, it was the "first ethnic manipulation in this new period marked by the founding of a multi-party state." C. Braeckman, *Terreur africaine: Burundi, Rwanda, Zaïre—les racines de la violence* (Paris: Fayard, 1996), p. 224.

16. C. Braeckman, *Le dinosaure,* pp. 24–25.

17. It was not until more than ten days after the events that the Kinshasa press reported: "Persistent echoes are circulating concerning an extremely troubling situation at the University of Lubumbashi." *Umoja,* May 23, 1990, cited in de Villers, "Zaïre, années 90," p. 147.

18. Following the election of Etienne Tshisekedi, a well-known opponent of the Mobutu regime who was born in Kasai, to the post of prime minister by the National Conference, the governor of the province of Katanga, Gabriel Kyungu wa Kumwanza, and the former prime minister Nguza Karl I Bond, both Katangans, orchestrated an ethnic cleansing operation aimed at sending the numerous Kasaians in Katanga back to their province of origin.

19. Bandeja Yamba points out that Governor Kyungu had favored the creation of several titles: *Le Lushois, Mukuba, Le Katangais, La Tribune, La Cheminée, Le Libérateur.* Bandeja Yamba, "Presse libre et propagande ethnique au Zaïre," cited in C. Beauregard and C. Saouter (eds.), *Conflits contemporains et médias* (Montreal: XYZ, 1997), p. 48.

20. See Journalistes en Danger (ed.), *République Démocratique du Congo: vers une nouvelle stratégie pour la liberté d'expression* (Kinshasa, October 2000).

21. *La Cheminée,* August 17–24, 1992, cited in Bandeja Yamba, "Presse libre et propagande ethnique au Zaïre," p. 50.

22. *Mukuba,* August 22, 1992, cited in Bandeja Yamba, "Presse libre et propagande ethnique au Zaïre," p. 51.

23. *Le Libérateur-Ujamaa,* December 26, 1994, cited in Bandeja Yamba, "Presse libre et propagande ethnique au Zaïre," p. 53.

24. Kasonga N. M., "La répression de la presse au Zaïre," p. 287.

25. Braeckman, *Terreur africaine,* p. 232.

26. On this subject, see Aimé Kayembe's analysis of the role of the Congolese media in the conflicts, in Institut Panos Paris, *La situation des médias en République Démocratique du Congo.*

27. Immediately after the presidential gift was announced, a group of editors met to form CASPROM, which was responsible for receiving and sharing

out the donation. Some opposition titles (*Le Potentiel, Le Phare,* etc.) refused this nebulous method and let the other publications (*Le Palmarès, La Référence Plus, L'Avenir,* etc.) share the money among themselves.

28. *Expansion Lubilanji,* May 12–19, 1998, cited in J. C. Willame, *L'odyssée Kabila: trajectoire pour un Congo nouveau?* (Paris: Karthala, 1999), p. 210.

29. V. Elongo Lulukunga, "Mutations politiques et pratiques journalistiques au Congo-Zaïre," DEA thesis, Université Libre de Bruxelles, 2004, p. 47.

30. Willame, *L'odyssée Kabila,* pp. 140–143.

31. Yet on July 30, 1998, to prevent a wave of panic following the announcement of Kabila's break with Rwanda, the Congolese minister of justice called together the Kinshasa press to inform them that the "state agencies would ensure the complete safety" of the Congolese Banyamulenge, Rwandans, Burundians, and Ugandans.

32. See C. Braeckman, *Les nouveaux prédateurs* (Paris: Fayard, 2003), p. 70.

33. He later became foreign minister, then vice president (as part of the presidential party) when transitional institutions were being established. On April 11, 2000, a Belgian judge issued an international arrest warrant against him for "inciting ethnic hatred." In February 2002, the International Court of Justice ordered the Belgian state to lift the warrant for Yerodia because, as a minister, he was protected by immunity.

34. See O. B. Diatezwa, "Politique, conflits et médias au Congo-Kinshasa," working document (2003), p. 13.

35. Interview with RAP21, *Newsletter* no. 21 (2003), p. 1.

36. *L'Avenir,* August 15, 2003.

37. Cited in Reporters sans Frontières, *Rapport annuel, 2002* (Paris).

38. Interview with RAP21, *Newsletter* no. 21 (2003), p. 1.

39. Cabinet meetings were rare and did not result in complete press releases, as each member of the government was totally ignorant about the running of the country in those sectors that were not his direct responsibility.

40. In the areas under the control of the RCD and the MLC, Ketumile Masire, the facilitator, made sure that journalists could be nominated locally to cover the work. In addition, Radio Okapi's special reporters were present throughout the negotiations, providing reports in five languages three times a day.

41. Reporters sans Frontières, *Rapport annuel, 2003.*

42. Journalistes en Danger, *Report on the Freedom of the Press, 2000* (Kinshasa).

43. Committee to Protect Journalists, *Attacks Against the Press, 2003.*

44. Braeckman, *Les nouveaux prédateurs,* p. 81.

45. Kizito Mushizi Njundiko, "Maendeleo: Une radio dans la guerre," in Institut Panos Paris and COTA (eds.), *Briser les silences: paroles d'Afrique centrale* (Paris: Karthala, 2003), pp. 108–109.

46. C. Braeckman, "Enjeux de la guerre et de le transition en République Démocratique du Congo," Conference for the Department of Information and Communications, Université Libre de Bruxelles, March 2004.

47. The Hirondelle Foundation had already been involved in Zaire in the management of Radio Agatashya, established in August 1994 with the collaboration of Reporters sans Frontières, in the Rwandan refugee camps at Bukavu.

48. This program owed much to the abilities of Jérôme Taunyia Ngongo, its longtime main presenter. He died in July 2004.

49. See Aimé Kayembe's position in Institut Panos Paris, *La situation des médias en République Démocratique du Congo,* p 83.

50. See Willame, *L'odyssée Kabila,* p. 220.

51. C. Biringingwa, "Au Sud-Kivu: le pouvoir fait des journalistes des griots," in Institut Panos Paris and COTA (eds.), *Briser les silences: paroles d'Afrique centrale* (Paris: Karthala, 2003), p. 111.

52. The Kinshasa Congolese already picked up Radio France Internationale and Africa Number 1 on FM, because those stations transmitted from Brazzaville, on the other side of the river. The BBC was interrupted from 1999 to 2001.

53. See the analysis in Willame, *L'odyssée Kabila,* pp. 190–192.

54. Journalistes en Danger, *La liberté de la presse en République Démocratique du Congo* (Kinshasa, 1999).

55. Kin Kiey Mulumba then settled in Kigali, where he launched *Le Soft des Grands Lacs,* a publication with regional ambitions that clearly benefits from the Kagame regime's support. Back in Kinshasa, he is still involved in local politics.

56. Reporters sans Frontières, *Rapport annuel, 2003.*

57. The Information, Press, and Audiovisual Commission met from June 22 to August 27, 1992.

58. It brought together 320 journalists, participants, and observers from Kinshasa, the provinces, and abroad, from May 13 to May 17, 1995.

59. The only dispute that arose from this law concerns the Mende amendment (named after the representative who introduced it), which forced journalists to reveal their sources of information. Following protests by professionals, who organized a march on December 21, 1995, to denounce the measure, the wording was modified: journalists were "only obliged to reveal the sources of information in the cases prescribed by the law."

60. R. Garreton, "Report on the Situation of Human Rights in the DRC" (Geneva: United Nations, 2001).

61. The printing shops of Terra Nova, Zaïre Printing Service, La Voie de Dieu, Imprimeries du Zaïre, and Umoja were bombed successively.

62. For example, no. 548 of *Potentiel* (1994) was completely destroyed.

63. A. Maja-Pearce (ed.), *Annuaire de la presse africaine* (Brussels: FIJ, 1996), p. 321.

64. Cited in Frère, *Voyage dans la presse zaïroise,* p. 21.

65. The AMI, created in 2003 by young Congolese who had returned from the United States, is another organization for defending freedom of the press that has drawn heavily for its inspiration on the experience of the JED.

66. African Media Institute, "Les entraves à la liberté de la presse en RDC," Kinshasa (2004), p. 52.

67. Lacking suitable medical care, he finally died in prison.

68. Radio Maendeleo, Radio Maria, and Radio Sauti ya Rehema ceased transmitting from June 2 to June 9, 2004, following the attack by the rebel forces on the town of Bukavu. Only Radio Okapi's local transmitter, located in the MONUC area, was able to continue transmitting during this troubled period.

69. K. Mushizi Nfundiko, "Maendeleo: une radio dans la guerre," in Institut Panos Paris and COTA (eds.), *Briser les silences,* p. 109.

70. Institut Panos Paris, *Africentr@lemédias* no. 6 (December 2002).

71. Journalistes en Danger, *Rapport 1999: La liberté de la presse en République Démocratique du Congo.*

72. The reasons for his arrest are extremely vague. First, Frédéric Kitengie was reproached for having interviewed the president of the Congolese football team, who was also the brother of a declared candidate for the presidency of the republic. Then Kitengie was accused of bad management dating from the time when he was director of information at the RTNC. Kitengie was finally released about ten days later.

73. See Journalistes en Danger, *Liberté de la presse: la grande illusion* (Kinshasa, 2000).

74. Modeste Mutinga was also beaten in New York by the presidential guard when he was taking part in the delegation accompanying President Kabila to a meeting of the UN Security Council on the situation in the DRC. Committee to Protect Journalists, *Democratic Republic of the Congo, 2000: Country Report.*

75. Emile Kakese Vinalu was finally pardoned by the head of state on January 5, 2001. When the RTNC announced his release, it intimated that in exchange for this presidential favor, the journalist should abstain from any future criticism of the regime.

76. Many magistrates in Kinshasa and the provinces contacted Journalistes en Danger to obtain a copy of the 1996 law, which they had never seen. The JED had to distribute about 150 copies of the text.

77. Reporters sans Frontières, *Rapport annuel, 2004.*

78. In addition to the recognized rebel movements, the Burundian rebels, Rwandan Interahamwe, Ugandan rebels, Mai Mai, and local self-defense must be considered.

79. Braeckman, *Les nouveaux prédateurs,* p. 165.

80. Journalistes en Danger, *Vers une nouvelle stratégie pour la liberté d'expression en RDC* (October 2000).

81. The paper *L'Avenir,* even though it was close to Kabila, also discovered in October 2000 that one of its computer technicians belonged to the military intelligence services.

82. Radio Elikya, Réveil FM, Radio Kituandi (of the Kibanguist church), Radio Malebo Broadcast Channel, Radio RTKM, Radio Sentinelle (of the Bethel City church), Antenne A, Canal Kin 1 and Canal Kin 2, and Télévision TKM.

83. Journalistes en Danger, *L'affaire RTKM: un espace de liberté pluriel confisqué* (March 11, 2001).

84. T. Tshivuadi, "L'affaire RTKM: misères d'une radio-télévision privée," in Institut Panos Paris and COTA, *Briser les silences,* p. 116.

85. The director of the RTNC's Goma office, Jean-Pierre Kulimushi, spent sixteen days in prison himself in October–November 2000; the RCD reproached him for having broadcast statements criticizing the behavior of RCD troops.

86. In August 1999, a member of Héritiers de la Justice (a Protestant NGO that was defending human rights in Bukavu) was arrested and detained, along with two journalists from Radio Maendeleo; he was accused of "helping the journalists to obtain military secrets."

87. In January 2006, Donat M'Baya and Tshivis Tshivuadi again had to flee the country after the JED released a report about the assassination of

Franck Ngyke, a political columnist from *La Référence Plus* who had been shot dead, along with his wife, in October 2005.

88. Maja-Pearce, *Annuaire de la presse africaine*, p. 321.

89. Elongo Lukulunga, "Mutations politiques et pratiques journalistiques," p. 56.

90. See Frère, *Voyage dans la presse zaïroise*, pp. 11–12.

91. Today, the main part of this financing is provided by the United Nations, the US Agency for International Development, the UK's Department for International Development, and the Swiss Agency for Development and Cooperation.

92. The radio station's management exclusively comprises expatriates who are paid on a United Nations salary scale; they can earn up to ten times more than their "overpaid" local colleagues.

93. Journalistes en Danger, *La liberté de la presse en République Démocratique du Congo, 1999*.

94. J. Nkambidio, "Statut et conditions de travail d'un journaliste congolais," in P. E. M. M. Kabeya (ed.), *Regards sur la presse congolaise: du Congo belge à celui de Kabila, sans oublier le Zaïre de Mobutu*, Palabres no. 10 (Paris: L'Harmattan, 2004), p. 101.

95. Formerly named the Institut des Sciences et Techniques de l'Information (ISTI), the regional training school IFASIC, created in 1973, was supported for many years by UNESCO and various bilateral aid agencies, but is now deprived of these external resources.

96. Formerly named the Studio-Ecole de la Voix du Zaïre (SEVOZA), the training center ICA, created in 1977, was used mainly for retraining OZRT staff. It has recently been equipped with digital technologies, with the support of the French embassy, and has developed modules open to the private media.

97. This private structure was created in 1986 by the then-director of the OZRT's Bukavu office.

98. C. Biringingwa, "Au Sud-Kivu le pouvoir fait des journalistes des griots," in Institut Panos Paris and COTA (eds.), *Briser les silences*, p. 112.

99. J. Kambale, "La presse congolaise fonctionne comme par inertie," in Institut Panos Paris and COTA, *Briser les silences*, p. 103.

100. The newspaper sellers spread out the day's various titles on the pavement, so that passers-by will often start up impassioned polemical discussions.

101. O. B. Diatezwa, "Politique, conflits et médias au Congo-Kinshasa," working document (2003), pp. 14–15.

102. See Institut Panos Paris (ed.), *La situation des Médias en République Démocratique du Congo* (Paris: Karthala, 2004).

103. Issuing a press card was the only official function still performed by the UPC. However, the card was granted to any candidate who paid the membership fee, without any check on the reality of his or her journalistic activity. The only material advantage gained by holding this card was free public transport, which is now practically nonexistent in Kinshasa and the provinces.

104. Among the provincial or regional groups are AEJIK, AFEM-SK, and RATECO.

105. Each major editor in Kinshasa also wished to develop his own NGO or foundation: Modeste Mutinga (*Le Potentiel*) directed Médias pour la Paix;

Ipakala Mobiko (*La Référence Plus*) directed Fondation Ipakala; and Michel Ladi Luya (*Le Palmarès*) directed Médias pour le Développement et la Paix.

106. For example, ARCO, created in 2000.

107. In 1996, UCOFEM was founded.

108. The National Press Congress did not wish to be seen as an initiative of the UPC, but it was mainly organized by the former executive of the UPC, with help from a few prominent members of the Kinshasa press and the financial support of several operators active in the media field in the DRC: the IPP, GRET, and NIZA. The cost of this operation was more than 200,000 euros. On the National Press Congress and the resulting change in the Congolese media landscape, see M. S. Frère, "RDC: les médias en transition," *Politique Africaine* no. 97 (March 2005), pp. 49–65.

109. Extracts from the UNPC's statutes.

110. OMEC had an extremely laborious birth. Some professionals thought that this type of control should be exercised exclusively by members of the corporation and not the public. Others wished to avoid the creation of a professional organization independent of the UPC whose disciplinary commission, exclusively comprising media owners and journalists, could establish itself as a censor. Yet others put forward regional arguments, fearing that OMEC would be "taken over by the Kasaians," who already have a very strong presence in the press ("Kasaians" run *Le Potentiel* and *Le Phare,* among other publications) and in professional organizations (the JED, FOPROMEDIA, Médias pour la Paix) in Kinshasa, and now in the Haute Autorité des Médias.

111. See Institut Panos Paris, *Africentr@lemédias* no. 23 (June 2004).

112. Note circulaire no. 001/CABMIN/PRESSE INFO/2004 "portant strict respect des consignes éditoriales en cette période de crise."

4

RWANDA

Journalists Before, During, and After the Genocide

IN ANY DISCUSSION of hate media, Rwanda and the deadly Radio Télévision Libre des Mille Collines (RTLM) immediately comes to mind. For months during 1994, a radio station, nicknamed Radio-Télévision–La Mort (Radio-Television-Death), prepared, encouraged, and supported the genocide of the Tutsi people, to the general indifference of the international community. Numerous and very detailed studies have since shown that RTLM was not acting alone, but was one element of a carefully organized system of interlocking media, so-called self-defense militias, political parties, and financial interests.[1]

More than a decade later, the Rwandan media is slowly recovering. It is still prey to multiple difficulties and scarred by the stigmata of the genocide. The shadow from this event has hovered for a long time over the attitude of the authorities, which are mistrustful of the liberty of the press. The shadow influences the behavior of journalists, the debates around the law regulating the sector, the material situation of the media, the professional environment, the reactions of the public, and even the attitude of foreign donors. Each of these variables, which influences the shape of the national media landscape and therefore the construction of democracy, is deeply marked by the memory of the genocide of 1994, in a traumatized nation where executioners and their victims still live together—a memory that is sometimes unavoidably manipulated. For a long time it will continue to shape the evolution of the Rwandan media, just as it remains a determining factor for the future political stability of the whole region.

Despite these difficulties, 2004 can be considered a turning point in the process of reconstruction of the media industry. That year, six privately owned radio stations have been authorized and five have started

RWANDA

Size	26,338 sq. km.
Population	9 million
Capital	Kigali
Ethnic groups	Hutu, Tutsi, Twa
Official languages	Kinyarwanda, French, English
Human Development	
Index ranking (2005)	159 (out of 177 countries)
Life expectancy	40 years
Literacy rate	64.0 percent

Chronology

1885–1916: German colonization.

1924: League of Nations, then Belgian Mandate.

1959: The Tutsi monarchy is overthrown by the "Social Revolution of the Hutu People," supported by Belgian authorities and the Catholic Church.

1961: Tens of thousands of Tutsi are massacred. Many Tutsi flee the country, settling mainly in Uganda, Burundi, and Congo.

1962: Independence. Grégoire Kayibanda, leader of the Parti du Mouvement de l'Emancipation Hutu (PARMEHUTU), becomes president.

1963, 1964, 1967, 1972, 1973: Massacres of Tutsi civilians.

1973: General Juvénal Habyarimana seizes power through a military coup. The Mouvement Révolutionnaire National pour le Développement (MRND) is the single party. A policy of ethnic discrimination is established through quotas in education and employment.

1980: Tutsi refugees continue to claim their right to return, but Habyarimana refuses, pretending the country is already overpopulated.

1988: Tutsi refugees in Uganda create the Rwandan Patriotic Front (RPF), a military and political organization.

1990: The RPF attacks the north of the country.

1991: Habyarimana accepts multiparty democracy, and a new constitution is adopted.

(continues)

1992: A government of national unity, including the new opposition parties, is established. Negotiations with the RPF start in Arusha, Tanzania.

August 1993: A peace agreement is signed in Arusha.

October 1993: The UN Security Council votes for the establishment of the United Nations Assistance Mission for Rwanda (UNAMIR).

April 6, 1994: Habyarimana is assassinated in a plane crash in Kigali. In the following hours, most opposition politicians (including the prime minister) and ten Belgian UN soldiers are killed. An interim government, comprising Hutu political extremists, is established. The systematic extermination of Tutsi starts in Kigali.

April 7–July 4, 1994: About a million Tutsi are killed by the Rwandan Armed Forces (RAF) and the Interahamwe militias backed by civilians, throughout the country.

April 21, 1994: The UN Security Council reduces the UNAMIR from 2,700 to 450 men.

June 23–August 21, 1994: France launches Operation Turquoise, to protect people in danger, but the mission also allows the people responsible for the genocide to escape to Zaire.

June 28, 1994: The UN recognizes the events in Rwanda as "genocide."

July 4, 1994: The RPF takes over Kigali. The RAF withdraws to Zaire, pushing 2 million Hutu to follow the military and the interim government in its retreat.

July 19, 1994: A government of national unity is established, with Pasteur Bizimungu as president and Paul Kagame as vice president.

November 1994: The UN Security Council establishes the International Criminal Tribunal for Rwanda (ICTR).

1996: Rwanda backs the Kabila rebellion in eastern Zaire and dismantles the refugee camps. Refugees either return to Rwanda, or hide in the Zairian forest. Tens of thousands are killed by the Rwandese army.

March 2000: Pasteur Bizimungu resigns as president and Paul Kagame assumes presidency.

May 2003: A new constitution is adopted through referendum.

August 2003: Kagame is elected president with 95 percent of the votes.

to broadcast in Kigali and in the rest of the country. The High Council of the Press, established in 2003, has conducted important monitoring and support with local media, including during the legislative election period. And the first graduates from the new School of Journalism and Communication of the University of Butare have started their media careers. Has the ghost of the RTLM been decisively buried?

Liberalization of the Media: An Overdue Opening

For decades two pillars of Rwandan society, the state and the Catholic Church, had exclusive rights over all information channels of the national media landscape. The Office Rwandais de l'Information (ORINFOR), established in 1974 to replace the Ministry of Information, exercised its authority over the whole of the media of the state: the Kinyarwanda newspaper *Imvaho* (The Truth) and the francophone newspaper *La Relève;* the Agence Rwandaise de Presse (ARP), which had exclusive access to information coming from abroad; and Radio Rwanda, created in 1961. Until the transition in 1991, ORINFOR was directly answerable to the presidency.

The church supported two publications: the monthly *Kinyamateka,*[2] created in 1933, and the bimonthly review *Dialogue,* founded in 1967 by a Catholic association. *Kinyamateka* was banned in 1968 by the government of Grégoire Kayibanda, even though the journal had previously published his papers. It became later the herald of the regime of Juvénal Habyarimana,[3] symbolizing the close collaboration between the state and the church in this small, very Christian country. In the 1980s, the tendency of the journal to occasionally adopt a more critical tone resulted in immediate calls to heel.[4]

In the same period, another publication, the monthly *Umunyamuryango Trafipro,* linked to a cooperative[5] and therefore to the emergence of a new civil society, tried to distinguish itself from the official voices, but its publication was suspended in 1985 after much pressure.[6]

Emergence of a Privately Owned
Press and Start of the War

In 1988 an independent newspaper, *Kanguka* (Wake Up), appeared. It was financed by a rich Tutsi businessman, Valens Kajeguhakwa, a former supporter of the Habyarimana family who had distanced himself from the regime. Under the direction of a southern Hutu, Vincent Rwabukwisi, the paper focused initially on local news and trivia. Gradually, it developed a policy of criticizing the corruption of the authorities, the gap between the rich and poor, and regionalism. Its growing popularity with an urban educated readership who had begun to manifest their disagreements with the regime, encouraged others to launch similar initiatives from 1990 onward. Between January and October 1990, ten or so new papers appeared, devoted mainly to expressing a growing fatigue with the long years of authoritarian and nepotistic rule.[7] *Kinyamateka* also developed a more critical tone under the direction of a young abbot, André Sibomana.

Those close to President Habyarimana became worried and launched another publication,[8] *Kangura* (Wake Him Up), largely inspired by *Kanguka* in form, but with ethnically oriented motives and an aim to defend the Hutu regime. Its publishing director, Hassan Ngeze, had been a freelance journalist for *Kanguka* while at the same time working as a bus driver delivering copies of the journal to the northwestern part of the country. He had only a primary school education, but this did not matter, since he rarely had to write. The majority of articles in *Kangura* came directly from the presidency, the Central Intelligence Service, or the Akazu (meaning "Little Hut": the entourage of the wife of the head of state, Agathe Habyarimana).

In July 1990 the authorities arrested Vincent Rwabukwisi, the publishing director of *Kanguka,* on his return from Nairobi, where he had gone to interview former king Kigeri V. At the same time, Hassan Ngeze was also arrested, and accused of disturbing public order. The two newspapers ceased publishing for some time, and the two prisoners were supported equally by Amnesty International and Reporters sans Frontières, which lent credibility to the professional legitimacy of *Kangura*'s director. In October, Rwabukwisi was sentenced to fifteen years imprisonment, while Ngeze was released.

In October 1990 the Rwandan Patriotic Front (RPF) launched an attack in the north of the country. The privately owned press initially aligned itself almost unanimously with the government. Some of the more zealous papers made ethnic references. *La Relève* carried extremely sharp headlines, accusing the *inyenzi* ("cockroaches") of being on the side of Yoweri Museveni, the Ugandan president, and his project of establishing a "Hima empire" in the region.[9] Five days after the start of the war in October 1990, the regime organized a fake attack on Kigali, which then justified the arrest of thousands of Tutsi as "accomplices" of the invaders. A number of journalists were among those arrested.[10]

Some privately owned newspapers at this time distanced themselves from the official account. But new, privately owned papers had few financial resources and could not, for example, travel to combat zones. The government could then give its own version of events at the front line. All contradictory versions were penalized and, from 1990 to 1992, more than forty journalists were arrested or detained arbitrarily, most of them under accusations of supporting the RPF.

With the authorization of a multiparty system in June 1991, the number of newspapers increased, reaching about sixty, most of them close to the new parties and expressing their viewpoints. It was essentially "a partisan press, without a code of conduct, practising defamation and denouncement."[11] The papers found a limited but enthusiastic readership among the small businessmen and civil servants who were eager for another version of events, for revelations, and for polemics.[12] *Urumuli rwa Demokarasi* (The Light of Democracy), *Le Démocrate,* and *Isibo* were close to the Mouvement Démocratique Républicain (MDR), the main opposition party.[13] Some titles were openly extremist and close to the former Mouvement Républicain National pour la Démocratie et le Développement (MRND) party or the Akazu: the magazine *Umurava* (Courage),[14] created by those close to the government; *Ijisho Rya Rubanda* (The Eye of the People); *Ijambo* (The Wise Word); *La Victoire-Turatsinze,* monthly of the Rwandan armed forces; *Umurwanashyaka* (The Militant), a bimonthly created by an active member of the Akazu; *Impanda-Echo des Mille Collines,* associated with the extremist Hutu movement; *Intera* (Forward); and *La Médaille Nyiramacibiri.* The papers of the RPF, *Rwanda Rw'ejo* (Rwanda of Tomorrow) and *Rwanda Review,* were also distributed clandestinely.[15] Other titles saw themselves as apolitical, such as the regional journal *Amakuru ki i Butare?* (What Is the News in Butare?) or the papers *Imbaga* (The Meeting) and *Ikindi* (Something Else). Most of these papers were written in Kinyarwanda.[16]

The regime allowed its profound contradictions to appear, betraying the divergences between external and internal pressures. On the one hand, the foreign partners required liberalization and democratic reforms as conditions for development aid, on which the country was completely dependant. On the other hand, the Akazu insisted on maintaining its privileges. The government pretended to make concessions, all the while reinforcing its grip on power.[17] In terms of the media, it showed a willingness to be open, by adopting in December 1991 a new law that was more liberal than the previous.[18] But it reinforced the repression of opposition papers and encouraged the most extremist.

Like the regime itself, this new law was ambiguous. It guaranteed freedom of the press and proclaimed, in Article 16, the freedom for any citizen to create and manage a radio or television station, provided the correct application procedures were followed. But on the other hand, it created a national press commission empowered to sanction or suspend any journalist who broke the law, and it set heavy penalties for offenses against the president of the republic. Other misdemeanors were defined in such an imprecise way that the text remained open to the most opportunist interpretations.

While the press enjoyed an apparent freedom, guaranteed by the law, barely half the newspapers survived (generally the most politicized), because of the huge economic and political difficulties facing them.[19] Meanwhile, the regime had to open the public media to the opposition political parties. Each party was granted a weekly slot of fifteen minutes on Radio Rwanda. But the regime, irked by this forced concession, dismissed the director of ORINFOR, Christophe Mfizi. He was replaced by a sympathizer of the Akazu, Ferdinand Nahimana, a professor of history who had defended a PhD thesis in Paris in which he rehabilitated the precolonial Hutu kingdoms.

Radicalization of the Media:
From Preparation to Support for the Genocide

Beginning in 1992, the steady advance of the RPF led to a radicalization of the media close to the regime. The militia of the MRND created its own paper, *Interahamwe*,[20] and the Coalition pour la Défense de la République (CDR), a radical party, launched a magazine, *Zirikana*. That same year saw the first assassination of a journalist, Straton Byabagamba from Radio Rwanda, a militant in an opposition party. He was killed by four CDR militants.

In 1992, Rwandan television began broadcasting three evenings a week and on weekends. Greater pluralism was tolerated on the screen, possibly because television remained an elitist media, accessible only to rich urban families. The professionalism of its editor in chief may have also contributed to its success in staying on the air. He tried to maintain a certain balance of information, despite some ethnocentric slips, in the name of patriotism. In April 1992, the creation of a coalition government allowed the opposition to gain control of the Ministry of Information, and Ferdinand Nahimana lost his post as director of ORINFOR. He was not replaced for five months, leading to a certain variability in editorial policy in the public media.

Also in 1992, Radio Muhabura (named for the volcano), a propaganda station for the RPF, started to broadcast from Uganda. It had very little access to the territory and transmitted only information that came from the military movement. It adopted a relatively formal tone like that of Radio Rwanda, with which it carried out a war of communiqués. It never detailed the abuses committed by the RPF, but neither did it call for violence. Since it transmitted only on shortwave, the radio's reception was poor in Rwanda. But it was listened to discreetly by those who, whether or not they were partisans of the RPF, wanted to know what was being said on the other side of the front line.[21] Its listeners had to be particularly vigilant: being discovered listening to Radio Muhabura was sufficient to be considered an "accomplice" of the RPF.

Faced with this competition for airwaves and increasingly suspicious that "its" national radio was being divested of its authority, the MRND hard-liners reckoned that it would soon be necessary to find "a more dedicated and effective channel for propaganda."[22] A group of President Habyarimana's associates then decided to establish Radio Télévision Libre des Mille Collines, which began broadcasting in April 1993.[23] Ferdinand Nahimana took control of operations. The station's shareholders included politicians from the MRND and the CDR, businessmen, and journalists from the public press. From July onward, even as the Arusha Accords were being signed, the radio station was able to transmit throughout the country, thanks to a series of relays from Radio Rwanda. The new station had considerable technical and financial resources and quickly gained a large audience, far beyond that of the moribund written press.[24] As journals close to the opposition succumbed to economic difficulties and repression, journalists from extremist papers were drawn en masse to the RTLM, which was soon broadcasting nonstop.[25]

At the beginning the RTLM offered mainly music and entertainment. After the assassination of President Melchior Ndadaye in Burundi in October 1993, it became immersed in politics, arguing that the generalized violence that reigned in the neighboring country could spread to Rwanda. It condemned the RPF and denounced the Arusha Accords, remaining faithful to the "Hutu power" ideology.[26] The Tutsi and their "accomplices," the Hutu political personalities of the opposition, were identified as being responsible for the difficulties facing the country. Among the accused were civil society leaders, human rights activists, journalists who had supported the peace process or criticized abuses by the MRND, the CDR, and their militias.

On April 6, 1994, the RTLM was the first to announce that the president's airplane had been brought down. The station lost no time in accusing the opposition Hutu, the RPF, and the Belgian contingent of the United Nations Assistance Mission for Rwanda (UNAMIR) of being involved in the attack. From the moment the interim government was created, the station broadcast twenty-four hours a day. It called for hunting down and eliminating the "cockroaches" and "snakes"—accomplices of the RPF who threatened to eradicate the Hutu of Rwanda. It supported, guided, and encouraged the work of the militias, which began by systematically executing the opposition leaders, then all Tutsi, who were characterized as an "enemy within" in collusion with the assassins of the president. The RTLM encouraged its listeners to participate in and join the ranks of the Interahamwe, on the grounds of legitimate defense. The station convinced the public that there was just one option: kill or be killed.

During the whole period of the genocide, the RTLM gave airtime to the most extremist of politicians, zealous civil servants, and members of the government who encouraged the population to do their "duty" by taking part in the killings. When the town of Kigali was finally taken by the RPF, on July 4, 1994, the station continued to broadcast from a mobile transmitter, which, following the population, had entered the zone protected by France's Operation Turquoise. The RTLM encouraged the essentially forced departure of civilians to Zaire, supporting the militias and the interim government, which had promised to leave to the RPF a territory emptied of its inhabitants. The RTLM's personnel and equipment came to rest at Bukavu, with hundreds of thousands of refugees. Taken hostage by the former Rwandan regime, these displaced populations would huddle together for almost two years.

In the camps, RTLM journalists met with their colleagues from Radio Rwanda, who had also joined the exodus. The national radio station had a less directly active role in the genocide, at least until May 1994. During the first days of the genocide, its more moderate journalists fled or were killed, resulting in a lack of direction for Radio Rwanda. But it was taken over progressively by the most extreme fringes of the interim government. The station broadcast communiqués demanding that the population stay at home or help the armed forces defend the country against its "enemies." However, it did not assist the militias directly in the daily organization of their macabre task.

By the end of July 1994, the Rwandan media landscape had been devastated: forty-eight journalists (including twenty-five Hutu) had been killed, most during the first days of the genocide.[27] Many others, aware of the threat, fled. Dozens of media professionals haunted the camps of Bukavu and Goma, and others soon found themselves behind bars.[28]

The Reign of Hate Media

At the initiative of Reporters sans Frontières, a team led by Jean-Pierre Chrétien, the specialist historian of the Great Lakes region, conducted and published a systematic analysis of broadcasts by the hate media before and during the genocide. What stands out is that, if the media cannot be considered the cause of the genocide, they were, along with the extensive arsenal of knives and machetes of the unemployed youth, one of the instruments of a carefully designed global strategy that aimed clearly to eliminate two elements of the Rwandan population: the opponents of the genocide ideology,[29] and the whole of the Tutsi people.

The Mechanisms of Ethnocentric Propaganda

Kangura was the first publication to openly and explicitly express itself against the Tutsi population. This was in a context where, by no coincidence, the emergence of a democratic political opposition was orienting the public debate on themes separate from ethnic references—the corruption of the authorities, illegal personal enrichment, and the like. From the time of its inception, the paper directly attacked the promoter of *Kanguka,* denouncing the Tutsi grip on commerce and business. After the RPF attack on Rwanda, *Kangura,* in its sixth issue (December 1990), published an "Appeal to the Conscience of the Bahutu," followed by the "Ten Hutu Commandments,"[30] a document that extolled hatred against and exclusion of the Tutsi. It identified them with the enemies who attempted to destabilize Rwanda, and denounced their so-called hegemonic tendencies. All Hutu who married Tutsi women or hired Tutsi secretaries were labeled "traitors," as were all Hutu who failed to preach this ideology.

Most of the tenets of this hate propaganda, which would lay the groundwork for the extermination and which would be taken up later by other papers and the RTLM, appeared in the "Ten Hutu Commandments."[31] The document contained the following strategies:

• *Rereading of history:* The distinction between Hutu and Tutsi was presented as an ancestral historical cleavage, with the latter being described as foreigners who had subjugated the Hutu for centuries. The "Appeal to the Conscience of the Bahutu" noted that the Tutsi kings "conquered the country of the Hutu, killed their monarchs and so enslaved the Hutu." The extremist media were to return systematically to presenting the "Hamite" origin of the Tutsi, which differentiated them radically from the Hutu "Bantu," who should call on the support of their "Bantu brothers" in their struggle (ninth commandment).

• *Ethnic evidence:* The sentiment of belonging, to the point of unashamed identification, was reinforced. "The Bahutu, wherever they may be, must be united in their solidarity and concerned by the plight of their brother Bahutu, firm and vigilant against their common Tutsi enemy" (ninth commandment). The principal identity was therefore to be ethnic, and to guide both the organization of society and individual political membership. The document stipulated clearly, "Strategic positions, whether political, administrative, economic, military or concerning security, must be entrusted to Bahutu" (fifth commandment).

• *Manichaeism:* According to the "Appeal to the Conscience of the Bahutu," there was, on the one hand, "a majority people,"[32] and on the other, a feudal minority that was trying to deny ethnic reality in order to continue "insinuating" itself into the majority. Democratic principles, therefore, meant the "the management of the *res publica* by the electoral majority" and not "equality between Hutu and Tutsi."[33] This distinction was characterized, in a way, as "Good" and "Evil"—the legitimacy of the majority, faced with the illegitimacy of the claims of the minority; the rights of the Hutu against the terrorist tactics of the infiltrators, the feudal Tutsi.

• *Manipulation of the facts:* Violence committed against the Tutsi was systematically presented as a defensive reflex by the Hutu in facing an aggressive enemy intent on "reinstating the minority and feudal power of the Batutsi." Citing 1959, 1962, and 1967, the dates of significant killings of Tutsi families, the "Appeal to the Conscience of the Bahutu" noted "the terrorism and the guerrilla tactics" of the Batutsi as they harassed the Hutu population.

• *Victimization:* The appeal claimed, "The Tutsi are bloodthirsty and power-mad and they want to impose their hegemony over the Rwandan people at gunpoint." The primary trigger for hatred was fear, with the extremist media returning constantly to the menace hanging over the Hutu, represented by the presence of the Tutsi in the country. Since 1959, "The Batutsi have not relinquished for a single day the idea of re-conquering Rwanda, exterminating the intellectuals and dominating the Bahutu farmers."[34] This strategy was also seen as part of a vast international plot. *Kangura* alluded to a "plan for the Tutsi re-colonization in Kivu and the central region of Africa," which was supposedly revealed in Zaire in 1962 and would have been put into practice with the seizure of power of Buyoya in Burundi, and of Museveni in Uganda. The threat was therefore permanent and "the Bahutu must be ready to defend themselves."

• *Dehumanization and bestialization of the enemy:* The seed was planted in the eighth commandment, which proclaimed, "The Bahutu must no longer have pity on the Batutsi." The RPF combatants, who called themselves *inkotanyi* ("brawlers" or "obstinate"),[35] were labeled *inyenzi* ("cockroaches"), a term that was applied to all Tutsi and extended to all political opponents.

• *Denunciation of all RPF ibyitso (accomplices):* The Bahutu must be "vigilant lest the Inkotanyi and their accomplices exterminate us," noted the introduction of the appeal in Kinyarwanda. These "enemies within" were the moderate Hutu politicians as well as the whole of the Tutsi population. For "the enemy is always there, among us and is only waiting for the right moment to try again to liquidate us."[36]

All the propaganda mechanisms necessary to lay the groundwork for genocide were contained in this sixth issue of *Kangura,* but the paper lacked two important elements to be truly effective: a popular tone, and the capacity to reach a large public. The RTLM possessed these additional assets and would use them to amplify the extreme ideology presented above.

The RTLM: From Words to Actions

The RTLM had a particular tone. It broadcast a lot of music, including Congolese popular songs and the extremist songs of popular musician Simon Bikindi.[37] It devoted a large amount of time to free programming, such as interviews with listeners or invited personalities. It was lively, amusing, and a clear departure from the official tone of Radio Rwanda or Radio Muhabura. Relayed rapidly across the whole of the country, it reached a large part of the Rwandan population, including the rural and illiterate masses, who did not have access to the written press but possessed small, cheap transistor radios.[38]

Aside from its format and scope, the RTLM possessed some particularly formidable features. First, it was directed by trained, experienced managers who could in turn rely on personnel from Radio Rwanda or the progovernment press. Behind its seemingly improvised and spontaneous façade, nothing was left to chance, from the choice of presenters to the selection of background music. Jean-Pierre Chrétien emphasized, "We are in the presence of well thought-out and ably executed propaganda, no improvised harangues of rabid fringe elements, but a breviary of hate carefully distilled by professionals in the audiovisual field."[39] Second, it expressed itself principally in Kinyarwanda. "The propagandists of the Rwandan genocide believed that their statements, notably those made in Kinyarwanda, would remain reserved for internal consumption, hidden from the eyes and ears of international opinion."[40]

Third, it had a talented team of presenters who played on their relationship with listeners, even though some of the "public" participation on the air was certainly staged. During the genocide the radio station was in permanent contact with the militias posted at the barriers, and with the night patrols. The radio announcers greeted and encouraged them, urging them to smoke hemp to give them courage and repeating the call to rob and pillage Tutsi property. It justified the massacres in the name of legitimate defense. It used nonstop humor, cynicism, and jokes to emphasize its rapport and complicity with the listener. Kantano Habimana, a presentation genius whose background as a sports commentator stood him in good stead, followed the massacre as if it were a football match, provoking constant mirth from his listeners. "Everyone, even we, listened to Kantano," recalled a survivor. "He was so funny that you could not stop yourself from following his broadcasts. Even if you were the one he was telling people to kill."[41]

This rapport and interactivity gave the station a real performative power. By speaking, it acted. Its words materialized, leading listeners to act. This power was already a characteristic of *Kangura,* which made accusations that provoked immediate consequences. Denunciations would result in executions by the militias of the persons identified. It was after the publication in the paper of a "listener's letter," complaining about the director of ORINFOR, that Christophe Mfizi was dismissed in 1990. In February 1991, a ministerial reshuffle had removed from their posts all who had been attacked by *Kangura,* leading a satirical publication to write that the reshuffle had been the product of a "journalistic decree" following "the request of the bi-monthly *Kangura.*"[42]

The RTLM was to push to the limit this real and immediate effectiveness of its broadcasts. Even before the genocide, the lists of "accomplices" it broadcast led immediately to the tracking down of opposition Hutu who were favorable to the Arusha Accords, as well as journalists and human rights militants who tried to denounce the violence aimed at the Tutsi. Once a person was identified, the militias created checkpoints in order to search the inhabitants of the area where the person lived, and violently attacked all those whose identity cards indicated they were Tutsi.

The fact that the same individuals directed and financed the militias, guaranteeing their impunity, and also supported the radio station, led to a complete complicity of the two "instruments." The station targeted those who denounced the militias, or "Network Zero,"[43] who then immediately became subject to persecution.

Beginning on April 7, 1994, the station's instructions became still more explicit. Rejoicing every day about the massacres of Tutsi families, journalist Valérie Bemeriki exclaimed, "Those people had to be killed and you have done it. The father should not just get a bullet in the head, he should be cut into little pieces."[44]

The RTLM was a real actor, at the center of events. It broadcast information that allowed the militias to organize themselves, to search each district for "accomplices," and to maintain a steady supply of arms. It provided updated lists of people who had already been executed and those who had still not been found. The RTLM asked listeners for clues to locate the "accomplices" and told them to contact the station so it could broadcast the addresses where they were hiding; it also broadcast license plate numbers of cars that people were using to try to escape.

The fourth important factor was that RTLM journalists knew they were completely free. They were guaranteed impunity,[45] as they worked within the propaganda framework drawn by the management. All excesses were permitted if they corresponded to the station's "editorial line." No subject was taboo: neither sex, nor scatology, nor perjury in what was traditionally a modest, reserved, and Christian society.

The station seized and perverted the Christian culture by claiming divine approval in the fight of "Good" against "Evil." At the same time, it encouraged attacks on churches said to be used as secret RPF bases. On July 2, 1994, on the eve of the taking of Kigali, Kantano Habimana declared in one of his long monologues, "These people, as my friend Gahigi says, are the Antichrist, they are very bad people. I do not know how God will help us to wipe them out. . . . But let us continue to exterminate them so that our little children will never again hear talk of the Inkotanyi."[46]

Apart from these internal features that made the RTLM an instrument of genocide, how can one explain the success of its propaganda? Several external factors appear to have contributed. There was no alternative in a radio landscape monopolized by official stations. The spread of disinformation in an atmosphere ripe for prejudice and intolerance had been simmering for a long time. People lived in an atmosphere that led each side to absorb, from their earliest years, a sense of their "difference" from the other, which led most to see themselves as fitting into one of the stereotyped categories. There was also a permanent and active connivance between the hate media and the extremist militias (the voice and the arm of the body, guided by the same brain). And finally, the generalized impunity was guaranteed to both those who called the people to "do the work" and those who were doing the executing.

Several factors have been cited to explain the abuses that were allowed to flourish: the journalists' lack of professionalism, the absence of adequate press legislation or a body to regulate the media, and the rewards offered to journalists who put themselves at the service of the highest bidders. All these factors, however, are not sufficient to explain the abuses. They have been present in many other contexts, but have not resulted in consequences as tragic as those observed in Rwanda in 1994.

An Absence of Alternatives: A Partisan Public Media and a Limited Foreign Media

If they were not listening to the RTLM, which media did Rwandans turn to for information? For a long time, the state media had provided the only news available to the Rwandan population. But in a largely rural and illiterate country, the national radio station was restricted to governmental communication. At Radio Rwanda, each news bulletin began with a speech from President Habyarimana.

After the first RPF attack in October 1990, Radio Rwanda put itself on a war footing. It broadcast anti-RPF propaganda and gradually all of the Tutsi population became the "enemies." In December 1990, a change of direction led to greater use of the airwaves for manipulation. In December 1991, Radio Rwanda broadcast a "communiqué" of the Rwandan Armed Forces (RAF) (its origins were not authenticated, but President Habyarimana authorized it), accusing the RPF of having infiltrated or supported newspapers, manipulating opposition parties, and stirring up violence and insecurity by preaching ethnic hatred against the Hutu.[47] Radio Rwanda broadcast more or less authentic communiqués or "documents," a practice used to discredit opponents or provoke violent popular movements. While declarations on RPF atrocities were broadcast daily, messages from human rights associations were not transmitted.[48]

In March 1992, following Radio Rwanda's repeated broadcasts of a communiqué from a so-called human rights group based in Nairobi announcing RPF preparations to eliminate a number of Hutu political personalities, tens of Tutsi families were massacred in the Bugesera region. Following this episode, which provoked an outcry within the opposition in Rwanda and throughout the international community, the director of ORINFOR, Ferdinand Nahimana, was forced to resign, leaving his post vacant for five months.

Radio Rwanda then went through a period of drifting editorial policy. On two occasions, in 1992 and 1993, its personnel (about fifty staff, including five Tutsi) went on strike, demanding greater freedom of expression, more resources, and a clearer editorial line. As underlined by Jean-Marie Vianney Higiro, the director of ORINFOR on the eve of the genocide (he fled the country on April 9, 1994), the radio staff had diverse political affiliations: "The Office reflected the political transformations taking place. . . . The fundamental problem remained the confusion between membership in a political party and the profession of journalist."[49] Pressure on the journalists increased, leading some to choose to resign while others accepted compromises in order to keep their jobs.

On April 7, 1994, Radio Rwanda urged "vigilance" and called on the population to "mobilise alongside the army." During the following weeks, the radio retained its official role, giving airtime to the interim authorities to broadcast their declarations. But gradually, most of the journalists who had remained at the station succumbed to the RTLM's influence and extremism, and were soon following its line.

As for the international media, their impact could only be limited. Before the genocide, no international media were broadcasting in Kinyarwanda. The international stations (the RFI, the BBC, and Deutsche Welle) used shortwave frequencies and were only listened to by French-speaking intellectuals. In 1990, the extremist paper *Kangura* had begun accusing correspondents of the Western media of being RPF agents. "There is an international network of disparagement of Rwanda," it stated, repeating the thesis of a vast international plot against the Hutu people. The tone was raised a notch with the attack of October 1990, following which it said that the foreign newspapers "like *Le Figaro, Le Soir* and *La Libre Belgique* undertook to soil Rwanda."[50] In fact, foreign journalists, and mainly the Belgian press, were starting to reveal the true nature of Juvénal Habyarimana's regime, which had previously been presented as a model in the region. Foreign journalists' denunciations of human rights violations provoked the regime, which took vengeance on the local press through arrests and intimidation. But the real impact of a not easily accessible written French press could only be limited.

During the genocide, few foreign media could keep correspondents on the ground, and the international news was dominated by other events judged more significant, such as the fatal accident of Brazilian racing driver Ayrton Senna and the South African elections.

"Coverage was minimal," comments Jean-Paul Gouteux, who has written on the "media abdication" of the French press.[51] The genocide therefore took place "behind closed doors"; the alarming articles, published by the Belgian press, passed completely unnoticed and did not even reach Rwanda. The few scraps of news broadcast by the international audiovisual media were automatically discredited by the RTLM, which viewed the foreign journalists as "whites (who) have been bought off by the Inkotanyi"; Radio France Internationale was said to be "improvised as a relay station for Radio Muhabura."[52]

After the Genocide:
A Traumatized Media Industry

In 1994 the RPF inherited a devastated country, strewn with more than a million dead bodies, where everything had to be rebuilt. In this context, the media industry was certainly not a priority. On the contrary, from then on, journalists were viewed with general suspicion and certain members of the profession were seen as accomplices to the unspeakable crimes that had been committed.

However, the public media quickly began broadcasting again. Radio Rwanda, which had lost all its staff, relied on journalists from Radio Muhabura and professionals who had returned from exile. Its watchwords were "national unity" and "reconstruction." Television also began to broadcast again, within limited time slots. Certain content was particularly sensitive, especially anything concerning refugees in Zaire and those who had been displaced within the country.

While the majority of print machinery had been destroyed,[53] and the profession had been decimated, some press initiatives timidly began to appear, including *Rwanda Rushya* (New Rwanda), *Le Messager,* and *Le Tribun du Peuple,* outlets that were independent or close to the RPF. *Kinyamateka* also resumed publishing, as did the state papers *Imvaho Nshya* and *La Nouvelle Relève,* which changed their titles slightly to mark the beginning of a new era.

In the refugee camps in Zaire, exiled journalists reorganized and created an association of Rwandan journalists. They attempted to continue publishing their extremist editorials through a news bulletin called *Amizero* (Hope), directed by Gaspard Gahigi, former chief editor of the RTLM. Hassan Ngeze, Kantano Habimana, and Valérie Bemeriki appeared among the cited authors, already forging the first arguments for the genocide denial theories. As Jean-Pierre Chrétien has noted,

"Perhaps never before has a genocide been the subject of such a rapid denial."[54] *Kangura* also started to reappear abroad.

Faced with the threat represented by this strike force, reorganizing just a few kilometers from its borders, the new Rwandan authorities were suspicious and anxious to control the circulation of news. In 1994 a humanitarian station, Radio Unamir, was authorized to broadcast, but two other projects were rejected.[55]

Arrest followed arrest, including within the public media, and some professionals were accused of having taken part in the genocide. Confusion reigned at the headquarters of some international associations for the defense of journalists and freedom of speech, which treated some of those who had been arrested on suspicion of participation in the genocide as prisoners of opinion.

Despite this unfavorable context, new papers sprouted: *Imboni* (The Pupil), *Ingoboka* (Unexpected Help), *Inkingi* (The Pillar), *Intaremara* (Valid), *Libération, La Patrie–Urwatubyaye* (Mother Country), *Rwanda-Renaître, Ukuri Gacaca* (Truth Gacaca), and *Umusemburo–Le Levain*. Ephemeral initiatives appeared and disappeared. In August 1995, twenty-eight papers, including a handful in English (many exiles returning from Uganda and Tanzania), were publishing.[56] Several foreign associations and aid programs tried to help with the rebuilding of the press.

From 1997 onward, murderous confrontations took place between the Rwandan army and the ex-RAF, which was distributing its extremist papers clandestinely. The climate remained tense. Official news was managed with a strategic and defensive objective. Some papers, locked into the ethnocentricity that the new regime was trying to eradicate, were accused of inciting hatred and "factionalism." In 1998, the minister of information reiterated that "all those who publish state secrets in the press, and their accomplices, will be punished according to the law." This meant, according to the terms of the penal code, "the death penalty in time of war and a term of imprisonment of 10 to 20 years in peacetime."[57] Added to the general mistrust of the regime were many material difficulties that discouraged goodwill toward returnees who had come back from abroad. An increasing number of journalists were going into exile or returning to exile, and private publications became rare. In 1998, only seven periodicals were appearing regularly.

Members of the profession set up the Association Rwandaise des Journalistes (ARJ)/Rwandan Association of Journalists and the Association Rwandaise des Femmes des Médias (ARFEM)/Rwandan Association of Media Women, in an effort to become more organized. UNESCO helped out by assisting in the establishment of the Maison de la Presse du Rwanda/Rwanda Press House. But these initiatives never really took off, because the journalists' lacked commitment and also because the most active members soon went into exile. In March 2000, Déo Mushayidi, director of the Maison de la Presse and editor in chief of the paper *Imboni*, left the country. He was followed by his publication director, Jason Muhayimana, and, a little later, by one of his colleagues, Jean-Claude Nkubito. While the exiles claimed that these departures were a result of pressure and threats, the regime saw them as mere excuses by would-be economic refugees who knew they would be more welcome abroad if they were political refugees. In other newspapers, these departures led to rumors of misappropriation of funds and divisive tendencies.[58]

As the regime shrunk to a hardcore of loyalists around Paul Kagame, who had become president in April 2000, two tendencies became apparent. On the one hand, the administration wanted to put in place a judicial framework to establish legal and regulatory conditions for media freedom and liberalizing the airwaves. On the other hand, in a country trying to rise above a logic based on ethnicity, ensuring security was a priority, especially given fears of a resurgence of hate-filled propaganda. On January 7, 2002, the minister of information, Désiré Nyandwi, reminded journalists that "the government has no intention of restricting the freedom of the press. Yes to the freedom of the press, but no to the aberrations which would plunge us again into the nightmare of 1994."[59]

It is true that the hate media played a horrific role, but it is worth remembering a statement from a document by the Ligue des Droits de la Personne dans les Grands Lacs (LDGL)/League of Human Rights in the Great Lakes Region: "The genocide was perpetrated at the instigation of authorities which encouraged, indeed, initiated, the emergence of these same media. A sovereign and responsible state has all the latitude needed to prevent the development of such media."[60]

This is what the new regime set out to do. On May 11, 2002, a new press law was adopted, after many years of negotiations and many amendments. Relatively permissive, it proclaimed that "the press is free" (Article 10) and that "censorship is forbidden" (Article 11). It opened the way to liberalization of the audiovisual media, which started to take shape after the establishment in 2003 of the Haut Conseil de la Presse (HCP)/High Council of the Press, which is responsible for guaranteeing and ensuring freedom of the press, commenting on authorizations for the creation of audiovisual media, and issuing as well as revoking press cards.

The current media landscape consists of two public sector newspapers, which are used to communicate government information. There are also several private publications, which are obviously favorable to the regime. The "independent" press (sometimes just as politicized as the private, proregime press), which is weak and lacks professionalism, and some media outlets close to the Catholic Church, complete this landscape. These periodicals are in English (*The New Times*, close to the regime),[61] in French (*Lenten, Rwanda Libération*, and *Le Soft des Grands Lacs*),[62] or in Kinyarwanda (*Umusemburo, Gasabo, Ingabo* [monthly of the Ministry of Defense], *Inganzo*, and *Ukuri*). Among the titles that claim to be "independent," the only ones to appear regularly are *Umuseso* (The Dawn) and *Umuco* (The Light). The Catholic press has been reduced to *Kinyamateka* (a weekly as of 1999) and two others that are wholly confessional: *Urumuri rwa Kristu* (The Light of Christ) and *Urunana* (Solidarity).[63] The private press agency Agence Rwandaise d'Information (ARI)/Rwanda News Agency publishes, besides a weekly, *Grands Lacs Hebdo*, a daily bulletin in French and English.

According to a Rwandan journalist, the progovernment papers "are accused of receiving unofficial payments and producing work which is complacent and requires a minimum of effort. They reproduce radio news or noncompromising dispatches dug up from the Internet and cover seminars and workshops in Kigali. Other papers, encouraged and supported by certain NGOs and embassies, dream of winning the prize for independent media. They dare to make some critical remarks about the regime and sometimes publish rumours or news, which is usually poorly handled since they cannot verify it."[64]

A report published in March 2004 by the HCP monitoring center noted that the private media were inclined to "make more analysis and to offer more views than the public media which often concentrated on a simple record of the facts."[65] A preliminary report published at the same time as the general elections in September–October 2003 noted that the media, whatever their affiliation, tend to favor only one version of the news—the version from the source they support (regime or opposition). They do not try to present different or contradictory points of view.[66]

The more prosperous newspapers are printed at the national printing house and benefit from advertising contracts with the state and with the big private companies close to the regime. The other publications regularly denounce this favoritism. Faced with high printing costs in Kigali, they print their papers in Kampala at an affordable cost, but this causes delays in appearance and administrative problems. *Kinyamateka* has its own printing shop, but print runs are small (under 4,000 copies)[67] and the readership is concentrated in Kigali.

Umuseso, considered the only paper critical of the regime, has been suspended several times. It has been through many internal divisions and a rapid turnover of personnel. Often carrying rumor, opinion, and unverified sensationalist news, it has a dangerous style that regularly flouts professional standards. Denouncing corruption at the highest levels of government and the army,[68] the paper complains of being disparaged and ostracized by the state and potential advertisers. An HCP report acknowledged that "some private media complain of being professionally discriminated against," for example, when they are refused access to certain public events to which they were not invited.[69] This lack of professionalism, combined with economic difficulties, state control of information, and internal quarrels, in a profession where division and suspicion persist, creates a context far from favorable for the healthy growth and development of the press.

ORINFOR, which has the same administrative structure as under the old regime, still oversees two public publications, as well as the national radio and television stations. Radio Rwanda broadcasts twenty-four hours a day, in Kinyarwanda, Kiswahili, French, and English. The national television broadcasts daily from 1 P.M. to 11 P.M., with programs in Kinyarwanda, English, and French. As government media, they prioritize institutional news and rarely give access to civil society, which is still underdeveloped. A July 2004 HCP report on the commemoration of the tenth anniversary of the genocide noted that "Radio Rwanda and TVR had not given a single report on the political opposition," nor adequate airtime to the civil population. They favor official speeches, contrary to the international media, which are more open to the points of view of citizens and the opposition.[70] However, the HCP has noted several times the willingness of the public audiovisual media to cover the whole country, which the private media cannot do. Since the death in 2000 of ORINFOR's director, Wilson Rutayisire (former director of Radio Muhabura), the military hierarchy is no longer present at this office.

In the private audiovisual area, six stations were approved at the beginning of 2004 by the HCP, five of which started to broadcast during the course of the year: Radio 10, Radio Flash, and Radio Contact (which essentially broadcast music and entertainment), the community station Radio Izuba in the province of Kibungo, and Radio Maria at Gitarama.[71] The sixth, Radio Salus, the station of the School of Journalism and Communication at the National University of Rwanda at Butare, started to transmit only in 2005, due to technical problems. Eight other stations were authorized in 2005.

The Rwandan media landscape is experiencing a gradual evolution toward pluralism, despite significant challenges. Those challenges include lack of resources in an economy that is struggling through reconstruction; lack of professionalism; the departure of the young graduates of the School of Journalism, who look for more rewarding careers outside the press; and regulatory frameworks that are still insufficient to allow a real diversification. As well, mistrust, manipulation, trauma, and the memory of the hate media remain, and still haunt the whole of the media industry.

Scars from the Genocide in the Press

And how could it be otherwise? How does one reconstruct a nation, a social fabric, pluralist institutions, and open media after a genocide, while the executioners and their victims continue to live side-by-side, listening to the same radio stations, reading the same publications? The Rwandan situation today is so complex that many foreign observers would like to simply gloss over this difficulty. In autumn 2003, a representative of an international media assistance program who was exasperated by the authorities' refusal to rapidly liberalize the radio sector, exclaimed, "But it's ten years now. It's time to turn the page and look to the future."

But what does a decade mean when recovering from a genocide? How does one go about shaping a completely new generation of professional, competent journalists? How does one restore confidence between the media and the political authorities, and between the media and their public, and also build up a news sector where material, financial, and human resources have been annihilated? Is it surprising that a decade later, under the permanent threat of a new war, haunted by the spectre of a genocide that some are waiting "to complete," and shaken by risky military adventures outside the country's borders, complete freedom of expression is still not guaranteed? Should it be regretted that some survivors still shudder when they hear a radio program being played in a neighboring courtyard and are unable to "look to the future"? Should it be shocking that some international NGOs, arriving in Kigali with a bagful of media aid projects, tidy sums in foreign currency, and the weight of their bad consciences (which are only equaled by their desire to do good), might be welcomed with reticence and coolness? The scars of the past are not easily healed.

Legal, Regulatory, and Institutional Framework

The first scar inherited from this past is manifested in the caution and slowness with which the new authorities began work on a new press law, a prerequisite for the development of independent media. The need for a new framework was obvious very soon after the genocide. The country needed to be put on its guard against the emergence of hate media. As Chad expert Gilbert Maoundonodji said, "All [reforms] concerning freedom of speech [seem] to be a prisoner of its past."[72]

But bringing a new law into being has been a long process. From 1994 to 2002, the regime used the absence of a legal and regulatory framework to justify slowing the liberalization of the audiovisual sector. The first version of the new law bore explicit traces of the genocide. Article 89 stated, "Whoever, in the context of the press, attempts to incite a part of the Rwandan population to commit genocide and with practical consequences, will incur the death penalty." President Kagame himself finally opposed this clause, and following his intervention this article, as well as the accompanying passages for Articles 88 and 90, were withdrawn from the law.

The final version of the law, adopted May 11, 2002, stipulates terms of imprisonment for violations of press laws such as defamation and invasion of privacy, but does not explicitly mention calls to commit genocide, which are dealt with in the penal code,[73] thus limiting the possibility of abusive interpretations. However, the law does include some quite severe clauses, stipulating, for example, that sellers and distributors of papers may be held responsible for the content of papers they handle in cases where the misdemeanor cannot be imputed to the director of the publication, the chief editor, or the author of the incriminating article. The law is otherwise relatively liberal and reaffirms freedom of the press (Article 10), defined as the prerogative to publish opinions and to collect, receive, and distribute information and opinions by means of the press. It stipulates that censorship is forbidden (Article 11).

The law also called for the creation of a regulatory body, the HCP, which was established in 2002.[74] However, the HCP has only an advisory capacity, with the final decision belonging to the Ministry of Information. The HCP is composed of nine members,[75] with a permanent administration of eight people. It has begun work in several areas, examining applications for private radio stations, granting press cards, and systematically monitoring the handling of news by the Rwandan media.[76] The HCP is also responsible for supervising equal access to the public media for candidates in election periods.[77] Its "monitoring" reports emphasize the predominance of official or superficial news in the local press, the absence of analysis, and the lack of diversity in media that limit themselves to giving just one point of view. The HCP also notes the tendency of the private press to drift into unsupported opinions and the privileged position accorded to the presidential party, the RPF-Inkontanyi.

The Ministry of Information, integrated as part of the Ministère de l'Administration Locale, de l'Information et des Affaires Sociales (MINALOC)/Ministry of Local Administration, Information and Social Affairs in 2000, is now again an autonomous ministry. In October 2003 it was associated with the cabinet of the prime minister and remains the decisionmaking body in matters of suspending or banning the media, granting licenses, and accrediting foreign journalists. It was also in 2003 that a new constitution was adopted; it stipulates that freedom of the press and freedom of information are recognized and guaranteed by the state.

What is critical, however, is not the law, but how the law is used, just as what is important is not the establishment of institutions, but how they operate. Whereas the law of 1991 and the old penal code explicitly forbade defamation and appeals to ethnic hatred, impunity and an absence of sanctions paved the way for genocide. This is the response given by the Rwandan authorities, too, when reproached for their overly scrupulous respect of the law.

Freedom of the Press vs. National Unity and Security

The difficult relations between the authorities and journalists, more precisely around the perception and the use of freedom of the press, constitute another legacy of past traumas. After the RPF victory in July 1994, the new minister of information, Jean-Baptiste Nkuliyingoma, from the MDR and a former journalist for *Imbaga,* had promised that the new administration would reestablish democracy and respect freedom of expression.[78] But this commitment was difficult to implement in a fragile context involving reconstruction of an entire nation.

From 1995 onward, criticisms of the RPF by some private media were badly received by the regime. International organizations for the defense of journalists became agitated following threats made against Edouard Mutsinzi, editor in chief of the paper *Le Messager-Intumwa,* and André Sibomana, who was still running *Kinyamateka.* Stormy relations ensued, full of suspicion and accusations between the Rwandan administration, which was then coming to grips with a complex, explosive internal situation, and the international foreign-based organizations, some close to certain exiles whose discourse was still ingrained with an ethnic dimension. These difficult relations certainly influenced the government's responses to the local publications, some of which felt supported and reinforced from beyond Rwanda's borders. The new regime thought that the need for national unity required minimizing criticisms of its policies.[79] But in 1995 the prime minister remarked, "In terms of national reconstruction, the role of the press has been more destructive than constructive."[80]

The return from Congo of former Rwandan public media professionals, beginning in 1996, increased tensions and resulted in a wave of arrests. Journalists of Radio Rwanda, or those who had worked for the station before going into exile, were arrested and accused of having directly taken part in acts of genocide.[81] Reporters sans Frontières, which preferred not to comment on many cases, did bring attention, on several occasions, to the situation of imprisoned journalists, whom the association maintained were not guilty.[82] The authorities replied that their imprisonment was not linked to their profession and that Reporters sans Frontières should not involve itself in their cases.

From then on, differing interpretations of situations, individuals, and their cases became almost systematic. For those on the outside, the regime became increasingly touchy, imposing silence on politically delicate subjects. For example, in 1997 the editor in chief of the bimonthly *Umuravumba,* Appolos Hakizimana, was shot dead a week after his paper referred to massacres carried out by the RPF.[83] And there was the imprisonment of Amiel Nkuliza, director of *Le Partisan,* from 1997 to 1999, condemned for "undermining the security of the state" after having published photographs of prisoners on the point of asphyxia at the central prison in Nsinda.[84] In August 2000, Radio Rwanda broadcast a communiqué criticizing the closure of the general assembly of the Ligue pour la Promotion des Droits de l'Homme au Rwanda (LIPRODHOR)/ Rwandan League for the Promotion and Defence of Human Rights in Rwanda that included allusions to conditions at Nsinda prison. The authorities immediately dismissed the journalist thought to be responsible for the communiqué.[85] For the Rwandan authorities, in each of those cases, the problem was the lack of professionalism, or the perverse intentions of political activists who were disguising themselves as journalists but whose agenda was other than that of providing the population with balanced and accurate news.

The reasons given for journalists' departures into exile also differed.[86] In 1999, John Mugabi, editor in chief of *Rwanda Newsline,* was arrested for denouncing the general secretary of the Ministry of Defense for taking bribes. The general secretary himself took the case to court, where the journalist was unable to produce evidence against the accusations. Saying he felt threatened for having questioned the involvement of the Rwandan army in the DRC, and accused of being in the pay of "negative forces,"[87] the journalist fled the country two years later to seek asylum in the Netherlands. He was followed by two of his close colleagues, which led to the closing of the paper. But the Rwandan authorities saw him as an economic refugee, who incidentally was a militant of a political party, disguised as an asylum seeker persecuted for his ideas. It was the same for other journalists who chose exile, such as Jean-Pierre Mugabe, publication director of the journal *Le Tribun du Peuple*,[88] who left for the United States; and Valens Kwitegetse, journalist for *Kinyamateka*, who went to Uganda.

Beginning in 2001, as defections within the state apparatus increased, certain newspapers suffered growing pressure. When Pasteur Bizimungu, former head of state, announced the creation of his new party (Parti Démocratique pour le Renouveau/Democratic Party for Renewal), the national correspondents of the foreign press (Thomas Kamilindi of the BBC and Lucie Umukundwa of the VOA) were threatened by the intelligence services and summoned to surrender tapes recorded during a press conference. Ismaël Mbonigaba, the publication director of *Umuseso*, which was part of the same group as *Rwanda Newsline*, was also harassed. In 2003, he spent a month in prison, accused of having "incited division and discrimination" for publishing an article announcing the candidature of Faustin Twagiramungu in the presidential election of August, accompanied by a caricature of the head of state that was judged to be "insulting."

Rumors about papers that had distanced themselves from the regime were widespread and reflected the many different interpretations as well as the existence of poorly defined underground networks. *Umuseso* noted that its editor in chief "is the subject of a demonization campaign orchestrated by government officials . . . , via the public and pseudo-independent media." The journal is regularly accused of factionalism, of revisionism, and indeed of denying the genocide, and is even suspected of putting out "propaganda for genocide."[89] Printed in Uganda for financial and practical reasons, it is regularly seized at the border. "The police wait at the border to welcome the journal *Umuseso* and escort it to the headquarters of the judicial police."[90] It is here that the decision is taken whether to ban one of its published articles or to seize the whole issue.

Even the relative calm of the current period, marked by fewer arrests and reprimands, is subject to different analyses. For the authorities, the calm signals an improved legal and institutional framework and a gradual maturing of the profession. For other observers, it is "hardly the result of a greater openness of the authorities but rather the lassitude and/or the resignation of a profession which prefers to adopt a low profile rather than be in conflict with an authoritarian regime."[91]

The issue of freedom of speech in Rwanda remains complex, because the word "free" has undeniably led to death on a massive scale, and there is still an ongoing discourse about "coming back one day to finish the job."[92] But it also must be recognized that, as a result, the space allotted to the media does not allow those who are willing to speak out, to do so freely. The Rwandan media have been capable of the worst. Therefore, they continue to be suspected of engaging in their past practices, even if those in charge have changed. As for the international media, they have sinned, at best, by omission faced with the unnameable, and at worst by "complicity in genocide."[93] Their intentions, motivations, or analyses are therefore deemed untrustworthy.[94] Suspicion will remain as long as the seeds of divisions are there—seeds that are encouraged by a wide control of the public space that is supposedly devoted to eradicating those divisions.

Journalists' Working Environment

Beyond a rigid political framework, journalists' working environment is profoundly marked by the country's tragic history, which is holding back the strengthening of the profession, whether in terms of working practices, material conditions, training of human resources, or organization.

The material constraints are no different from those found in other enclosed, impoverished, and largely illiterate countries where the potential market for the written press is relatively restricted. They differ, however, in degree. Rwanda is a state where war has destroyed all the printing resources, where genocide and massacres have decimated the profession, and where the economy has been devastated. The director of the occasional monthly *Ubumwe,* John Sendanyoye, recalled, at the tenth anniversary of its publication, the difficult conditions facing the majority of the Rwandan press. It lacked premises and permanent personnel, had a print run of 1,000 copies, only half of which sold, and had to print its issues in Uganda to cut down on costs.[95] This lack of security leads to permanent problems of survival and consequently, a potential vulnerability to political manipulation. Ousted from his journal following an internal split, Ismaël Mbonigaba declared, "I am worried about the very probable compromising of the editorial line of the journal . . . , since the journal, in order to survive and prosper, has to put itself under the protection of strong men, which I have always resisted since the creation of *Umuseso*."[96]

Self-censorship is very common in the media in Kigali, as if the journalists were afraid not only of incurring the wrath of the authorities, but also of their own power to do harm. A publication director declared in 2001, "It's the journalists themselves who have laid down their arms."[97] As Eustache Rutabingwa, former director of the Rwanda Press House, remarked, the golden rule for Rwandan journalists has become, "Be prudent without being cowardly."[98]

One form of this prudence consists in hiding behind official sources, which is a process that dominates the media, as noted in the HCP monitoring reports.[99] The HCP has called on Rwandan journalists to develop their contacts "with diverse and contradictory sources."[100] If the so-called independent press complains of being confronted with a tradition of withholding information at the level of certain officials,[101] the HCP reproaches it for being too familiar with "armchair journalism," and little inclined to undertake on-the-ground investigation,[102] which leads it to be content with spreading rumors.

Journalist training also suffers from a heavy legacy. Until 1996, Rwanda had no school of journalism, and before the genocide the majority of journalists of the official media had either received initial training in Zaire, the Soviet Union, or Belgium, or been trained on the job. The professionals of the new private press generally do not have access to training, just a university degree or a desire to express themselves.

Beginning in 1994, the new regime insisted on the need for training. In 1996, with the encouragement of Laurent Nkusi (who later became minister of information), the School of Journalism and Communication was established at the University of Butare. The curriculum was initially very theoretical, and the first year's graduates had no practical experience. Gradually, with the support of several financial partners (the French embassy, UNESCO, the European Union), the school is now acquiring equipment so it can provide training that is grounded in professional practices, and has launched its own radio station. However, the school is confronted with the double problem of recruiting students (with the profession of journalist being poorly regarded) as well as teachers. Not only is there no tradition of teaching journalism in Rwanda, but many professors who would have been qualified were killed in the genocide. The teachers of the diaspora, who have returned to lend a hand, have sometimes been discouraged by the difficult working conditions and have left again. Moreover, most of the best Rwandan journalists who could have taught, have given up employment in the media for better-paid work at international organizations or UN agencies. The profession does not attract people. Added to the wretched financial conditions offered and the material difficulties of producing quality work, the lack of credibility among the public is not an incentive for the young to take up the career.

Finally, the professional associations are not likely to bring journalists together around common objectives with a shared solidarity. The memory of the former Union des Journalistes Rwandais (UJR), which was close to the Habyarimana regime, and the Association des Journalistes Professionnels du Rwanda (AJPR) is still in everyone's mind. Created in 1991, they were powerless to control the excesses of their own members, even after a charter of deontology and rights of journalists was adopted in 1993. Had not the AJPR, during a seminar only weeks before the genocide, broached the problem of the responsibility of the hate media, without daring to clearly accuse the RTLM?

All the postgenocide initiatives targeted toward uniting media professionals have quickly fallen into lethargy. The Rwandan Association of Journalists, created in 1995, which has had a series of presidents, is not active, has little credibility, and is little known among journalists. It has since formulated a new code of conduct, which was renewed in 2005. The Rwanda Press House, initiated in 1996 with the support of UNESCO, had been intended as a place for professionals to obtain vocational training and documentation, and to meet colleagues. However, it has never functioned satisfactorily. Journalists have little interest in the organization, which is split by the divisions and mistrust that reign in this milieu. Several of its directors have resigned, one after the other. These various initiatives have benefited from financial and material resources, sometimes significant,[103] from international NGOs and financial backers. Their lack of success is therefore not due to lack of financial security.

The profession has not been able to regroup and organize itself because, apart from low salaries paid to journalists and their lack of motivation to join voluntary organizations, the milieu is still divided on many levels. The splits are political, linguistic (those from the English-speaking diaspora who have returned do not have the same professional approaches as the French-speaking journalists), and generational. There is virtually no collegial spirit, and mistrust prevails between colleagues, weakening cooperation and isolating members from each other and from professional bodies.

A Traumatized Public: What Are the Media For?

Today, an overwhelming majority of the Rwandan population mistrust the media. They despise journalists, whom they consider spokespersons for the government or political parties, or manipulators whose job is not to inform but rather to make a living by passing on messages.

In theory, the media are a tool of democracy to help public opinion formulate its visions for society. But what can be said of "public opinion" in a country where people hesitate to express themselves in debates and where the media hardly give them the opportunity? The HCP monitoring report on media coverage of the general elections of October 2003 is revealing. As a general rule, the Rwandan media "concentrated on the principal personalities and ignored the rest of the population."[104] Some months later, a repeat study conducted during the commemoration of the tenth anniversary of the genocide reached the same conclusion: "The ordinary citizens do not have enough opportunity to give their view on the circumstances of their lives after the genocide,"[105] with the media being absorbed in ceremonies and official speeches.

A crisis of confidence persists between the Rwandan public and their media, which leads many to turn to the international media, especially the BBC and the VOA, which broadcast daily hour-long news bulletins in Kinyarwanda.[106] However, it should be emphasized that, if the public audiovisual media still give little voice to the citizenry, the development of community radio outside Kigali could generate new habits. Radio Izuba has already established ten or so "listeners clubs," each bringing together about twenty people, and eventually equipped them to take part in radio programming.[107] The station receives numerous letters from listeners.

As for the "independent" newspapers, they are relatively expensive (100–500 Rwandan francs; US$.20–1.00) given the low buying power of most Rwandans. The papers inspire little confidence, with the courts having demonstrated several times that they have published unverified information that turned out to be untrue. It is open to debate whether the public buy certain papers for credible information or merely entertainment. For example, in 2001, *Umuseso,* the best-selling of the local papers published in Kinyarwanda, which prints sometimes up to 6,000 copies, was seized three times following the publication of "a page of sexual education, judged to be quasi-pornographic, which its many readers were very enthusiastic about. In November, the Minister of the Interior succeeded in forcing the journal to drop this feature under threat of a definitive suspension and sales fell to 3,500 copies."[108] It seems likely that "pornography" rather than the paper's political analysis was partially responsible for its success.

Multiform Support from the Northern Partners

In March 1994 the Belgian Embassy in Kigali organized a conference on "objectivity in political reporting," which was attended by all the Rwandan media. The RTLM was represented by its editor in chief, Gaspard Gahigi, who harshly criticized the "gutter press" as being "clearly disingenuous in its intentions." Many participants were critical of their colleagues' subjectivity and dishonesty, but according to the workshop report, published some months later by the review *Dialogue,* no participant had the courage to point a finger at the RTLM and its role.[109] This incident speaks volumes on the blindness of certain foreign partners and on the dubious usefulness of this type of gathering, so favored by NGOs supporting the Southern media with their programs of development assistance.

Numerous bilateral organizations (French and British foreign aid, the Dutch embassy), multilateral organizations (UNESCO, the United Nations Development Programme [UNDP]), and also NGOs (Reporters sans Frontières, Media Action International, the Hirondelle Foundation, the Institut Panos Paris, Internews, Article 19) are involved in the reconstruction of the Rwandan media and are creating an environment more conducive to local initiatives.[110] Ranging from material and financial assistance to journalist training to the reinforcement of professional associations and national regulatory bodies, various methods have been used to try to raise the level of professionalism and organize the Rwandan press over the past decade.

Not all these projects have been free of problems and tension. Some NGOs, considered by the authorities to have ambiguous motives, have been expelled or denied authorization. Others have negotiated projects but, following a change of heart on the part of local partners once they were launched, have not succeeded. Administrative hitches and many procedural delays have prevented initiatives to send Rwandan journalists to regional and international professional exchanges.

The authorities seem to have become as suspicious of the media's partners as they are of journalists. Here again, the memory of the pre–April 1994 behavior of some of these organizations, added to the naiveté or angelic innocence of some of them when faced with the complexity of Rwandan society, may explain the authorities' reticence.

Conclusion

In 1945, after World War II, the French authorities, deeply affected by the trauma of collaboration, decided to reaffirm their grip on the media, which had become political instruments before and during the conflict. The state-run Agence France Presse replaced the private Havas agency; newspapers published during the occupation were banned; new press cards were issued, taking into account the attitude of each journalist during the war; the property of publishers and printers who had collaborated was seized; the majority of printing organizations were nationalized, and distribution was set up as a state monopoly. Only gradually did the media begin to recover their autonomy. From 1954 onward, journals were able to buy their own printing presses. In 1957, the AFP became autonomous, but it was not until 1982 that the state gave authorization for the establishment of the first private radio stations on French soil, though there had been undeniable pluralism in the period between the world wars.[111]

It is worth remembering that for any country emerging from the trauma of war, let alone from a genocide, the authorities will consider information and its control to be strategic. It should also be remembered that the whole process of normalization can only unfold very gradually over a number of years, even decades.

Two events of great symbolic importance for Rwanda have taken place recently, and they represent the foundations necessary for this normalization to occur. First, in December 2003, at the International Criminal Tribunal for Rwanda (ICTR) at Arusha, a verdict was given in the "hate media" trial. The main actors from the RTLM were classed as criminals liable to life imprisonment.[112] Ferdinand Nahimana, promoter of the RTLM; Jean-Bosco Barayagwiza, member of the RTLM's organizing committee and adviser to the Ministry of Foreign Affairs during the genocide; and Hassan Ngeze, former publication director and editor in chief of *Kangura,* all pled not guilty.[113] Ferdinand Nahimana and Hassan Ngeze were sentenced to life imprisonment, Jean-Bosco Barayagwisa to thirty-five years in prison. Georges Ruggiu, the Italian-Belgian RTLM presenter, had already been tried in June 2000; he pled guilty and was sentenced to twelve years in prison.

The fundamental importance of the outcome of this trial cannot be overestimated. It is a necessary step that allows survivors, who heard the names of their friends and family, now dead, read on the air, to at last feel that a certain justice has been done, even though an association for journalists' rights has expressed the fear that "the authorities, including those in Rwanda, use this verdict as a pretext for repressing further the legitimate criticisms voiced by the press."[114]

Second, in 2004, five private radio stations began to broadcast in Rwanda. The government also renewed the BBC's authorization to broadcast on FM in Kigali, and authorized the extension of broadcasting to other towns.[115] This is not negligible progress in a country that now has a level of radio pluralism more developed than in states such as Gabon, the Central African Republic, Congo, or Cameroon (see corresponding chapters in this book), which have hardly been subjected to the same foreign pressure to legally authorize private radio stations.

Undeniably, painful problems remain. Press enterprises are evolving in a difficult economic context that leaves them open to political pressures from all sides. Journalists are not sufficiently trained and rely on "passive" journalism (they use only official sources, do not have a balanced investigative approach, and self-censor). The legal framework could be less defensive and more permissive (improving, for example, journalists' material circumstances and establishing forms of public assistance for the private press). However, one can hope that, for the whole of the Rwandan situation, time will slowly but surely do its work. No foreign support, whether large-scale or targeted, can replace the slow process of restoring the confidence and sense of fraternity among media professionals, of affirming the credibility of journalists in the eyes of the public, and of constructing relations of mutual respect between public authorities and the industry.

Notes

1. See the indispensable work J. P. Chrétien (ed.), *Rwanda: les médias du génocide* (Paris: Karthala, 1995).
2. This monthly (whose name means "who brings the news"), which for a long time was the only regular publication of the country, played an important role in the campaign for political representation for the Hutu, preparing and supporting the "social revolution" of 1959. Grégoire Kayibanda was its editor in chief from 1955 to 1958.
3. LDGL, "La problématique de la liberté d'expression au Rwanda: cas de la presse" (June 2002), p. 3.
4. In 1980 the journal was given new management, led by the Abbot Sylvio Sindambiwe. He tried to give the journal a wider remit, but suffered such pressure and threats that he finally resigned; he was later killed in a suspicious road accident.
5. The word *tafipro* was an abbreviation for "travail, fidélité, progrès" (work, loyalty, progress). The word *umunyamuryango* means "of the family."
6. Chrétien, *Rwanda,* p. 20.
7. LDGL, "La problématique de la liberté d'expression au Rwanda," p. 3.
8. A first attempt had made some months earlier—*Intera* (Forward), edited by Ananie Nkurunziza—though it did not manage to assert itself.
9. See *La Relève,* October 19–25, 1990.

10. Sylvestre Nkubiri of *Kinyamateka,* Alphonse Rutsindura of *Amakuru ki i Butare,* and Ignace Ruhatana of *L'Opinion.*

11. F. Reyntjens, *L'Afrique des Grands Lacs en crise: Rwanda, Burundi, 1988–1994* (Paris: Karthala, 1994), p. 172.

12. Chrétien, *Rwanda,* p. 29.

13. The MDR subsequently split into a moderate wing and a reactionary and aggressive wing, the latter close to the extremist parties identified with "Hutu Power." The partisan journals lined up with this split: *Isibo* and *L'Ere de la Liberté* on the side of the MDR-Twagiramungu; *Umurangi* and *Ibyikigihe* (Today) on the side of the MDR-PARMEHUTU. See Reyntjens, *L'Afrique des Grands Lacs en crise,* p. 172.

14. Edited by Janvier Afrika, who would become one of the rare repentants of "Network Zero" and a precious informer on the functioning and strategies of the Akazu.

15. Close to the RPF, Alexandre Kimienyi also edited *Impuruza* (Call to Fight), from the United States.

16. Filip Reyntjens sees in them a clear difference compared to the press of neighboring Burundi, which at the same time is essentially in French and of better quality. Reyntjens, *L'Afrique des Grands Lacs en crise,* p. 174.

17. Jean-Pierre Chrétien emphasizes how the Habyarimana regime functioned from the very start on two levels of discourse. It spoke of "balance" (meaning ethnic quotas) in "communal self-centered development," to distract attention from the illegal trafficking that was enriching the inner circle; and of "work" when it came to ordering massacres. When civil society showed itself, and the political opposition made itself heard, in terms not based on identity but centered on a critique of management of the state, the Habyarimana regime diverted attention toward "ethnic" explanations of the crisis. All along, it pretended to be accelerating the process of democratic reform, all the while preparing, secretly, for war.

18. Before that, the legal framework comprised only a legislative timetable that was adopted on March 5, 1922, and that was barely completed with later decrees adopted in 1929, 1944, and 1980. See Institut Panos Paris (ed.), *Afrique centrale: des médias pour la démocratie* (Paris: Karthala, 2000), p. 174.

19. *Kangura* never had problems of survival: the journal had a print run of 10,000 copies in 1991, and was printed without charge at the national printing house.

20. The Interahamwe militia (The Ones Working Together) was originally a youth organization of the MRND, created in 1991 in response to the youth movements of the opposition political parties, which had just been legalized. Progressively, with the radicalization of the MRND and the creation of the CDR, these young people were organized into "self-defense" militias throughout the country, and received arms and military training.

21. C. Braeckman, *Rwanda: histoire d'un génocide* (Paris: Fayard, 1995), p. 166.

22. L. Kayinbanda, "RTLM Was Not an Amateur Enterprise," in M. Ben Arous (ed.), *Médias et conflits en Afrique* (Paris: Panos Afrique de l'Ouest–Karthala, 2001), p. 68.

23. After the adoption of the law of 1991, several applications for new privately owned radio stations had been submitted. The special commission

authorized to issue the operational licenses, comprising representatives of several ministries, sat only once, during which it authorized only one station: the RTLM.

24. In early 1993 the review *Dialogue* noted that only twenty-six declared periodicals had published "at least 5 issues during 1992," which gives an indication of the irregularity of the publications. Cited in Reyntjens, *L'Afrique des Grands Lacs en crise,* p. 172. This year was marked by numerous cases of violence against journalists, some of whom went into hiding. On the eve of the genocide, only twelve titles were still appearing.

25. Several members of the personnel of *Umurwanashyaka* joined the RTLM, such as Gaspard Gahigi (a former director of national radio and former correspondent of the AFP) and Kantano Habimana. Valérie Bemeriki, who worked on *Interahamwe,* and Ananie Nkurunziza of *Intera,* joined as well, alongside journalists from ORINFOR.

26. "Hutu Power" is a radical current that arose in 1993 within several political parties, including the democratic opposition. Its defenders were opposed to the Arusha Accords, and have called for the unity of all Hutu against the Tutsi.

27. The association Reporters sans Frontières, which has identified them, cannot confirm whether they were killed for their ethnic origins, for their political opinions, or for having exercised their profession as journalists.

28. In 1996, 1999, and 2001, the Rwandan authorities published a list of "criminals of the first category" (planners, inciters, supervisors, and organizers of the genocide, as well as authors of sexual violence, all liable to the death penalty), which contained about 2,900 names, including those of 29 journalists.

29. Within the political opposition to the Habyarimana regime, there were some important divergences regarding the "Tutsi question." Some personalities who were hostile toward the MRND were not necessarily against the idea of the "final solution"—that is, the extermination of the Tutsi.

30. This text was criticized by the Belgian press, which denounced its racist tone. In 1991 it was made known to the whole of the scientific community who were interested in Africa, thanks to historian Jean-Pierre Chrétien, who had it published in *Politique Africaine* no. 42. But the publication "hardly attracted much attention at the time," Chrétien regretted two years later. Chrétien, *Rwanda,* p. 16.

31. Presented as coming from external Bahutu, this document would be referred to extensively during the trial, in Brussels on the basis of the universal jurisdiction of Belgian courts, of Vincent Ntezimana, considered one of its possible authors. See L. de Vulpian, *Rwanda: un génocide oublié? un procès pour mémoire* (Brussels: Editions Complexe, 2004), pp. 137–142.

32. The motto of *Kangura* is "the voice which strives to awaken and guide the majority people."

33. It is this same Manichaean analysis that *Kangura* applies to the Burundi situation, in which it interferes with an occasional "international edition." Moreover, in April 1991, it was at the demand of the Burundian government that Hassan Ngeze was arrested a second time: the authorities of the neighboring country were no longer able to tolerate the continual appeals to ethnic hatred against Tutsi that the journal was sending to the Hutu of Burundi.

34. In another issue, *Kangura* emphasized that the Tutsi "is never satisfied until he manages to eliminate you" (February 1992).

35. The term could equally be translated as "fighters": it evokes individuals who struggle tirelessly until they reach their final goal.

36. The hypothesis of the "final solution" is already implied in such a statement. It was to be clearly spelled out in January 1994 by *Kangura,* which predicted: "If they again lift their head, it will no longer be necessary to go and fight with the enemy in the maquis. We will start rather by clearing out the enemy within."

37. It broke, therefore, from the programming of Radio Rwanda, which was centered on popular songs written in Kinyarwanda (except for the music of Rwandan exiles). During the genocide, certain compositions of Simon Bikindi in Kinyarwanda, calling for the vigilance of the Hutu and for the elimination of the Tutsi, were played up to ten times a day.

38. In 1989, about 415,000 radio receivers were counted in Rwanda, about one per thirteen inhabitants. Chrétien, *Rwanda,* p. 57. The massive distribution of transistor radios and batteries has also been organized with the establishment of the station in 2003.

39. J. P. Chrétien, "Rwanda: la propagande du génocide," in R. de la Brosse (ed.), *Les médias de la haine* (Paris: Editions La Découverte, 1995), p. 26.

40. Chrétien, *Rwanda,* p. 16.

41. Interview with Yolande Mukagasana, November 2004.

42. *Libre Afrique,* cited in J. P. Chrétien, "Presse libre et propagande raciste au Rwanda," *Politique Africaine* no. 42 (June 1991), p. 114.

43. Network Zero was established by the more radical extremists of the regime, those close to Agathe Habyarimana's family.

44. Cited in Chrétien, *Rwanda,* p. 72.

45. While several complaints of defamation were made against RTLM journalists at the start of 1994, none of these actions have been brought to conclusion.

46. Cited in Chrétien, *Rwanda,* p. 50.

47. See Reyntjens, *L'Afrique des Grands Lacs en crise,* p. 185.

48. See M. Alexis and I. Mpambara, "The Rwanda Media Experience from the Genocide," International Media Support assessment mission (March 2003), p. 10.

49. J. M. V. Higiro, "Distorsions et omissions dans l'ouvrage *Rwanda: les médias du génocide," Dialogue* no. 190 (April–May 1996), p. 167.

50. *Kangura* no. 6 (December 1990), cited in Chrétien, *Rwanda,* p. 284.

51. J. P. Gouteux, *La nuit rwandaise: l'implication française dans le dernier génocide du siècle* (Paris: L'Esprit Frappeur, 2002), p. 223. Following the publications of Jean-Paul Gouteux on the subject (*Un génocide secret d'État* [Paris: Editions Sociales, 1998] and *Le Monde: un contre-pouvoir?* [Paris: L'Esprit Frappeur, 1999]), the newspaper *Le Monde* brought action against him in two trials in 1999, which the great French daily lost.

52. Cited in Chrétien, *Rwanda,* pp. 285–286.

53. Before the genocide, there had been three large printing works: the national printing house, the educational printing house, and the printing works of Kinyamateka.

54. Cited in de la Brosse, *Les médias de la haine,* p. 55.

55. These were the projects Radio Agatashya of the Hirondelle Foundation, and Human Rights Radio of the CLADHO. A request from Radio Unité of the diocese of Kabgayi was also rejected.

56. Reporters sans Frontières, *Rwanda, L'impasse? la liberté de la presse après le génocide, 4 juillet 1994–28 août 1995* (Paris, September 1995), p. 20.

57. Cited in E. Palmans, "La liberté de la presse au Rwanda et au Burundi," in *L'Afrique des Grands Lacs, Annuaire 2002–2003* (Paris: L'Harmattan, 2003), p. 53.

58. These defections occurred in a context marked by the successive resignations of major political personalities who were distancing themselves from the regime (the president of the National Assembly, the prime minister, and finally the president of the republic).

59. *Grands Lacs Hebdo,* January 15–22, 2002.

60. LDGL, "La problématique de la liberté d'expression," p. 13.

61. Essentially, titles run by journalists returned from a long exile in Uganda or Tanzania, and some French titles being run by exiles returned from Burundi or Zaire/Democratic Republic of Congo.

62. Edited by Tryphon Kin Kiey Mulumba, Mobutu's last minister of information who later became spokesperson of the RCD Goma. Based in Kigali, he launched *Le Soft des Grands Lacs* just before the presidential election in Rwanda. See Chapter 3.

63. *Dialogue* is now published in Brussels, where its driving force, Father Guy Theunis, is based.

64. J. Ruremesha, "Rwanda: le fantôme des médias de la haine plane sur la presse," *Syfia International Bulletin* nos. 2–10 (May 2002).

65. HCP, Rwanda Media Monitoring Project, "Analysis on Professionalism in Rwandan Media" (Kigali, March 2004), p. 7.

66. HCP, Rwanda Media Monitoring Project, "An Analysis of Media Coverage of the First Multiparty Legislative Elections After the Independence of Rwanda" (Kigali, November 2003), pp. 11–12.

67. *Kinyamateka* claims a weekly print run of 5,000 copies; *Umuseso* gives a figure rising sometimes to 10,000.

68. Denunciations of corruption are frequent in other Rwandan media. At the end of 2004, three high-ranking officials (including a cabinet director and the vice president of the Supreme Court) were obliged to resign following accusations of corruption.

69. HCP, Rwanda Media Monitoring Project, "Analysis on Professionalism in Rwandan Media," p. 26.

70. HCP, Rwanda Media Monitoring Project, "Media Coverage of the 10th Commemoration of 1994 Genocide in Rwanda" (Kigali, July 2004), p. 17.

71. Two other confessional stations, one Catholic, the other Protestant, had to provide complementary information.

72. G. Maoundonodji, "Etude sur le pluralisme radiophonique au Rwanda," working document (Institut Panos Paris, 2004).

73. LDGL, "La problématique de la liberté d'expression au Rwanda," p. 16.

74. In May 2005 the HCP had already granted 104 cards to news professionals.

75. Three of them are elected by the private press (one represents the public media, two come from civil society), and three are designated by the government.

The president of the body, until May 2005, was Privat Rutazibwa, director of the ARI, who sits on the HCP for the private press alongside abbot Dominique Karekezi (director of *Kinyamateka*) and Casimiry Kayumba (director of *Ukuri*). Privat Rutazibwa withdrew after several clashes with the minister of information, Laurent Nkusi.

76. The HCP has conducted four systematic studies, including one on the coverage of the general elections of 2003; a study of the ten-year commemoration of the genocide, in April 2004; as well as an overview report on the question of professionalism in the Rwandan media and the practical difficulties of press management.

77. During the general elections of 2003, each candidate was given fifteen minutes airtime on national radio and television to present his program.

78. A. Maja-Pearce (ed.), *Annuaire de la presse africaine* (Brussels: FIJ, 1996), p. 266.

79. Journalism said to be "of national unity" is not new: with the gaining of independence, this idea allowed the justification of state control over the media in newly born African countries, with arbitrary borders, where such a nation was still to be constructed. See M. S. Frère, *Presse et démocratie en Afrique francophone* (Paris: Karthala, 2000).

80. Reporters sans Frontières, *Rwanda, L'impasse?* pp. 8–9.

81. Gédéon Mushimiyimana, Joseph Ruyenzi, Albert Baudouin Twizeyimana, Ladislas Parmehutu, and Telesphore Nyilimanzi were all employees of ORINFOR. For journalists, as for other political personalities or those of civil society, the situation was especially complex, because those imprisoned for genocide maintained that they were in fact prisoners of opinion: the debate could only be settled by a judge, hence the importance of the courts.

82. Dominique Makeli and Tatiana Mukakibibi were among those considered "not guilty" by Reporters sans Frontières.

83. Accused of participating in genocide, he had been arrested in 1996, but was released without any further investigation.

84. Reporters sans Frontières, "Rwanda: des pressions discrètes et ciblées: le président Paul Kagame est un prédateur de la liberté de la presse" (November 2001), p. 8. In December 2000, *Le Partisan* also published one of the most famous negationist editorials.

85. See LDGL, "Rapport sur la situation des droits de l'homme dans la région de Grands Lacs: Burundi, Rwanda, RDC," May 2002, p. 135.

86. There have also been some disappearances of journalists, but about which there can be no certainty. So, in 1995, Manasse Mogabo, journalist at Radio Unamir, left his home one morning never to be seen again. Some months later, it was the turn of Emmanuel Munyemanzi, head of the production service of the national television station, who vanished after being accused of sabotage by the director of ORINFOR following a technical incident that occurred during the recording of a political debate.

87. Term used in the Lusaka Accords to identify, among others, the Interahamwe. See F. Reyntjens, "Rwanda, Ten Years On: From Genocide to Dictatorship," *African Affairs* no. 103 (2004), p. 181.

88. The ambiguity of this individual and his political contacts is described by Jean-Paul Gouteux in *La nuit rwandaise,* pp. 270–276. Considered a sympathizer

of the RPF, particularly Major Lizinde, *Le Tribun du Peuple* commented in August 1997 that "the revolution" had failed, and went as far as to compare the abuses of the government (misappropriation of funds, nepotism, clientism, corruption, and absence of patriotism) to those of the Habyarimana regime. See Reyntjens, "Rwanda, Ten Years On," p. 189.

89. I. Mbonigaba, "Un flambeau au gré des vents dans l'après-génocide," in Institut Panos Paris and COTA (eds.), *Briser les silences: paroles d'Afrique centrale* (Paris: Karthala, 2003), pp. 128–129.

90. Ibid., p. 130.

91. LDGL, "La problématique de la liberté d'expression au Rwanda," p. 16.

92. An expression that indicates the extermination of the Tutsi.

93. See Gouteux, *La nuit rwandaise.*

94. In 1996, Ghislaine Dupont, correspondent of the RFI, was attacked in her hotel room. At the start of 1997, Reuters correspondent Christian Jennings was expelled from Rwanda. Foreign correspondents are tolerated, but if their coverage of events doesn't satisfy the regime, they are issued a warning; three warnings leads to expulsion.

95. "Rwanda: les 10 ans du journal Ubumwe," in Institut Panos Paris, *Africentr@lemédias* no. 11 (May 2003), p. 6.

96. Cited in Palmans, "La liberté de la presse au Rwanda et au Burundi," p. 57.

97. Cited in Reporters sans Frontières, "Rwanda: des pressions discrètes et ciblées," p. 9.

98. Cited in Ruremesha, "Rwanda."

99. The HCP's March 2004 report on professionalism of the Rwandan media indicated that close to 60 percent of the sources used in the analyzed media (public and private) were institutional. HCP, Rwanda Media Monitoring Project, "Analysis on Professionalism in Rwandan Media."

100. HCP, Rwanda Media Monitoring Project, "Analysis on Professionalism in Rwandan Media," p. 34.

101. Ibid., p. 26.

102. Ibid., pp. 25–26.

103. From 1996 to 2000, UNESCO paid the rent and bills and provided the equipment at the Rwanda Press House. However, at the end of this five-year period, the press house was still not functioning. See D. Mushayidi, "La Maison de la Presse du Rwanda: quel rôle? quelle viabilité?" in Institut Panos Paris, *Afrique centrale: des médias pour la démocratie,* pp. 172–173.

104. HCP, Rwanda Media Monitoring Project, "An Analysis of Media Coverage," p. iv.

105. HCP, "Media Coverage of the 10th Commemoration."

106. The hour-long broadcasts of the BBC in the Kirundi-Kinyarwanda language (at 7 P.M. every day), and of the VOA in the Kirundi-Kinyarwanda language (at 5:30 A.M. every day), are very successful, according to Solange Ayanone, former programming director of Radio Izuba.

107. Radio Izuba received help from the US Agency for International Development for its installation: a subsidy of US$180,000 allowed it to start broadcasting in March 2004 in relatively comfortable circumstances. In May 2005 the station employed twenty-eight people, half of whom were women.

108. Ruremesha, "Rwanda."

109. The record of this meeting was published by the review *Dialogue* in November 1994 (no. 175). However, the former director of ORINFOR, Jean-Marie Vianney Higiro, who was present at the workshop, has since pointed out that there were indeed some contributions that denounced the program content of the RTLM, but that these contributions were not documented in the published notes. Higiro, "Distorsions et omissions," p. 160.

110. This large number of partners is no doubt explained by the intense guilt felt by these structures, specialist or not, about having done nothing, before April 1994, to denounce the RTLM.

111. Until 1980, the only authorized radio stations in France were the public stations (Radio France, France Inter, France Culture, France Musique, and the regional stations) and four "peripherals" that had their studios in France but broadcast on longwave from neighboring foreign territories (Radio Monte Carlo, Radio Luxembourg, Europe 1, and Sud Radio).

112. Two other journalists charged with participation in the planning of the genocide, Valérie Bemeriki, formerly of the RTLM, and Joël Hakizimana, are presently in prison.

113. On his personal website, Hassan Ngeze presents himself as a journalist "persecuted for having exercised his right to free speech." See http://www.hassanngeze.s5.com.

114. Committee to Protect Journalists, *Attacks Against the Press, 2003.*

115. Since 1998, the BBC, Voice of America, and Deutsch Welle have been broadcast on FM in Kigali.

5

REPUBLIC OF CONGO

The Press Among
the Militias

DESPITE ITS EXTENSIVE oil reserves, the Republic of Congo is one of the poorest countries in the world. It is typical of many troubled postcolonial countries that are undermined both internally and externally. The 1990s were especially turbulent and violent, though the decade started with a move toward democracy after thirty years as a one-party state. The country was then torn apart by three successive civil wars in the space of five years. With a war taking place in the heart of Brazzaville, the Congolese media did not make it through this troubled decade without a few knocks and mishaps. The written press experienced two periods of growth, separated by periods of almost total extinction, while the audiovisual media were both the site and the instrument for settling political accounts.

The Painful Birth of a Privately Owned Press

A Heady Feeling of Freedom

Beginning in 1990, when censorship was abolished and the press was liberalized, dozens of new titles appeared, particularly during the 1991 National Conference, the transitional period, and the 1992 presidential election. These political papers appeared irregularly and were remarkable for their freedom of tone, the audacity of their caricatures, and the derision with which they treated the government and its major figures. The weekly *Madukutsiékélé*, popularly known as *Maduku,* was run by newly graduated students. The first to adopt a satirical tone, it had a real success during the National Conference. It was followed in 1991 by *La Rumeur* (which later

119

REPUBLIC OF CONGO

Size	342,000 sq. km.
Population	4 million
Capital	Brazzaville
Ethnic groups	15 (Kongo, Téké, Lari, Mbochi, etc.)
Official language	French
Main local languages	Lingala, Kikongo, Téké
Human Development Index ranking (2005)	142 (out of 177 countries)
Life expectancy	52 years
Literacy rate	82.8 percent

Chronology

1910–1960: French colony (French Equatorial Africa).

1960: Independence. Fulbert Youlou becomes president.

1963: A popular revolution brings Alphonse Massamba-Débat to power.

1968: Military coup. Alfred Raoul is appointed president.

1969: Military coup. Commander Marien Ngouabi becomes president. The country turns officially to Marxism and becomes the "Popular Republic of Congo."

1977: Ngouabi is assassinated. Colonel Jacques Yhomby-Opango becomes president.

1979: Military coup. Colonel Denis Sassou-Nguesso is appointed president by the central committee of the country's single party, the Parti Congolais du Travail (PCT).

1991: Sassou-Nguesso, under international pressure, allows a national conference to be held.

1992: A new constitution recognizing multiparty democracy is adopted by referendum. Pascal Lissouba wins the presidential election over Denis Sassou-Nguesso and Bernard Kolélas, mayor of Brazzaville.

November 1993: Civil war breaks out between the Zulus (Lissouba's militia) and the Ninjas (Bernard Kolélas's militia), later supported by the Cobras (Sassou-Nguesso's militia).

(continues)

became *La Rue Meurt*) and *Le Choc,* then in 1992 by *La Colombe, Le Forum, Maintenant,* and *La Ruche.* The survival of these papers was very precarious, "as shown by the irregularity of their publications, their restricted circulation, their meagre profits and the poverty of their agents."[1]

January 1995: A reconciliation government is established, including Lissouba's party (Union Panafricaine pour la Démocratie Sociale [UPADS]) and Kolelas's party (Mouvement Congolais pour la Démocratie et le Développement Intégral [MCDDI]). Sassou-Nguesso goes into exile.

June 1997: On the eve of presidential election, Sassou-Nguesso tries to seize power with the support of Angolan troops. A second civil war starts. Lissouba and Kolélas are forced into exile.

August 1998–December 1999: Fights continue in the south of the country and in the districts of Brazzaville occupied by southerners.

2001: An inclusive national dialogue is held. Lissouba and Kolélas refuse to join.

January 2002: A new constitution is adopted by referendum, and Sassou-Nguesso is elected president for seven years.

March 2003: A peace agreement is signed between the Ninjas and the government, but the militias remain armed.

Despite their fragility, these sixty or so newspapers brought a new tone to a scene formerly dominated by the state's audiovisual media. The government paper, *Mweti,* had folded, and the only private paper, *La Semaine Africaine,* was linked to the Catholic Church. Until 1990, this weekly, founded in 1952 and published by the episcopate, enjoyed great success,[2] but harsh censorship ensured that its tone was extremely measured. When the often impertinent private political papers appeared, the public suddenly deserted *La Semaine Africaine,* causing its circulation to drop by about half.[3]

The diversity and audacious tone of these new private papers were a result of their close ties with parties or politicians. The papers that managed to survive and make a place for themselves owed their existence to surreptitious financing from political or business groups that also protected them. In 1993, the opposition, caught up in the media frenzy, launched Radio Alliance, which transmitted for only a few days, as the government had no wish to liberalize the audiovisual sector. When the first war started, in 1993, the papers quickly took sides, supporting either the government or the opposition: the militia of newly elected president Pascal Lissouba, the Zulus, versus the Ninjas, the militia of Brazzaville mayor Bernard Kolélas, the latter of which was later backed by the former president, Denis Sassou-Nguesso, and his Cobras.[4]

After the 1993 war, the press remained extremely politicized: *Le Temps, La Corne Enchantée, L'Alternative, L'Espoir,* and *Le Canard de Mercredi* were close to Pascal Lissouba and his Union Panafricaine pour la Démocratie Sociale (UPADS). *La Rue Meurt* supported Bernard Kolélas's Mouvement Congolais pour la Démocratie et le Développement Intégral (MCDDI). *Le Choc, Aujourd'hui, Le Rayon, Le Flambeau, La Référence, La Liberté, Le Messager,* and *Le Gardien* flirted with Denis Sassou-Nguesso's Forces Démocratiques Unifiées (FDU).[5] These titles waged pitched battles against each other, continuing to ignore each other's opinions until the second war broke out, in 1997.

This time, the war was deeply rooted in the geography of the districts of Brazzaville, which was not without consequences for the newspapers. One of the town's particular features is that it has "a very contrasting geography of ethnic and regional origins" and that "the main political parties continued to pursue a strategy of geographical roots that they conducted in the rest of the country."[6] This meant that the home territories of the political parties and their respective militias were clearly delimited, with each paper setting up its office in the area dominated by its faction.

At the end of the 1997 war, after Denis Sassou-Nguesso's victory, almost all the newspapers disappeared. The exceptions were those favorable to the winner: *Le Choc, La Rue Meurt,* and *Le Flambeau.* Also remaining was *La Semaine Africaine,* which people close to Sassou-Nguesso accused of being a mouthpiece for the opposition.

Democratic Convalescence

The 1998 war completed the devastation of the media landscape, confirming even more clearly the divisions among journalists. Nevertheless, beginning in 1999, the appearance of new papers marked the second springtime of the Congolese press: *Le Pays, Les Echos du Congo, Cocorico, Le Coq, L'Autre Vision, Vision pour Demain, Les Dépêches de Brazzaville, Thalassa, L'Elephant, L'Humanitaire, Lumière Equatoriale, Présence Économique, Le Paysan,* and *L'Observateur,* among others.

Local journalists saw many of these publications as "gutter press and scandal sheets."[7] Some, however, demonstrated a degree of professionalism, such as *Tam Tam d'Afrique* (created in June 2000 by the former local correspondent of Agence France Press), *Les Echos du Congo,* and *Le Défi Africain. La Semaine Africaine,* with the wisdom that comes with age, has tried to help rebuild a professional ethos based on journalistic concerns rather than political ones. Though it makes an effort to be neutral, it still betrays a certain closeness to the regime in power.

The government relies on its weekly *La Nouvelle République* (which appears irregularly) and especially on *Les Dépêches de Brazzaville,* a luxury publication published by a private agency. The paper was created in 1998 by a French journalist who was an adviser to the presidency, to polish its image. The Agence Congolaise d'Information (ACI), created in 1960, has started working again after having suffered particularly badly during the 1997 war, when its offices were destroyed; it now publishes a weekly bulletin.

President Sassou-Nguesso, now feeling sufficiently secure, even allows some papers financed by those close to his regime (such as *Le Pays,* now defunct, or *Epanza Makita*), to criticize the management methods of certain dignitaries. As the saying goes, "Those who truly love know how to punish."

Control of the Audiovisual Sector

The audiovisual scene is extremely limited. Until 1998, the sector was a state monopoly, in spite of the National Conference having proclaimed its liberalization. It was limited to Radio Congo, Télé Congo, and their local stations, particularly at Pointe-Noire. The Agence Intergouvernementale de la Francophonie (AIF) had also helped to install four local community stations, at Nkayi, Mossendjo, Etoumbi, and Sembé.[8]

There was still a certain degree of pluralism, however. Radio France Internationale had been broadcasting on FM from Brazzaville since 1992, followed by Africa No. 1 and the BBC. The many FM stations broadcasting from Kinshasa were also picked up on the other side of the river (and still are).

After the failure of their first experiment with an opposition private radio station, Radio Alliance, in 1993, Sassou-Nguesso's forces set up Radio Liberté, a militant station that broadcast from a radio car during the 1997 war. A pirate television station, Télé Congo Liberté, soon followed, with the same aim of countering the omnipresent governmental propaganda in the state media. These roaming stations, set up thanks to the ingenuity of a few radio technicians (Radio Congo agents who were marooned in the districts under the Cobras' control), were never hit by enemy fire.

Though some people were calling for its closure, Radio Liberté continued to broadcast even after the end of the fighting, installing its head office in the sixth district of Brazzaville, the fiefdom of Sassou-Nguesso's partisans. Its former presenters, who came from the state media, have returned to their previous employers. The lead writer, Ekia Akoli Wamené, for example, has become director-general of Télé Congo.[9] The station is still financed by people close to the regime, who occasionally try to retake control, but it is now trying to gain credibility with the public by opting for a less partisan editorial line.

During the 1999 war, Pastor Ntumi's rebel movement also set up a clandestine station, Radio Royale, which broadcast periodically in the Pool region, though its transmissions have now stopped.

Some other initiatives have seen the light of day in the past few years: Radio Océan at Pointe-Noire, Radio Louvakou at Dolisie, and Digital Radio in Brazzaville. The latter, owned by a general in the Congolese armed forces (Norbert Dabira), along with a private television station (Digital Radio Télévision; DRTV), is essentially commercial and does not dabble much in politics.[10] The national radio station has also developed a local station, Canal FM, born from the old station Radio Rurale. The network of local community radios has also grown with the establishment (generally by ministers or the district authorities) of Radio Moka, Radio Nkeni, and Radio Lekena. The Catholic Church had opened Radio Kintouari at Pointe-Noire before launching Radio Magnificat in Brazzaville in March 2006.

Public television is still in a dominant position, but the widely received Kinshasa television stations enjoy a great deal of success, especially the Congolese preachers, who are finding new "followers" on the other side of the river.

The Media at War

In 1999 an observer noted: "These days, one reads the Congolese papers with fear. All they talk about every day are preparations for the fourth war. . . . And when politicians, who are always looking for controversies, read that they get excited. They think that what the journalists are saying is based on reality when really they're often just making it up to sell papers. What's strange is that it always starts like that. Then war breaks out."[11] According to this view, the Congolese newspapers are "birds of bad omen" that see evil coming from afar, or are even provoking it. Yet they are not just playing a Cassandra-like role. They have closely followed politicians' dangerous, destabilizing activities, rather than provoking them.

During the transitional period, Prime Minister André Milongo warned journalists, "We are going through sensitive times. You bear a heavy responsibility, which means that you must not allow yourself to be the mouthpieces of parties or to be corrupted into bending the wills of your fellow citizens to those of the politicians."[12]

The wars in Congo were "wars of opprobrium" as well as wars of armed combat. The most monstrous accusations were used to discredit the enemy. For example, in August 1997, when Bernard Kolélas was not yet involved in the conflict, *La Rue Meurt* published a caricature titled "Two Savages in the Town," showing Lissouba as a monkey and Sassou-Nguesso as a cobra, at whom the human figure of Kolélas cast a distant look. The paper's tone changed when Kolélas joined the conflict, with each paper echoing the positions taken by its patron. In February 1999, the same paper called for the massacre of French expatriates. The small circulation of these papers, however, limited their negative effects.

With their more powerful broadcasting capabilities, Radio Congo and Radio Liberté indulged in a real war of the radio waves, each of them offering airtime to victims who described the atrocities they suffered at the hands of the other side. Radio Liberté accused government forces loyal to President Lissouba of "carrying out ethnic cleansing." The next day the French television station, France 3, repeated this information, then made no further mention of it, having no doubt realized that it had fallen into a trap of misinformation.[13] While Radio Congo broadcast numerous messages inciting violence in the northern districts of Brazzaville, Radio Liberté encouraged "cleansing" of the southern districts.

Only the Catholic weekly *La Semaine Africaine* made a priority of publishing articles on ways to end the conflict. It showed the ravages of war and promoted a solution by dialogue.[14] When voices from civil society tried to support the idea of resolution by negotiation, the paper gave prominence to accounts and opinion columns from this pacifist fringe. In April 1999 the paper noted, "The Congolese political classes have good reason for continuing to fight each other, as each side tries to impose its will by force. In spite of all the destruction, the deaths, the homeless populations and the weariness of the international community, the warring leaders can see no need for dialogue."[15]

Insurmountable Material Difficulties

Despite *La Semaine Africaine*'s thoughtful approach and its appeals to reason, it was not spared by the wars, and its neutrality was sorely tried. In 1993 the paper had to disguise its vehicle by removing its logo from the door,[16] because it had not taken sides at a time when everyone else was declaring their allegiance. In 1997 the fighting affected the area where *La Semaine Africaine*'s editorial office was located and the paper had to suspend publication for a month, before moving, thanks to the army's protection, to the Bacongo district. The district was then in the hands of Kolélas's Ninjas, who made sure the premises were secure. At first, this district was spared by the fighting and still had electricity and a working print shop, but the respite did not last. Because Kolélas was on Lissouba's side, this part of town was also affected by the fighting, and the paper had to negotiate with the local militias for protection.[17] At the end of the war, with Sassou-Nguesso's victory, the paper returned to its usual offices in the town center.

Not only did the very strong "regional-ethnic" character of the town's districts make it difficult for journalists to get around easily, but they also

had constant problems obtaining access to the fighting. "We could not report from the scene of conflict," explained Joachim Mbanza. "If you walked
around with a camera, you would be exposed to the wrath of the militia men
who did not appreciate journalists."[18] What else could journalists do except
rely on rumor and the stories of people who succeeded in getting "to the
other side"?

The paper was extremely isolated during the war. Since all the other papers had stopped publication, *La Semaine Africaine* was the only one still in
print and had no sources of professional support. Many journalists fled the
country and took refuge in Kinshasa on the other side of the river, where correspondents from the foreign press were working.[19] Some journalists hid in
the forest until the end of 1999 to escape the fighting. "Almost all the papers,
whatever their opinion, were reduced to silence. Those which attempted to
confront the current misfortunes were dissuaded by the Draconian strictures
of the state of emergency. The readers went to earth in their tribal ghettos."[20]

A Patronage Press

One reason for lapses in the Congolese press during the war was due to the
motivations of the people in charge of it. From the moment of their establishment, the Congolese media were part of a patronage network central to
the Congolese state. These private networks even had a role in the redistri-
bution of public funds.[21] Since the civil service and "public" services, as
well as the private sector, were not entirely under state control, it is not surprising that the media companies were part of the same system. The Congolese press under Lissouba is a striking example of a patronage press.
Newspapers were at the service of Lissouba, who used them to promote the
interests of a series of clients often bound to him by regional or ethnic ties.

As well, the Congolese press is to a large extent (up to 90 percent) run
by journalists who are also state employees who work in the state media,
among other areas. There are no paid employees in the privately owned
press, with the notable exception of the editorial staff of *La Semaine
Africaine*. Permanent delays in the payment of salaries in the civil service
place these journalists in a very uncomfortable position. Consequently,
many of them look for jobs in the offices of the ministers, obviously by
demonstrating political sympathies.[22] In addition, their precarious financial
situation tempts journalists into making extensive use of "advertorials," in
which a journalist writes an article favorable to a sponsor in return for a
small payment. What is known in other countries as "brown envelope,"
"gumbo,"[23] or "plugging," is called "camorra" in Congo. Such practices in
a country where the political parties are the main sources of media funds
often lead to politicization of newspapers.

The Media Environment

Periods of conflict systematically lead to violations of journalists' rights and to the state taking control of the media. In such a context, where legal guarantees are weak and professional associations do not exist or are divided, the private media organizations can be easily swept away by war.

Legal and Regulatory Framework

The 1992 constitution recognized freedom of the press. In 1996, a new press law was adopted, but media professionals criticized it because of the restrictions it imposed on their freedom. Forty-six of the 160 articles in the new press law focused on sanctions for press offenses.[24] The law obliged the papers to deposit their publications in several places before putting them on sale, and even demanded that journalists, editors, printers, and newspaper sellers register their home addresses with the court. The police then made visits to verify that the addresses were correct, which led to intimidation of the media professionals.

The 1996 law also provided for heavy penalties, including imprisonment (up to five years) and up to 5 million CFA francs (US$10,000) for violations of the press law, such as defamation, insults, or incitement to ethnic violence. It also authorized the court to order the destruction of any printing facilities used to print inflammatory papers. In August 1996 the government suspended all publications that did not conform to the new law. They could only reappear (which they did the following week) after having put their affairs in order.

In 1997, Denis Sassou-Nguesso's new government adopted an act that abrogated the 1992 constitution, but kept in force the provisions relating to freedom of expression. Article 17 stipulated that the "exercise of individual and collective rights and freedoms, in particular, the freedom of movement, opinion, religion, expression, association, procession and demonstration," were guaranteed. However, the 1996 law remained in force. In November 2001, a new law on freedom of information and communication was adopted. There were few changes from the 1996 law, with the exception being that prison sentences were no longer stipulated for insults and defamation, only for incitement to violence, racism, and riots.

The fact that the judicial instruments were ineffective in limiting the lapses of the media during the period preceding the wars can be attributed to the lack of an effective regulatory body, among other things. The Conseil Supérieur de l'Information et de la Communication (CSIC), which was noted in a law from August 1994, was not established until April 1997, just a few weeks before the second war broke out. At the end of the fighting, the adoption of the 1997 act led to the suspension of all constitutional institutions, including the CSIC. The new law of 2001 provided for the creation of the Conseil Supérieur de la Liberté de la Communication (CSLC), whose members were appointed in August 2003. But at present, the CSLC, whose members took oath only in May 2006, has no resources or head office. It is provisionally occupying a room in the parliament building.

Control of the State Media

The transitional process has not led to real pluralism in the state media, because journalists practice self-censorship. Though at the beginning of the period of political openness there was a certain degree of freedom in the tone of national radio, it did not last.[25] Since 1992 the radio and television stations have been subjected to systematic incursions by armed men (presidential guards, paratroopers) who seize the microphones to broadcast their political demands. With changes in power and shifts in alliances causing promotions and demotions on political grounds, personnel changed constantly, often under the taint of ethnoregionalism.

Immediately after Pascal Lissouba came to power, "purges" hit the national radio and television stations. Journalists suspected of being close to the former president, Sassou-Nguesso, were excluded, while others resigned.[26] The trade unions denounced several times "the confiscation of freedom of expression, which has led to systematic censorship of the activities of political parties other than UPADS."[27] The excluded journalists organized sit-ins and campaigns to reclaim their right to broadcast, but their programs were progressively removed from the schedule. For five years, simply referring to the country's former strongman could get a journalist in trouble. In 1994, two Radio Congo journalists were held by the police for granting him an interview. They were freed thanks to their managers, who claimed that they were responsible for this initiative.[28] A few weeks later, one of their female colleagues was interrogated for having mentioned the role the former president played in the South African transition.

Naturally, as soon as Sassou-Nguesso came back to power, the mechanism went into reverse. Many journalists close to Lissouba went into exile or took refuge in the provinces. "A real witch hunt was organized," commented Reporters sans Frontières.[29] In the state media, people close to the former regime were hunted down by armed men.[30] The situation has improved today, but many journalists are still not free.

"Censorship has changed sides, but is still present. Whole currents of public opinion can rarely express themselves in the audiovisual media," Reporters sans Frontières noted in 2000. Allusions to former president Lissouba are still risky. In May 1999, a journalist for the Congolese national television station, Maurice Lemaire, was arrested and accused of sending documents to people close to Lissouba, who was then in exile. It is noteworthy that the 1996 law, still in force at the time, obliged journalists in the public media to support the government. In 1996 the government demanded that journalists in the state media who also worked for privately owned papers make a clear choice between these two jobs, or risk being sacked from the civil service.

Constant Violations of Journalists' Rights

Fear of repression and retaliation was another reason for the media to align themselves with politicians, the only people who could protect them. Immediately after the election of Pascal Lissouba, the opposition papers became victims of judicial harassment. *La Rue Meurt, Le Forum,* and *Le Gardien,* all associated with the opposition, were hauled before the courts. In June 1995 and November 1996, two publication directors (Asie-Dominique de Marseille of *Le Choc* and Médard Gauhy of *Alternative*), who had been condemned to long prison sentences for defamation, violently denounced the "judicial onslaught" against the "independent" press.[31]

The Lissouba regime's methods could be even more summary. In June 1993, Alain Shungu, who worked for the privately owned daily *Aujour-d'hui,* close to the Parti Congolais du Travail (PCT), was kidnapped and placed in detention. In November of the same year, four soldiers machine-gunned the home of a former national radio journalist, Clément Massengo, killing his wife and daughter. The journalist was suspected of directing the Radio Alliance station. The same day, the army used rockets to attack buildings in the Bacongo district, a fiefdom of the opposition, in the hope of destroying the station's secret base.[32] Beginning in 1995, arrests increased rapidly and punitive raids were launched against newspaper sellers.[33]

When the second war came, the growing number of violent acts went unpunished. In August 1998 the Ninjas assassinated Fabien Fortuné Bitoumbo, a journalist for Radio Liberté and the weekly *Le Gardien,* who was accompanying the minister of mines and industry to Mindouli, 150 kilometers south of Brazzaville. The former editor in chief of *La Rue Meurt,* a paper associated with Bernard Kolélas, had begun to work with media close to Sassou-Nguesso; this shift no doubt provoked the Ninjas' anger. In September 1998 the premises of *La Rue Meurt* were ransacked by the police, but the paper quickly reappeared.

The violence and pressure did not end with the war. In May 1999, Hervé Kiminou-Missou, the Africa No. 1 correspondent for Angola, was arrested at the Pointe-Noire airport on his way to Cabinda. His identity papers noted that he was born in Pascal Lissouba's region, and he was accused of spying. In 2001 the director of *Le Flambeau,* Prince Richard N'Sana, was arrested for having published a "best wishes message" from the former president that urged people to "mobilize to defeat the dictator."[34] This editor is now a politician close to President Sassou-Nguesso.

Pressure has also been put on the international media. In November 1993, Radio France Internationale's correspondent, who covered the confrontations, was expelled for broadcasting "false information."[35] The following year, the minister of communications, Albertine Lipou Massala, accused the foreign media of "favouring the opposition" and demanded that Congolese journalists in the public media who worked for the foreign press "choose unambiguously"; the pretext was that "they cannot serve two masters at once."[36] The situation has not improved much under Sassou-Nguesso. From February to mid-July 1999, Africa No. 1 was banned from broadcasting on FM from Brazzaville. It was reproached for having given a disproportionate amount of airtime to opponents of the regime in an open-mike program called *The Listeners' Magazine.* The government of Sassou-Nguesso, whose daughter married the president of Gabon, Omar Bongo, exercised such pressure on the Libreville radio station that three journalists of Africa No. 1 who held dual nationality (Congolese and Gabonese) were sacked. After long negotiations and the nomination of a new correspondent close to the regime in Brazzaville, the pan-African radio station has obtained permission to start broadcasting on FM again.

Today, the government wavers between the stick and the carrot, as it alternates between trying to control and trying to reconcile the whole of the local press. In 2000, after the general assembly of the Union Internationale des Journalistes et de la Presse en Langue Française (UIJPLF) was held in Brazzaville, the head of state agreed to give 300 million CFA francs (US$612,915) to the privately owned press, to be shared among the papers, the foreign press center, and the documentation center. There have been serious problems with the sharing of the money, leading to numerous disputes and contributing to further divisions among the press.

Weak Professional Associations

Congo's network of professional bodies is very weak. The only organization with a minimum of resources is the Centre de Ressources pour la Presse (CRP), created in 1994 with the support of UNESCO and Ouest Fraternité.[37] The CRP provides journalists with access to computing resources, basic documentation, and workshops and training sessions conducted by the professional associations.

During the Communication Convention of May 1992, a few months before the presidential election, Congolese journalists adopted an ethical and professional charter, but it has never been applied. The Observatoire Congolais des Médias (OCM) was established in February 2003; it is chaired by Bernard Mackiza, former editor in chief of *La Semaine Africaine,* and is supported by the Swedish Life and Peace Institute and the Institut Panos Paris.

Conclusion

The privately owned Congolese press has no doubt been a victim rather than a player in the country's successive political crises. Several times and for months on end, it has been at the mercy of violent militias, facing a recurring cycle of vengeance and reprisals as power changed hands. Today, it is confronted by a strong centralized power that has an increasingly tight stranglehold on the sector. In this situation, the alternative is clear: compromise or disappear. It will certainly take some time for the press to become organized and affirm its independence on the basis of real professionalism without relying on political support.

The audiovisual sector, still almost completely monopolized by the state media, has been subject to ruthless confrontations and seizures by the state and military. Radio has been used by all sides as a nonconventional weapon in the Congolese civil wars, equally affecting listeners, journalists, and the internal organization of media structures.

From the democratic opening in 1991, through episodes of armed conflict, to the current situation of precarious peace, Congolese journalists have never worked in a favorable context. They have never had an opportunity to work in a truly pluralist political and professional environment, nor have they been able to affirm their financial and editorial independence. Peace, the media, and the profession still need to be brought together.

Notes

I thank Joachim Mbanza, publishing director of *La Semaine Africaine,* for his meticulous proofreading, criticisms, and comments.

1. J. C. Gakosso, *La nouvelle presse congolaise: du goulag à l'agora* (Paris: L'Harmattan, 1997), pp. 11–12.

2. The monthly *Le Chemin,* published by the Protestant Church, appeared in 1982. However, it does not offer general information.

3. J. Mbanza, "Un journal dans la tempête de la guerre civile," in Institut Panos Paris and COTA (eds.), *Briser les silences: paroles d'Afrique centrale* (Paris: Karthala, 2003), p. 68. A general assembly of the readers was organized in order to

solicit their opinions on the necessary changes to the paper, and a financial and administrative audit was conducted to help the title to restructure. J. Mbanza, "Gérer un journal en période de crise politique: le cas de *La Semaine Africaine*," in *Rapport de l'atelier gérer un journal en période de crise* (Dakar: AMJ, AIF, UJAO, OSIWA, March 2002), p. 18.

4. The main militias involved in Congolese wars were the Cobras (Sassou-Nguesso), the Vampires, the Zulus, the Aubevillois, the Cocoyes and the Mambas (Pascal Lissouba), the Ninjas (Bernard Kolélas), as well as the Faucons and the Requins, close to smaller political parties.

5. Including the old PCT and other political parties close to Sassou-Nguesso, the FDU became the FDP in 1997.

6. E. Dorier Apprill, "Jeunesse et ethnicités citadines à Brazzaville," in *Politique Africaine* no. 64 (December 1996), p. 73.

7. Reporters sans Frontières, *Mission Report in the Republic of the Congo* (Paris, September 1999).

8. Three of the rural local stations have stopped transmitting, two because of the war, their infrastructures having been wrecked, and the third because of natural catastrophe.

9. Reporters sans Frontières, *Mission Report in the Republic of the Congo*.

10. Institut Panos Paris, *Africentr @lemédias* no. 5 (November 2002).

11. S. Mangaya, "Congo-Brazzaville: tristes dérapages de la presse congolaise," *ANB-BIA (African News Bulletin/Bulletin d'Information Africaine) Supplement* no. 399, November 1, 2000.

12. Cited in Reporters sans Frontières, *Rapport annuel, 1993* (Paris), p. 108.

13. Y. Koula, *La démocratie congolaise brûlée au pétrole* (Paris: L'Harmattan, 1999), pp. 67–68.

14. Mbanza, "Un journal dans la tempête de la guerre civile," p. 70.

15. *La Semaine Africaine,* April 19, 1999, p. 3, cited in Institut Panos Paris (ed.), *Afrique centrale: des médias pour la démocratie* (Paris: Karthala, 2000), p. 103.

16. Mbanza, "Un journal dans la tempête de la guerre civile," p. 69.

17. Mbanza, "Gérer un journal en période de crise politique," p. 18.

18. Mbanza, "Un journal dans la tempête de la guerre civile," p. 70.

19. Reporters sans Frontières, *Rapport annuel, 1998,* p. 34.

20. Gakosso, *La nouvelle presse congolaise,* p. 51.

21. M. E. Gruenais, "Congo: la fin d'une pseudo-démocratie," *Politique Africaine* no. 68 (December 1997), p. 129.

22. Reporters sans Frontières, *Rapport annuel, 1995,* p. 116.

23. The "gumbo" is a vegetable that is used in sauces so the food will "slip" in the throat.

24. E. Gauvrit, "Congo: l'épreuve des urnes," in *L'Afrique Politique, 1997* (Paris: Karthala, 1998), p. 313.

25. See Gakosso, *La nouvelle presse congolaise,* pp. 14–15.

26. In November 1992, the director of news, the editor in chief, and three other journalists from Radio Congo, all considered to be close to the PCT, resigned because they thought it was impossible for them to "exercise their functions according to rules of ethics." Reporters sans Frontières, *Rapport annuel, 1993,* p. 109.

27. Cited in Reporters sans Frontières, *Rapport annuel, 1993*, p. 109.

28. A. Maja-Pearce (ed.), *Annuaire de la presse africaine* (Brussels: FIJ, 1996), pp. 99–100.

29. Reporters sans Frontières, *Mission Report in the Republic of the Congo*.

30. Institut Panos Paris, *Afrique centrale*, p. 105.

31. Gauvrit, "Congo," p. 313.

32. Reporters sans Frontières, *Rapport annuel, 1994*, pp. 137–139.

33. M. E. Gruenais, "Congo: la fin d'une pseudo-démocratie," *Politique Africaine* no. 68 (December 1997), p. 131.

34. Reporters sans Frontières, *Rapport annuel, 2002*.

35. Reporters sans Frontières, *Rapport annuel, 1994*, pp. 140–141.

36. Cited in Reporters sans Frontières, *Rapport annuel, 1995*, p. 117.

37. Ouest Fraternité is an overseas aid association created and run by staff of the Ouest France Group, which publishes the regional daily paper with the largest circulation in France.

6

CENTRAL AFRICAN REPUBLIC

A Fragile and Ill-Used Media Sector

CENTRAL AFRICAN MEDIA are among the continent's least well-known. They are overlooked by aid and support programs and suffer from the permanent state of crisis in the country. The brief dawn of optimism, in 1993, released unprecedented dynamism in the sector. But the politico-military reverses, economic crisis, and precarious state of daily life, combined with government repression, have undermined even the most determined initiatives. Even more than elsewhere, the media and its professionals seem to be in crisis: "Inadequate professional and technical quality, coverage limited to the town of Bangui, slack handling of information with a marked lack of analysis, limited financial means (no subsidies, no head office, no advertising revenue and a high selling price),"[1] according to Tchakpe M'Brede, the former president of the Union des Journalistes Centrafricains (UJCA).

Fragile Pluralism in the Media

The privately owned press first appeared in the Central African Republic (CAR) in 1991, when the political scene was being liberalized. It developed timidly, and by 1993 there were forty-nine titles, most of them publishing irregularly and with limited circulations (200–3,000 copies). They included *Afric'Events* (founded in 1991), *La Tortue Déchaînée* (1992), *Le Bouclier* (linked to the Central African League for Human Rights), *Délit d'Opinion,* and *L'Etendard de la Patrie* (1993). Printed on two pages of A4 paper, these periodicals were particularly appreciated in intellectual circles. In addition, a few titles (*Le Conventionnel, Le Progrès,* and *Le Républicain*) were associated with the new political

135

CENTRAL AFRICAN REPUBLIC

Size	622.984 sq. km.
Population	3.7 million
Capital	Brangui
Ethnic groups	100 (Gbaya, Yakoma, Sango, etc.)
Official language	French
Main national language	Sango
Human Development	
Index ranking (2005)	171 (out of 177 countries)
Life expectancy	42 years
Literacy rate	48.6 percent

Chronology

1910–1958: French colony of Oubangui-Chari (French Equatorial Africa).

1958: The territory joins the French Union, and Barthélemy Boganda is elected prime minister of the Central African Republic (CAR).

1959: Boganda dies in a plane crash. David Dacko succeeds him as prime minister.

1960: Independence. Dacko becomes president.

1965: Colonel Jean-Bedel Bokassa seizes power.

1972: Bokassa proclaims himself "president for life."

1976: Bokassa proclaims the "Central African Empire."

1977: Bokassa has himself crowned "Emperor Bokassa the First."

1979: Dacko overthrows Bokassa in a coup backed by France. The republic is restored.

1981: Presidential election confirms Dacko as the head of state, but the results are disputed by his defeated challenger, Ange-Félix Patassé, and the country plunges into instability. General André Kolingba seizes power and restores order, banning all political parties.

November 1986: Kolingba is confirmed as president for six years by referendum.

1992: Kolingba, under international pressure, allows a national debate that leads to the reestablishment of multiparty democracy.

August 1993: Patassé wins the pluralist presidential election.

April and May 1996: Mutinies break out in the army.

January 1997: The Bangui Accords lead to the formation of a government of national unity. The Mission Interafricaine de Surveillance des Accords de Bangui (MISAB), a pan-African monitoring force, is established, with French material support.

(continues)

1998: MISAB is replaced by the United Nations Mission in the Central African Republic (MINURCA).

1999: Patassé is reelected president, but the election is contested by Kolingba's supporters. MINURCA is replaced by the United Nations Observation Bureau in the Central African Republic (BONUCA).

May 2001: Kolingba attempts a coup, but Patassé resists, backed by Libya and Congolese soldiers from Bemba's Mouvement de Libération du Congo (MLC).

October 2002: François Bozizé, former head of the Central African armed forces, attempts a coup but fails.

March 2003: Bozizé seizes power in Bangui with the support of the Chadian army. A transition period starts.

May 2005: Bozizé is elected president, ending the transition.

parties, but appeared very irregularly. In face of this new competition, *E le Songo,* the old government monthly, changed into the weekly *Be Africa Sango,* and then ceased publication.

However, the economic and social conditions were so unfavorable that the privately owned press found it difficult to survive and to publish regularly. The Central African Republic is one of the poorest countries on the continent, with a literacy rate in French below 30 percent. Most of the population is struggling just to survive, the health and education infrastructures are in ruins, and the civil servants are paid several months late. It is hardly surprising that the privately owned press was so fragile from the start.

When he was first elected president, Ange-Félix Patassé was conciliatory toward the new papers. In his inauguration on October 22, 1993, he promised to "rebuild the country on the ruins left by the previous regime," to "protect and consolidate democracy," and to "give all citizens bread, peace and freedom."[2] But most of the papers, run by self-taught people, chose to oppose the new government, accusing it of corruption, incompetence, and bad management. As the country's political situation deteriorated, the government leaders became annoyed and took increasingly summary measures against the journalists whom they designated as "poachers," accusing them of lack of professionalism.[3] Though initially the criticism was aimed at journalists close to the former regime, the threats and intimidation soon extended to the whole of the privately owned opposition press, which was suspected of being in the pay of political parties.

New titles however, continued to appear, including *Le Coup d'Oeil Centrafricain* and *Le Novateur* (the first aborted attempt at a privately owned daily) in 1994, and *Nouvelle Vision, Beafrika, Le Peuple,* and *Vouma–La Mouche* (The Fly) in 1995. Other dailies followed, including *Le Citoyen* in 1996; *Le Démocrate, Le Confident,* and *L'Hirondelle* in 2002; as well as numerous periodicals that appeared only sporadically (*Le Quotidien de Bangui, L'Echo de Centrafrique, Les Dernières Nouvelles, Le Patriote, L'Action, Sabango, Le Globe, Temps Nouveaux, Le Centrafriqu'Un, Fraternité Hebdo*). With a usual print run of 500 copies, the four dailies could increase to 2,000 in "hot news" periods, but they were distributed only in the capital and were even limited to certain districts of Bangui. With a maximum of twelve pages, they tended to publish press releases and facsimiles of official letters.[4]

The titles controlled by the Patassé government were not much more regular. *Centrafrique Presse,* a privately owned weekly close to the president, and the bulletin of the Agence Centrafricaine de Presse (ACAP), both appeared sporadically. *Le Forum de l'Unité,* a government publication that succeeded *Be Africa Sango,* was the only title that was offset-printed in tabloid format, but it was rarely on the market.

When François Bozizé seized power in March 2003, ending the ten-year rule of the Central African Republic's first democratically elected government, he could not rely on the support of any specific paper, because no paper had openly supported the armed rebellion. Yet because of numerous confrontations with the previous government, which the papers now characterized as "tyrannical," the privately owned press was mostly favorable to the coup. The papers' support became even stronger with Bozizé's promises to restore the constitutional state and respect freedom of the press. *Le Citoyen* and *Le Confident* openly welcomed the change, even if they were already asking questions about whether this new government was really transitional. Only *Centrafrique Presse* immediately went into radical opposition, referring to the country's new strongman as the "the self-proclaimed Bozizé" and denouncing the dictatorial "real nature" of the "putschist government."[5] *Le Forum de l'Unité* ceased publication, and several journalists close to Patassé then fled the country. The other papers gradually resumed their critical tone when faced with the transition government's recurrent shortcomings and increasingly restrictive behavior.

The audiovisual landscape in the CAR has long been dominated by Radio Centrafrique (founded in 1958) and Télé Centrafrique (1974), which are entirely under government control. Although the Central African radio scene has theoretically been liberalized, it lacks an appropriate regulatory framework. There is little variety, because those who could potentially initiate projects do not have the funds to create broadcasting infrastructures. The first private initiative was Radio Notre Dame, a religious station created in 1995 by the Catholic diocese of Bangui that also broadcast news, discussions, and programs on civic education and human rights.[6]

In August 1998, Radio MINURCA, associated with the United Nations peacekeeping force, started to broadcast, but closed down in February 2000 when the UN mission came to an end. However, a few months later, in June 2000, a new station, Radio Ndeke Luka (Bird of Opportunity), was created with the Radio MINURCA team with the aim of supporting the peace process. The station, managed by the Hirondelle Foundation (Switzerland), receives support from many foreign aid agencies. It broadcasts in Sango and French, and its stated objective is to contribute "to the consolidation of peace, the re-building of the Central African Republic and the economic and social development of the sub-region by broadcasting impartial, useful and professional information."[7] The station also aims to promote the work of the UN agencies and the NGOs present in the country. At first, it transmitted continuously from Bangui on FM, but since 2003 it can also be listened to throughout the country for one or two hours a day on shortwave.[8]

In May 2001, another religious radio station was founded, Radio ESCA, also known as the Voice of Grace. It is linked to the Baptist Church and financed by American Evangelical churches, and its programs center mainly on religion. It was followed in July 2001 by Radio Evangile Néhémie, sponsored by members of a French Baptist church.

Additional local community radio stations were created in the provinces with the support of the Agence de Coopération Culturelle et Technique (ACCT), which became later the Agence Intergouvernementale de la Francophonie (AIF). These stations were placed under the control of the Ministry of Communications. They include local radio Mambéré Kadéï in Berberati (founded in 1993), Radio Linga in Bambari (1995), and Radio Maigiaro in Bouar (1996), which is now barely functioning. There are also a few Episcopal radio stations: Radio Beoko (Unity) in Bambari, Radio Siriri (Peace) in Bouar, and Radio Ndoyé (Love) in Bossangoa, established in 1996. Africa No. 1 and Radio France Internationale also transmit on FM from Bangui, the first since 1995 and the second since 1997.

Television remains a de facto state monopoly, because no private entrepreneurs have braved the financial risks involved in establishing a station. Although the authorities do not hesitate to delay the start of an event in the hope that the cameras will arrive, Central African television has a very restricted coverage. Many viewers in Bangui cannot even receive the station's broadcast, because of a defective transmitter.[9] Satellite reception of foreign television channels exists, but is very limited, given the lack of financial resources in Bangui.[10] As well, the national press agency (ACAP) has no correspondents in the provinces, no longer receives foreign news services, and ceased publication of its bulletin in September 2004.

Outside the country, people close to former president Patassé, currently in exile in Togo, continue to manage media that oppose Bozizé's regime. Patassé's former spokesman and publishing director of the *Centrafrique Presse,* Prosper N'Douba, runs a virulent website from France.

The Media During the Crisis

In a country marked by permanent politico-military instability and a multifarious and persistent economic crisis, the Central African media work under enormous difficulties as they attempt to consolidate and become more professional. However, they continue to try to defend human rights and provide a forum for free expression where the government can be criticized.

A Poverty-Stricken Private Press

The greatest weakness of the privately owned press lies in its poverty, which is inevitable in such an economically devastated environment. "The papers are not economically viable, which means that journalists are easily victims of the 'brown sealed envelope' syndrome."[11] In other words, the media let themselves be influenced by politicians who want to communicate self-promoting information. Moreover, "you cannot really talk about newspaper companies in the CAR. The paper's staff usually consists of one person, who is the editor, the publishing director and who writes all the articles."[12] In 2005, only two titles, *Le Citoyen* and *Le Confident,* had a head office. *Le Démocrate* and *L'Hirondelle* managed to appear every day, though they had neither an office nor computing equipment. The advertising market in the country is practically noninexistent, as the private companies fled following the pillaging that took place during the mutinies and coups.

The public media are not much better off. The state media's employees are considered part of the civil service, which means that salaries are paid several months late and that delays accumulate. At the start of 2005, some civil servants had not been paid for forty months. The age and dilapidated state of the equipment give rise to serious doubts that the national radio and television stations will continue to broadcast in the medium term. Even now, their transmitters can hardly cover Bangui. In 1995, Reporters sans Frontières found that "80 percent of the national radio's equipment is not working."[13] In February 2004, the Bozizé government's minister of communications, Parfait Mbay, recognized that "national radio broadcasting is characterized by the obsolescence of its technical equipment, some of which dates from 1958. . . . The Central Africa Press Agency is only a press agency in name. . . . The Central African television has only one camera for reporting, making it impossible to cover several national events simultaneously."[14] Currently, radio and television share the only service vehicle, bought in 2004. Before that, journalists and technicians traveled on foot, in taxis, or at the expense of event organizers.

In July 2003, thanks to a Japanese government subsidy, national radio and television were able to start restoring their war-damaged offices. Recent support from UNESCO and the French embassy allowed them to acquire a minimum of digital equipment (two computers) just before the 2005 presidential and legislative elections. In order to reach the whole country during the electoral process, the national radio broadcast was retransmitted a few hours a day on shortwave from Paris, via Radio France Internationale. More recently, the European Union (EU) accorded a grant to Radio France Internationale to support local radio stations inside the country.

The economically deprived press of Central Africa receives some foreign support, but it must deal with the ceaselessly shifting situation in the country. As Patrick Bakwa, editor in chief of the daily *Le Confident,* pointed out, "There are international NGOs with development plans ready and waiting for the independent press but, because of the constantly changing political situation, they are not ready to apply them. They are waiting for the situation to stabilise."[15]

As for the radio sector, interested financial partners support Radio Ndeke Luka, which has an annual budget of about half a million euros.[16] Bilateral and decentralized aid agencies (French and Swiss), and multilateral aid agencies (the AIF), collaborate with UN structures (the United Nations Observation Bureau in the Central African Republic [BONUCA], the UN Population Fund, and the UNDP) to mobilize these resources. However, as always in this type of project, the station faces the combined challenges of sustainability and the need to successfully hand itself over to an entirely local management and production team.

The Hirondelle Foundation tried to transfer the station to locals after the departure of the expatriate station manager in 2005, and is still trying to define and implement the most suitable plan for its gradual withdrawal, but human and financial resources are lacking.

Recurrent Repression of Journalists

Additional obstacles to the development of the Central African press are political violence and permanent instability. Though the government was relatively tolerant toward the privately owned press during the first years of Patassé's rule, the public media regularly censored declarations by the opposition parties. When the new regime held press conferences, it soon started to exclude "from the list of the journalists invited those who were too close to the former president (André Kolingba) and those who might ask uncomfortable questions."[17] Soon, journalists from privately owned papers who were too-pointed in their criticism of corruption in government institutions and the presidential circle, found themselves in court under accusations of defamation; some were sentenced to long prison sentences. In 1996, Marcel Mokwapi, publishing director of the first privately owned daily, Le Novateur, was jailed for several weeks, then sentenced to six months in prison for having published an article stating that the prime minister "wished to protect at all cost a close relative involved in a financial scandal."[18]

Beginning in 1996, the successive mutinies and upheavals within the army led the authorities and the police to use greater and more diverse violence against journalists. Faced with continuous instability, the government broadened the range of taboo subjects and increased its armory of repression well beyond legal procedures.

In May 1996, Raphaël Kopessoua, editor in chief of Vouma–La Mouche, was beaten by mutineers he was trying to photograph.[19] In February 1997, Richard Bagouma, publishing director of Nikpa, was caught and tortured by the security services, who accused the press of being manipulated by the political opposition. His colleague, Jean-Rigobert Maka Gbossokoto, editor of the satirical newspaper La Tortue Déchaînée, received death threats for having harshly criticized the government, and the director of Le Novateur spent three months in prison for having published an article on the arbitrary detentions and abuses committed by the presidential guard.

In 2001, after the failed coup attempt by former president André Kolingba, repressive measures became even harsher. In July, the police seized the printing equipment of the Groupement des Editeurs de la

Presse Privée Indépendante de Centrafrique (GEPPIC), which printed many local papers. The government targeted, in particular, *Le Citoyen,* a new private daily edited by Maka Gbossokotto, for criticizing the presidential guard's attitude toward civilians during the events of May 2001. The editor was accused of "creating hatred in the population," and members of the presidential guard threatened to kill him and his wife.

A few weeks later, a collaborator from *Le Citoyen,* lawyer Assing-ambi Zarambaud, was arrested for his involvement in the attempted coup. But representatives of human rights associations think that the real reason behind the arrest was the series of articles Zarambaud had written for the paper denouncing the government's retaliatory measures against the Yakoma community, André Kolingba's ethnic group, who were seen as sympathetic to the rebels. At that time, 80 percent of the presidential guard were from the Kaba ethnic group, from the north of the country, and were close to President Patassé and his party, the Mouvement pour la Libération du Peuple Centrafricain (MLPC).

The director of Radio Notre Dame, Father Tonino Falagoista, was also arrested, in October 2001, for denouncing the treatment of the Yakoma during and after the events of May 2001 in a dispatch sent to the Missionary Service News Agency (MISNA), a Catholic organization based in Rome. Many journalists from the Yakoma community, who were well-represented in the privately owned as well as in the public press, were considered to be close to Kolingba's Rassemblement Démocratique Centrafricain (RDC), and were threatened. Fearing reprisals, they fled the country or went into hiding.[20]

The situation worsened after the failed putsch on October 25, 2002, which marked the start of the rebellion by François Bozizé's men. Other belligerents had come onto the scene, and Patassé's regime was no longer alone in threatening journalists. At the end of October 2002, Prosper N'Douba, spokesman for the Central African presidency and publishing director of *Centrafrique Presse,* was kidnapped and held for five weeks by General Bozizé's partisans. In December 2002 the rebels took the town of Bossangoa and broke into the diocesan radio station Ndoyé, where they killed its main presenter, who was on air at the time. The station was damaged and stopped broadcasting.

Violations of human rights became commonplace. Violence carried out against civilians with total impunity was the rule rather than the exception. For journalists, the taboo subjects now included the presence of the various armed groups within the country and the violent acts they carried out against the civilian population, as well as those committed by the police.

In February 2003, Joseph Bénamssé, correspondent for the BBC and the Associated Press, was questioned for having broadcast a report about Rwandan troops among the Congolese MLC rebels supporting Ange-Félix Patassé. Once again in February 2003, Marthurin Momet, publishing director of the privately owned daily *Le Confident,* was arrested and held in detention following the publication of a series of articles denouncing the violent acts committed against the civilian population by Jean-Pierre Bemba's MLC rebels. He was accused of "undermining the State's internal and external security" and "inciting hate" because he criticized the government's inability to control abuses committed by its allies.[21]

After seizing power on March 15, 2003, General Bozizé presented himself as a representative of a popular uprising aimed at restoring the constitutional state in the Central African Republic. In a speech in June, the new president said, "Today, no one can deny that Central African citizens are free to express their opinions without fear of imprisonment. The press is free to criticize the actions of the governing classes."[22] Many journalists welcomed the change, and some exiled writers decided to return to the country.

The honeymoon did not last long. The new government also had its forbidden topics, which included questions about its ability to ensure the country's stability and also relations with its Chadian "sponsors." In July 2003, Faustin Bambou, publishing director of *Les Collines du Bas-Oubangui,* was questioned at length by the police and then by the director of public prosecutions for having criticized the privileges granted to a Chadian businessman by the government.

A few days later, Ferdinand Samba, director of the paper *Le Démocrate,* was arrested for having disseminated "alarming and incorrect" information when he mentioned an attack by Patassé's troops on the town of Kaga Bandoro. In September 2003, a heavily armed militia leader entered the offices of the daily paper *Le Citoyen* after it published an article explaining that Bozizé did not have complete control over the militias that had brought him to power.[23]

Finally, the new president, just like his predecessor, quickly became intolerant of personal criticism. In February 2004, Judes Zossé, publishing director of *L'Hirondelle,* was arrested and accused of "defaming the head of state" for having published in his paper an article titled "Bozizé the Great Cashier, the State's Tax Collector," taken from the opposition's website Centrafrique Presse. The article insinuated that General Bozizé had placed taxes collected in the provinces into his personal account. Zossé was condemned to six months in prison, becoming the first journalist to be incarcerated for criticizing the new head of state.

Hostilities were then openly declared between the privately owned press and the new government, with the exception of a few titles, such as *Les Dernières Nouvelles,* which was clandestinely financed by Bozizé and his acolytes. In July 2004 the director of public prosecutions and the appeals court in Bangui called the privately owned press titles to order by accusing them of making "offensive remarks" about the authorities. "Attacks on the head of state and the ministers have reached unacceptable proportions . . . the papers are simply compendiums of lies and rumours," said the prosecutions director.[24]

The previous day, the minister of communications, Lieutenant-Colonel Parfait Mbay, had also accused the privately owned press of "serious abuses," reckoning that these papers were "being used to tarnish the image of the most prominent figures in the government." He reminded media professionals that "newspapers must . . . tell the truth and nothing but the truth, but always bear in mind the fact that not all truths should always be told."[25]

The "Voice of the Voiceless"

When the various authorities accuse the privately owned press for its lack of professionalism, its subservience to the political opposition, and its ethnic biases, the media defend themselves by saying they are only at the service of their clientele, an impoverished population whose basic rights are trampled. This is why, for example, they defended the Yakoma, on several occasions, when the community was threatened by the ethnically based strategies of Ange-Félix Patassé.[26] The media were then immediately accused by the government of being puppets of the political opposition, in particular of Kolingba and his RDC, and of resorting to "tribalism." In December 1999, during a speech before parliament, President Patassé declared, "Measures will be taken against the press that tends to incite rebellion, tribal warfare and hatred."[27]

When Kolingba launched his attempted coup from exile in 2001, the press denounced reprisals taken against the Yakoma. The daily *L'Hirondelle* noted in edition no. 297 (May 2001) a red list of people to be executed, drawn up by the Central African presidency. This publication caused a great scandal, even though the source of the document has never been authenticated.

Far from accepting the accusations of "tribalism," the papers emphasized their wish to "give a voice to the voiceless." In the same vein, they reported on social movements by publishing notice of the strikes that had become endemic in the civil service. In 2002, *Le Confident* did not hesitate to openly support a strike notice issued by teachers whose pay was thirty months in arrears.[28] It must be said, however, that the voiceless in question were, above all, members of the political opposition, and that articles about the population's social problems are rare in the Central African press. As for the people in the rest of the country, they are completely neglected, because none of the media have the technical and financial resources to maintain correspondents outside Bangui.[29]

The privately owned papers also claim the role of "watchdogs" and the right to politically accuse people in charge of public affairs who do not carry out their work correctly. In June 2004 the managing director of Energie Centrafricaine (ENERCA), Jean-Serge Wafio, was sacked after *Le Citoyen* published a series of articles accusing him of misappropriation of funds. On July 8 the paper's director was taken into police custody after the sacked senior manager filed a complaint against him.[30]

Self-censorship, due to fear of judicial or police reprisals, is very common. In October 2002, at time of Bozizé's attempted coup, "most local journalists admitted refraining from criticizing the authorities' brutal reprisals against Bozizé's supposed partisans."[31]

Finally, in confused political situations involving massive violations of human rights with total impunity, the media often become the only recourse for the abused. In October 2003, five members of the presidential guard stopped a woman in the street and took her back to their camp, where they raped her, one after the other. The victim's fiancé, who went to the camp to demand her release, was severely beaten and tortured. This couple then turned to Radio Ndeke Luka to tell their story. After the station decided to broadcast this information, the highest authorities summoned the director and asked him for proof of the accusations. When the station produced the proof, the authorities did assume responsibility, and arrested the five soldiers and discharged them from the army.

On December 10, 2000, World Human Rights Day, the United Nations bureau in the Central African Republic polled people on the streets of Bangui and found that Radio Ndeke Luka was deemed "the best defender of human rights in the CAR."[32] This radio station is certainly unique in the country. It has important resources, has a well-trained and regularly paid staff, and is undoubtedly listened to more than any other station in Bangui, as is evident from the number of letters and telephone calls received from listeners. Its international supporters, however, do not protect it from government repression, and its journalists and presenters are regularly threatened. The crucial role that

Radio Ndeke Luka played in times of unrest, when no other media were available, must also be stressed. During the attempted coup of May 2001, when the public media could not transmit, the government had to appeal for calm using Radio Ndeke Luka, until Radio Centrafrique again became functional, on June 13. During the coup of March 2003, Radio Ndeke Luka ceased transmitting for only twenty-four hours, and was the only source of credible and verified information on current events. In the opinion of local observers, it is currently the only daily source of rigorous, impartial, useful, and professional information for the Central African population.

An Unfavorable Media Environment

Legal and Regulatory Framework

For a long time, the legal framework kept the CAR press under tight control; long prison sentences and heavy fines were handed out for press offenses. People could be held in police custody or preventive detention for long periods without charges or investigation. Yet the new constitution, adopted in 1995, guaranteed freedom of expression and freedom of the press. The law made the founding of newspapers subject to prior authorization by the minister of communications, but it was always granted.[33] At that time, an observer remarked, "The privately owned press can work in relative freedom in the Central African Republic. . . . Its influence is so marginal that the government can afford to ignore it."[34]

In 1998, Law 98/006, concerning the general organization of freedom of communication in the Central African Republic, and Law 98/005, concerning the organization and working of the Haut Conseil de la Communication (HCC), were adopted. Article 15 of Law 98/006 declared, "The journalist has a right to freely investigate all matters concerning public life and to discuss the actions and declarations of any public or private institution." In fact, it was quite liberal when it came to the conditions for creating media companies, but it set out a long list of press offenses and reminded journalists of their duties and responsibilities. In this way, it interfered in self-regulation of the media left free by the professional organizations. As the Central African journalists did not have their own professional code of ethics, it was left to the law to decide which practices were unprofessional.[35]

In January 2003, a few weeks before the coup that led to the downfall of Ange-Félix Patassé, these two texts were amended, but without any major changes. In 2004, after Reporters sans Frontières, the Committee to Protect Journalists, and local journalists had pressured the Central African government for revision of a criminal law that provided for penalties and imprisonment of up to five years for defamation, a new press law decriminalized press offenses. The judiciary did not support this initiative. According to a judge of the appeals court in Bangui, some journalists have adopted a "suicidal attitude." "They happily malign, insult, and defame and, after all that, reject any idea of legal proceedings."[36]

The HCC had a short experience. In 1998, during the legislative elections, an independent electoral commission ensured that political parties had equal access to the public media. The next year, it was the turn of the HCC to ensure equity of the state media. But its life was soon over, for in August 1999, President Patassé dissolved it, reckoning that its members were more concerned with material considerations and their salaries than with exercising their functions. In 2005, a newly remodeled HCC, based on an updated ordinance and including four representatives of the profession, was established in haste on the same day that the presidential campaign started. Soon after the election, a debate arose about the legitimacy of this "transitional" council to keep working after the end of the transition period. Most of its members were replaced, but the new HCC established in 2006 has not yet found a real place in the media landscape.

Paralysis of the State Media

The state media are far from embracing the ideas of openness and pluralism. After the first free elections that brought Ange-Félix Patassé to power in 1993, the state media remained strictly governmental, mainly devoting their energies to covering the official activities of the president and his executive. It was not uncommon to hear "the whole of government press releases, header included, read out on the radio."[37] Furthermore, the directors of radio and television were traditionally members of the party in power. The new regime did not hesitate in carrying out a kind of "cleansing" by transferring executives considered close to the RDC.[38]

In 1997 the state media made slight concessions to the notion of political pluralism and broadcast a daily program giving airtime to the political parties represented in the National Assembly. It was the first time the opposition had access to the public media, though the activities and positions of the president's party, the MLPC, continued to benefit from much wider coverage. The program was closely monitored by the authorities. In April 1998 the Ministry of Interior ordered that the broadcasting of a televised debate organized by a new party, the Union Nationale pour la Démocratie et le Progrès en Centrafrique, should be interrupted. The party was immediately suspended for three months, for "sectarianism" and "tribalism."

In 1998, following the political disturbances, the minister of communications set up a control commission that was responsible for checking information before it was broadcast on radio or television. The journalists' association immediately protested this measure, which the authorities rescinded several days later.

In May 1998, a radio journalist was dismissed for having accused advisers in Patassé's circle of corruption and bad management. In January 1999, Christian Noël Panika, a radio journalist (and correspondent of the RFI and the AFP), was in turn suspended for three months by the director-general for having broadcast a press release from the Association Nationale des Etudiants Centrafricains (ANECA) without the approval of the minister of communications. Another radio journalist, Sylvie Jacqueline Benguere, was in turn "suspended off-air until further notice" in October 1999, for not having read all of the congratulation messages addressed to President Patassé on his reelection. The punishment was lifted three months later.[39] In November 2000, Christian Panika, also a union militant, was suspended from his functions as a presenter, for "disobeying line management." *Seventh Day,* a very popular open-mike program hosted by Raphaël Kopessoua, during which politicians responded to questions asked by listeners, was also taken off the air, because too many criticisms of the government were being heard.

At the start of December 2002, the opposition was finally allowed to reappear on state media, from which it had been virtually excluded after the presidential election in 1999. "Roaming microphone"–type programs were organized in order to give airtime to all the political currents in the country.[40] After the Bozizé coup of March 2003, some journalists in the state media tried to profit from the burgeoning era of freedom to such an extent that Prime Minister Abel Goumba declared he was "surprised by the behaviour of the official press that he had asked to support the transitional government."[41]

Apart from the opposition's difficulties in gaining access to public broadcasting, an additional problem is the omnipresence of the military in the daily lives of national radio and television. For more than two decades, the Central African state media have been under armed guard. Because control of the state media is always an issue during attempted putsches, the center of Bangui is always a scene of panic whenever gunfire is heard near the national radio station. Although the national television station, located in an avenue on the outskirts of the city center, has always been spared by the various mutinies and violent disturbances, the radio station has systematically been the target of protesters anxious to broadcast declarations over the airwaves.[42] This was again the case in June 2004, when a group of soldiers started firing in the air near the radio station, causing anxiety in the population, though it was only a scuffle between soldiers.

During the attempted coup of May 2001, the military presence in the two public audiovisual media was reinforced, and remained that way until March 15, 2003. As the mutineers had broken the radio transmitter during the early hours of combat on May 28, the authorities, with the help of national radio staff, installed an alternative station, Radio Paix et Liberté, that transmitted directly from the head of state's residence.[43]

The outbreak of open rebellion against the government, from October 2002 to March 2003, led to extremely tight control over the editorial boards, which were instructed not to allow François Bozizé to speak, under any circumstances. "The authorities have informed me that I am no longer allowed to make declarations to the press because it seems that they are sensational," Bozizé declared to the AFP.[44] In January 2003 an announcement was made that a new statute would be adopted to give the public audiovisual media financial and administrative autonomy within a new structure, the Office de Radio Télévision de Centrafrique (ORTCA). But this project has not yet been implemented, due to a lack of financial and political will.[45] Without autonomous management, the public media remain entirely under the thumb of the executive, and under the vigilant guard of the military.

The Absence of the International and Foreign Media

The international media do not pay much attention to the Central African Republic. Only a few specialized French media show any interest. Yet Ange-Félix Patassé's regime, basking in the glory of being the first democratically elected government in the country, demonstrated several times its sensitivity to criticisms by foreign journalists. In January 1999, two journalists, Stephen Smith of *Libération* and Géraldine Faes of *Jeune Afrique,* were prevented from entering the country at the Bangui airport a few months after Smith had published an article on Patassé's involvement in the diamond trade.

In November 2002 the authorities jammed the frequencies of Radio France Internationale and Africa No. 1, the international radio stations broadcasting on FM from Bangui. President Patassé accused the French radio station of too-favorable coverage of the rebels: "If you continue, I will take RFI off the FM band in Bangui," he threatened. Subsequently, the minister of communications denied there had been any official jamming of the broadcaster's frequency, affirming that "storms and heavy rain" could have caused the interference.[46]

Weak Professional Associations

The Central African privately owned press might have better resisted the many repressive measures and accusations of lack of professionalism if it had shown more solidarity by forming a strong and united professional association. Unfortunately, this has not happened. There are seven generalized or specialized professional associations, but only four main ones. All, however, are subject to internal dissent and operating difficulties. The Union des Journalistes Centrafricains, created in 1993, has always had one overriding drawback: the majority of its members belong to the state media, which means that, as civil servants, they cannot take part in any struggle to defend the profession.[47] The Fédération Syndicale des Travailleurs de la Communication (FSTC), created in 1993, is also mainly made up of public service journalists who want to reinforce the protection given by their status as civil servants.

The Groupement des Editeurs de la Presse Privée Indépendante de Centrafrique, created in 1996, has defended journalists under attack and improved working conditions of the press at every possibility. In 1998 the US embassy provided it with two powerful photocopiers on which to print all its papers. However, management problems soon appeared, as some editors used equipment and consumables without paying their bills. Some of the equipment disappeared, and some was damaged during the coup of March 15, so GEPPIC has had to return to using private printers.[48] It has sometimes carried out acts of collective professional solidarity, as in July 2004, when GEPPIC suspended publication of privately owned press papers to protest against the arrest of Maka Gbossokotto, the director of *Le Citoyen*. But GEPPIC is also subject to leadership quarrels that hinder its activity. The new executive, nominated in March 2004, has only limited credibility.

The Association Centrafricaine des Editeurs de la Presse Indépendante (ACEPI) is a parallel structure created by editors who also occupy posts as civil servants and whose papers rarely appear. They created their own association because the law bans state employees from engaging in private commercial activities, and these press promoters have been refused admission to GEPPIC, which contests their legitimacy on the market.

Conclusion

As in all countries in conflict, the media in the Central African Republic have been subject to the full gamut of political, military, and economic pressures: accusations of treason, shortages of raw materials, an impoverished public, no advertising revenue, rampant pillaging that has destroyed the economy, permanent uncertainty, exclusion from the outside world, lack of contact with the country's internal regions, destruction of equipment, professional divisions, lack of training, and the like. But even more than elsewhere, the media in the Central African Republic have faced all these challenges on their own.

Only the Hirondelle Foundation, following in the footsteps of the United Nations, has decided to intervene in this particularly fragile and landlocked field. The lack of professionalism with which the Central African media are often charged seems inevitable, given the total lack of financial and human resources. But at least its potential negative effects are limited, because of the short circulation of CAR media. They make up for all these difficulties, however, with an iron will to survive, which at least guarantees the existence of some degree of pluralism.

Notes

I thank Mathurin Momet, Christian Aimé Ndotah, and Lucienne Maka Gbossokotto for their critical proofreading and comments.
    1. "L'expérience du journalisme en Centrafrique: de la théorie au vécu quotidien," in the seminar report "The Collection, Processing, and Broadcasting of Information During an Electoral Period in a Post-Conflict Situation and a Context of Transition," UNESCO–Ambassade de France, Bangui, May 24–29, 2004.
    2. M. Koyt, M. F. M'bringa Takama, and P. M. Decoudras, "République Centrafricaine: les vicissitudes du changement," in *L'Afrique Politique, 1995* (Paris: Karthala, 1996), p. 245.
    3. There is no school for training media professionals in the Central African Republic, only one-time seminars organized by some funding agencies.
    4. There is no *Journal Officiel* in the Central African Republic; therefore, many laws and decrees can only be read if they are published in the general press.
    5. *Centrafrique Presse,* June 9, 2004.
    6. Due to technical problems, Radio Notre Dame stopped transmitting from December 2003 to August 2005.
    7. Extract from the Radio Ndeke Luka charter.
    8. In Bangui it broadcasts twenty-four hours a day, seven days a week, and within a radius of 200 kilometers around the town. Faced with financial problems, because it was not allowed to charge for the press releases and announcements

that it broadcast, the station had to reduce its shortwave transmissions to the whole of the country, beginning April 1, 2005, from two hours to one hour a day.

9. In 1993 the estimated number of television sets for the whole country was 5,000. Reporters sans Frontières, *Rapport annuel, 1996,* p. 101.

10. A local private company, Turbo Satellite Media, offers a bundle of fifteen foreign channels accessible by subscription with a decoder. It claimed 400 subscribers in Bangui in April 2005.

11. A. Maja-Pearce (ed.), *Annuaire de la presse africaine* (Brussels: FIJ, 1996), p. 258.

12. Institut Panos Paris (ed.), *Afrique centrale: des médias pour la démocratie* (Paris: Karthala, 2000), p. 89.

13. Reporters sans Frontières, *Rapport annuel, 1996,* p. 101.

14. AFP dispatch, February 16, 2004.

15. RAP21, *Newsletter* no. 99 (AMJ), February 28, 2003.

16. Running the radio station costs 300,000 Swiss francs (US$242,813) a year. In addition, retransmitting for two hours on shortwave costs 200,000 Swiss francs (US$161,875) a year.

17. Reporters sans Frontières, *Rapport annuel, 1995,* p. 99.

18. Reporters sans Frontières, *Rapport annuel, 1997,* p. 98.

19. Reporters sans Frontières, *Rapport annuel, 1997,* p. 98.

20. Including the directors of the following papers: *Le Démocrate,* Ferdinand Samba; *L'Hirondelle,* Judes Zosse; *Les Collines du Bas-Oubangui,* Faustin Bambou; *L'Avenir,* Fouguet Kolodo; and *Pari du Développement,* Michelino Komane.

21. He was finally released after the coup of March 15, but his paper's office had been sacked and pillaged by the rebels.

22. Cited in the Committee to Protect Journalists, *Attacks Against the Press, 2003,* 45.

23. Ibid., p. 46.

24. AFP dispatch, July 9, 2004.

25. AFP dispatch, July 8, 2004.

26. Most of the political parties have ethnic and regional bases. Patassé's MLPC has the support of the north (the Sara and Baya peoples), former president Dacko's MDD is strong in the west, and Kolingba's RDC is popular in the southeast. Patassé instituted ethnic rebalancing because the civil service and the army had been dominated by the Yakoma, members of Kolingba's ethnic group, until then. He excluded them from the presidential guard, and transferred them to the national army, so that he could be surrounded by his own people, the Kaba, a subgroup of the Sara.

27. Central African League for Human Rights, *Annual Report, 1999,* p. 7.

28. *Le Confident,* November 26, 2002.

29. When Bozizé's troops were advancing, from October 2002 to March 15, 2003, the media in Bangui had very little reliable information on what was happening in provincial towns, and were unable to follow the progress of the rebels.

30. AFP dispatch, July 12, 2004.

31. Committee to Protect Journalists, *Attacks Against the Press, 2002,* p. 1.

32. Radio Ndeke Luka, "The Reference Points," working document, 2004.

33. Reporters sans Frontières, *Rapport annuel, 1996,* p. 101.
34. Reporters sans Frontières, *Rapport annuel, 1997,* p. 97.
35. GEPPIC drew up a text that has been used to establish an ethical and professional practice monitoring committee, the OLPCA.
36. Cited in Institut Panos Paris (ed.), *Afrique centrale: des médias pour la démocratie,* p. 95.
37. Reporters sans Frontières, *Rapport annuel, 1994,* p. 116.
38. Thus, in 1994, Emmanuel Piama and Guy Tampon, director and editor in chief of *E le Songo,* respectively, were removed in favor of a new team. However, they remained in the civil service.
39. Central African League for Human Rights, *Report, 1999,* p. 7.
40. Reporters sans Frontières, *Rapport annuel, 2003,* p. 1.
41. Cited in ibid.
42. In 1993, soldiers from the presidential guard occupied the radio station and demanded payment of their salaries, which were in arrears. In 1996, the mutineers laid siege to the radio station and entered by force in order to read a press release presenting their demands. A month later, during a second mutiny, soldiers seized control of the transmitter, located eight kilometers from the town center, and partially damaged it.
43. Reporters sans Frontières, *Rapport annuel, 2002,* p. 1.
44. Cited in ibid.
45. A proposed special status for journalists in the public media was recently rejected because the proposed salaries were very high.
46. Committee to Protect Journalists, *Attacks Against the Press, 2002,* p. 1.
47. In November 2004, a new board of the UJCA, enlarged to include the privately owned press, was nominated, chaired by Maka Gbossokotto, publisher of *Le Citoyen.*
48. Only the daily *Le Citoyen* has its own printing equipment.

7

CHAD

Media Resistance
in the Midst of Turmoil

CHAD'S HISTORY SINCE independence has been marked by an impossibility to establish a constitutional state and maintain peace in a country where rebel political and military movements have always proliferated and where there have been periods of extreme tension in relations with neighboring states. None of the various Chadian leaders have managed to govern the country in a consensual manner without excluding certain communities. None have succeeded in completely suppressing the armed rebellions fighting against the central government. For almost thirty years, the Chadian media, mostly limited to governmental structures, were used by authoritarian regimes against guerrilla movements within their territory. When Idriss Déby, who himself came from an armed rebel movement, took power in 1990, he declared, "No journalist will be prosecuted" and "From now on, the newspapers are free."[1] Immediately, a privately owned press developed, followed in 1997 by free radio stations, drastically modifying the information scene in the country.

But these media are confronted by a double challenge. On the one hand, Chad has an unfavorable socioeconomic situation, with a poor and largely illiterate population (despite the official figures, barely 20 percent of the population can read French) spread over a vast landlocked country, which leads to high prices for all the raw materials used by media companies and a market that is structurally weak. On the other hand, its government is on its last legs and hostile to criticism. After many negotiations and armed campaigns, it has managed to eliminate and weaken the rebellions that contested its authority, though without achieving any consensus.

155

CHAD

Size	1,284,000 sq. km.
Population	9.75 million
Capital	N'Djamena
Ethnic groups	200 (Tubu, Sara, Arabs, etc.)
Official languages	French, Arabic
Human Development	
Index ranking (2005)	173 (out of 177 countries)
Life expectancy	48 years
Literacy rate	25.5 percent

Chronology

1910–1960: French colony (French Equatorial Africa).

1960: Independence. François Tombalbaye, belonging to the Christian elite from the south, becomes president.

1962: Tombalbaye bans political parties and imposes a one-party state.

1965: The Front de Libération National du Tchad (FROLINAT) is created in Sudan, supported by the Muslim population of the north of the country.

1975: General Félix Malloun, a southerner, overthrows Tombalbaye and becomes president.

1979: Goukouny Oueddeï, from FROLINAT, seizes power and becomes president.

1980–1981: Fighting explodes in N'Djamena between two FROLINAT factions led by Oueddeï and Hissène Habré.

1982: Habré seizes power and installs authoritarian and repressive regime.

1990: Idriss Deby, Habré's former military adviser, overthrows Habré.

1993: A national conference is held, leading to a political transition and democratic reform.

1996: Deby is elected president of the republic, but opposition parties contest the poll results.

2001: Deby is reelected president. Massive frauds are again suspected.

2004: The National Assembly ratifies a constitutional amendment that increases the number of terms a president can serve.

2005: A new constitution is adopted by referendum.

2006: Deby is reelected president.

Emergence of Pluralism in the Media

For a long time, the privately owned press in Chad consisted of just one paper, the cultural publication *Tchad et Culture,* created in 1960. In 1989, *N'Djaména Hebdo* (now a biweekly) appeared, signaling the era of pluralism. Beginning with Idriss Déby's rise to power in 1990, about thirty initiatives were launched, coinciding with the emergence of democratic demands throughout the continent. Though most of the publications did not survive, some took root: *Le Progrès* (1993), *L'Observateur* (1997), *Le Temps* (1995), and *Notre Temps* (1999) managed to survive, alongside their predecessor. Circulations are low (2,000–5,000 copies), and the publications are mainly distributed in the capital, though they try to maintain a presence in some provincial towns (Moundou, Sarh, Bongar, Abéché).

The privately owned newspapers, with the exception of *Le Progrès,* which is close to the government,[2] campaign for political change and present a reasonably similar editorial content without strong divergent tendencies. They focus on events in the capital, and more specifically on political polemics and denouncing abuses of power. Because there are no well-established opposition parties on the political scene, the NGOs and privately owned press form the backbone of the opposition to the current regime. Since 1990 the newspapers have been much more consistent in their positions than most of the political parties, who have shown "extreme fluidity" in their alliances, resulting in some "spectacular conversions."[3]

As a magistrate pointed out, "The leaders of the opposition, who should be stimulating political discussion, prompt the media to take their place, in a sort of struggle by proxy. The Chadian press has become the only forum where concerns about both human rights and social questions are expressed."[4] This has meant that criticism of the government is the prime occupation of journalists. Anyone attempting to deviate from systematic opposition and adopt a more balanced position is immediately suspected of having been bought off by those in power.

This essentially accusatory role was evident in 1996, at the time of the first "free" elections and, more specifically, at the time of the constitutional referendum in March, when some newspapers asserted that the "no" camp had in fact won and that the announced victory of the "yes" camp was due to fraud. At the time, most observers agreed that in this case vote rigging had been limited,[5] and accused most of the papers of a form of systematic opposition. Seven years later, however, during the Justice Convention, some magistrates admitted that they had been bought off by the regime in power.

The presidential elections (1996, 2001, and 2006) and legislative elections (1997 and 2002) were opportunities for the press to criticize the regime. "Today, we can think of politics as a farce, with a final scene that we know in advance," was written in *N'Djaména Hebdo* just before the legislative elections of 2002, in which the presidential party, the Mouvement Patriotique du Salut (MPS), won 100 of 115 seats.[6]

It is very difficult for the newspapers to provide more varied content, because they have little knowledge of what is happening in the rest of the country. They do not have funds to carry out investigations outside the capital, nor do they have any local correspondents.[7] In addition, their circulation is mainly limited to N'Djamena, because of a lack of reliable distribution networks, difficulties in coverage, and the small potential clientele in the provinces. These factors mean that 70 percent of the newspapers' print runs never leave the capital.

Radio stations started to develop in 1997. The first was La Voix du Paysan, a community station, founded by a Catholic NGO located in Doba. Dja FM, the capital's first private radio station, was founded in N'Djamena in 1999, followed in 2000 by FM Liberté, founded by ten civil society associations including the Chadian League for Human Rights. Today there are about a dozen stations in the country. Given the prohibitive cost of a license for a commercial private radio station (5 million CFA francs per year [US$10,215]), most stations are registered as community stations. They often remain dependent on external finance from Catholic and secular development agencies, among others.

The main international radio stations are also now present on FM in N'Djamena and some provincial towns: Radio France Internationale, the BBC, Africa No. 1, and Voice of America. Cameroon Radio Television (CRTV) can be picked up in areas near Cameroon. In addition, there are the satellite television channels, including at least a hundred Arab channels.

The Media and Local Antagonisms

The Press and North-South Antagonism

According to Claude Arditi, "The profound antagonism between north and south in Chad has been gradually built up by a process of reducing the complexity of ethnic identities and socioeconomic contexts to this single opposition."[8] This antagonism is now deep-rooted, as demonstrated by the results of the constitutional referendum of 1996. Though contested, the results were particularly striking. In the nine northern districts, the "yes" camp won with scores of 82–96 percent, while in the five southern districts the "yes" camp's score was well below 20 percent. These results seem to show that rejection of the government is based on a regional rather than an ethnic or tribal dynamic, as the south covers a considerable number of different communities.

Have the media participated in or contributed to this reduction of complexity in intercommunal and politico-economic relationships in the north-south dichotomy? According to Arditi, "the local press regularly reports on conflicts between farmers and herdsmen or disputes within the school system between people of the north and the south; in these articles, the members of each side develop their arguments."[9] But the reporting does not try to explain the deeply rooted origins of the violence, nor does it point out how heterogeneous, diversified societies have sometimes formed images of themselves through creating an oversimplified binary opposition. The press notes that conflicts among school students are almost always provoked by students from northern communities, particularly those close to the government, and that in conflicts between farmers and herdsmen, the latter are generally the aggressors.

Faced with one of the most potent sources of tension in Chad, some observers reproach the press for offering shallow analyses and simplifying disagreements to reinforce stereotypes. Others, however, accuse the media of a "southern" bias, because journalists who criticize the government are mostly from the south. Only *Le Progrès* is run by journalists from the north, and its former publishing director also has connections in Islamist circles. Among the radio stations, FM Liberté, the first private radio station in N'Djamena, is also considered by the government to be "southern"-driven, since it is known for denouncing human rights violations.

Despite these labels, which the journalists contest, the media have never gone so far as to incite hatred of the other community. The worst that can be said is that the opposition press sometimes uses disparaging terms for ethnic groups, such as the diminutive term *zak* to refer to the Zaghawa community, to which President Déby belongs. It also sometimes publishes letters from readers that are extreme in tone, such as one from a contributor to *Notre Temps* who wrote in 2002, "You seem to have forgotten that your ancestors were the slaves of our northern ancestors."[10]

The weakness of the private newspapers seems to stem from their taking for granted the distinction between a dominant north and a marginalized, despised south, without trying to present a more balanced view. But how do we distinguish between those who diligently reinforce this north-south divide, which is also exploited by the government, and those who are simply reporting on a situation that is, in fact, unbalanced?[11]

The preponderance of journalists from the south in the privately owned press is even more visible because the public audiovisual media use a recruitment policy that systematically favors journalists from the north. Few, if any, of these northern recruits are ready to denounce this favoritism, for fear of reprisals against a "northerner" suspected of complicity with the "southerners." Consequently, only the latter criticize the government's discriminatory methods.

The north-south antagonism is also expressed in linguistic and religious debates, which are frequently covered in the media. For example, the press gave wide coverage to the polemic on the introduction of Arabic as an official language by the constitution of 1996. The northern Muslim populations thought that the language in question was classical Arabic, whereas the southern Christians, who are not familiar with the Quran, saw it as the Arabic dialect normally spoken in Chad, usually called "Chadian." "The Southern-oriented newspapers," explained Chadian journalist Brahim Moussa, "think that Arabization is a way for the government to proceed with the rampant Islamization of the country. Whereas for *Le Progrès,* for example, the policy of making Arabic a working language is only logical, because it is an international language spoken by a large part of the population and in all the country's markets."[12]

These linguistic differences lead to disputes about religion and also to antagonisms between herdsmen and farmers. The religious quarrels focus on, among other things, the organization of social life and the administration of justice. Faced with traditional justice as carried out in the north of the country, the newspaper *Notre Temps* reminded readers, "Chad is a multi-ethnic and multi-confessional country, a secular state with a constitution that does not recognize either the 'dia' or collective punishments and penalties."[13]

Conflicts Between Herdsmen and Farmers

Quarrels between Sara and "Arabs," often related to the damages done by herdsmen's livestock in farmers' fields, are frequent and sometimes murderous in the south of the country. The Chadian press is not indifferent to this problem and mentions it regularly, even if it lacks the resources to make inquiries in the field.

Most of the papers that are critical of the government show marked sympathy for the Sara farmers. "Farmers aggressed by herdsmen," ran a headline in *N'Djaména Hebdo* in May 1997; "Herdsmen must keep their herds in the north," *Notre Temps* echoed in November 2002.[14] "This conflict between herdsmen and farmers is a favorite theme of the so-called Southern media, which accuses the authorities of helping the herdsmen by supplying them with weapons."[15] Some observers have jumped to the conclusion that the privately owned press shows sympathy for the Sara because the publications are owned and run by southerners, but the editors in question reply that it is simply compassion for the victims that shapes their handling of the news. Once again, they are revealing real injustices. While the state compensates victims of conflicts between farmers and herdsmen in the north and center of the country, farmers in the south never benefit from this remuneration.

The newspapers also denounce the persistence of "slavery," such as children being bought from their parents in the south for 5,000 CFA francs (US$10.20) to guard the herds.[16] In a country where the major politicians are also large livestock farmers—sometimes the owners of immense herds—the organization of the agropastoral areas is a major issue that the government can exploit for its own ends. This means that the authorities see any criticism of the way the sector is managed as a maneuver by the political opposition.

Radio stations have taken some initiatives in the field to try to restore peace in localities where intercommunal conflicts have broken out. The community radio station Terre Nouvelle, in Bongor, with the support of the Deutsche Gesellschaft Jür Technische Zusammenarbeit (GTZ), has installed relays in several small towns in the west of Chad, specifically towns, such as Pala, that have been the scene of conflicts between "natives" and "newcomers," with the avowed intent of preventing conflicts and building peace.[17]

Armed Rebel Movements in the North and East

In October 1998, Youssouf Togoïmi, the former minister of defense, launched the Mouvement pour la Démocratie et la Justice au Tchad (MDJT), based in the Tibesti mountains. This new movement was yet another addition to the other rebel factions already active in the north (Laokein Bardé's Forces Armées pour la République Fédérale [FARF]) and the Lake Chad region (Brahim Mallah's Mouvement pour la Démocratie et le Développement [MDD]). Local and international journalists are generally forbidden access to conflict zones. In any case, the local media do not have the resources to cover a rebellion taking place hundreds of kilometers from the capital.[18]

The privately owned press, nevertheless, tried to give leaders of rebel movements an opportunity to express themselves. Some people saw this as legitimizing outlaws and spreading their propaganda. For others, it was a democratic action that allowed all the players to express their points of view. In 1998 the government initiated several court cases for defamation against newspapers that had published interviews with Youssouf Togoïmi. In September 2002, when the death of the rebel chief was announced, the progovernment media celebrated the disappearance of "an obstacle to peace," while the privately owned media were much more circumspect.

Journalists who risk publishing information on clashes with the army may open themselves to reprisals by the government. In January 2001, members of the armed forces harassed Michaël Didama, publishing director of *Le Temps,* after the paper had published an article on the rebellion and a press release from the MDJT that suggested that the number of army casualties was considerably greater than the official figures.[19]

Generally speaking, the privately owned media have regularly denounced the brutal behavior of government forces, which has led other media, including the progovernment newspaper *Le Progrès,* to say that the independent newspapers "tend to systematically condemn the government and absolve the rebels."[20]

The attention (and relative understanding) that the privately owned newspapers give to the rebels shows that, over and above north-south differences, the constant theme of their editorial line is criticism of the regime. The members of Togoïmi's movement are all "northerners," but the media are interested in their cause because they oppose Idriss Déby's regime. In September 2003, when the MDJT rebels took the town of Bardaï, the privately owned press's main headlines stressed the setbacks suffered by the loyalist troops, whereas *Le Progrès* gave prominence to the internal disputes in the movement since the death of its leader.

The privately owned press is always skeptical about peace agreements, often signed after negotiations, that bring financial advantages to the new allies. The public media, on the other hand, always noisily express triumph. Does this mean that the privately owned press does not want peace, or that it is being realistic when it comes to agreements that seem to have little chance of lasting?

A Two-Sided Media Environment

Public Media Under Control

The extremely critical tone of the private media is in marked contrast to that of media under state control: Radiodiffusion Nationale Tchadienne (RNT), established in 1955; Télévision Nationale Tchadienne (TVT), created in 1987 with no real legal status; and the Agence Tchadienne de Presse (ATP), formed in 1965, responsible for the news bulletin *Info-Tchad,* which was only irregularly published. Because of the obsolete and defective transmission equipment, many parts of the country no longer receive the RNT transmissions, while the TVT only covers the town of N'Djamena for a few hours a day (6 P.M. to 11 P.M.).

All the state media suffer from a lack of material resources, lack of motivation of their personnel, lack of independence (the three media are simply civil service departments in the Ministry of Communications), and the extremely political nature of nominations.[21] Self-censorship is practiced continually, encouraged by the threat of defamation suits[22] and the presence of intelligence service agents among the radio's personnel. RNT managers sometimes refuse to broadcast press releases from the opposition, even after having been paid official rates for the airtime.[23]

Despite all these difficulties, in the past few years journalists in the public media have attempted to organize themselves to demand an improvement in their status and also greater editorial freedom. The challenge comes mainly from television, which has younger and more reactive staff than does radio. In 2002 the Collectif des Agents de la Télévision (CATEL) gave notice of a six-day strike to demand the rehabilitation of two journalists who had been punished by management for having criticized the prime minister on the air. The two journalists were restored to their positions after they sent a letter of apology to the management. In May 2003, after another forty-eight-hour strike, the employees succeeded in their demands for new equipment. In July 2004 the employees once again went on strike, for more than a month, in order to obtain a reevaluation of their status. The public radio and press openly dissociated themselves from the movement, which they stigmatized as "a strike by 'southerners,' and a few northern opponents."[24] The government has managed to break several strike movements by exploiting regional feeling, mainly among freelance journalists, many of whom are in the public sector only on the basis of ministerial recommendations.

TVT journalists are subject to constant pressure from the authorities. In August 2002, journalists surprised customs officers from the mobile squad as they were molesting an adolescent who had picked up soap that had fallen from their vehicle. The journalists filmed the incident. A quarrel then broke out between the customs officers and the journalists, which the latter also filmed and decided to broadcast on the evening news. A few moments before the broadcast, the minister of communications banned the piece due to heavy pressure from customs officials.[25]

Last but not least, television suffers from major technical problems. It was only in 2004 that a Radio China Taiwan International aid mission got the RNT's shortwave radio transmitter working again. It had ceased transmitting in December 2002, depriving Chadians living outside the capital of all access to national information.[26] In remote areas, where there is no local FM station, the RNT is the sole source of information.

Attacks on Freedom of the Press

Relations between the privately owned press (with the exception of *Le Progrès* and the "northern" radio station, Al Nassr) and the government are extremely conflictual. Chadian journalists are subject to intimidation, harassment, pressure from police and the military, and arbitrary measures (questioning, searches, imprisonment, and unjust condemnations), generally directed toward writers who criticize the regime's major personalities. In a country where it is not uncommon to see the police beat journalists who are attempting to cover official events, access to information is not guaranteed. For this reason, people often must depend on rumor, which leads to defamation suits.

Taboo subjects are mainly the rebellion in the north and anything that touches on the president and his circle. Merely allowing a representative of the opposition to express a point of view can also be grounds for police action. For example, in May 2004, FM Liberté was threatened with closure for having broadcast an editorial that was seen as offensive because it challenged the constitutional review that would give Idriss Déby a third mandate. In February 2004, the director of Radio Brakos, a private radio station transmitting from Moissala (600 kilometers from N'Djamena), was questioned and severely beaten for having allowed the broadcast of an interview with a Chadian opposition politician.

Police action for defamation is frequent. Because those claims always originate from the government and not from private citizens, they can be seen as instruments of pressure used by the executive (which also manipulates the judiciary) against the privately owned press. In 1998 and 2000, *L'Observateur* and *N'Djaména Bihebdo* were prosecuted and condemned for "complicity in defamation" because they reported remarks made in public by Chadian politicians. They were judged to be "co-responsible" for those remarks, and one of the publishing directors was imprisoned.[27] In another incident, a retired civil servant (who was not part of the editorial team) was sentenced to imprisonment in 2002 after writing a letter that was published by *N'Djaména Hebdo* in its opinions column. The complaint that led to his arrest was made by the Libyan ambassador in Chad, because the letter had denounced attacks on Chadian nationals living in Libya and the authorities' lack of interest in them.

Generally, the punishments are disproportionate to the offenses committed. During a meeting between journalists and magistrates organized in May 2003 by the Institut Panos Paris, Sobdibé Zoua, counsel for the Chadian bar association, declared, "Some gentlemen of the press, even when it has been established that the facts with which they are charged are offences, try to justify themselves in the eyes of public opinion by portraying themselves as martyrs." To which a media professional replied that they were not claiming impunity, but wished to "re-establish a just balance between a fault and the penalty that punishes it."[28] Chadian justice has sometimes taken such remarks into account. In June 2004, the court condemned the Chadian

state to pay 6 million CFA francs (US$12,258) in compensation and inter-
est to the radio station FM Liberté for damages the station suffered during
its closure from October 21 to December 9, 2003, on official grounds of "illegal operation" and "deviant behavior."

Outside the capital city, community radio stations are also subject to
pressure and intimidation by local authorities, ranging from the police com-
missioner to the heads of civil service departments, including brigade commanders and all public office holders, who try to silence criticism with
threats.[29] In April 2003, journalists from the Brakos community radio station
started a three-day strike to protest the local authorities' interference in the
management of the station. The authorities had threatened the station after
it had denounced customs officers and police who were guilty of pillage
and violating civilians' human rights.[30]

Finally, the government has tried to pressure the media by sending journalists on field trips at times of heightened tension, to seduce them into
changing their minds on sensitive issues. In 2000, at the time of the massacres at Bardaï, and in 2001, when an opposition politician died under
suspicious circumstances on a road in the country's interior during the presidential campaign, journalists were taken to the locations of these events
and handed envelopes containing generous quantities of cash. The journalists refused the bribes.

An Open Legal and Regulatory Framework

Though the Chadian private media are in a difficult situation, the legal
framework within which they operate is one of the most favorable in the
region. Law 029/PR/94, of August 22, 1994, concerning press regulations
in Chad, recognizes freedom of the press, without prior authorization or security. It is supplemented by Law 43/PR/94, of November 8, 1994, concerning audiovisual communication, and by Law 12/PR/94 of April 3, 1994,
pertaining to the creation of the Haut Conseil de la Communication (HCC).
The new constitution, adopted in 1996 after a long transitional period following the National Conference in 1993, institutionalizes freedom of the
press and opinion. In reality, this freedom remains fragile, in light of the
constraints imposed by the economic situation and by strained relations with
the government.

The constitution recognizes the existence of the HCC, which as an independent administrative authority has wide powers to organize the media
sector. However, it cannot always exercise its powers freely, and it is subjected to much pressure from the executive. Nevertheless, it was generally
considered to be the most functional of all its peers in Central Africa until

April 2001, when, on the eve of the presidential election, the HCC adopted a decision banning political debate in broadcasts by private radio stations and comments in the news bulletins. Article 35 of this decision, which provoked an outcry, stipulated that the radio stations "which do not conform to this decision will be suspended for the whole of the election campaign." This was the first such intervention by the HCC in the radio field.[31] FM Liberté, the most popular private radio station in N'Djamena, refused to bow to this injunction and, after stormy negotiations with the HCC, obtained permission to cover the electoral campaign.[32] Relations between the HCC and the media then deteriorates.

In February 2002 the HCC suspended FM Liberté for three weeks following its broadcast of a report on the riots at the University of Ngaoundéré in the north of Cameroon, during which Chadian students were injured. Retaliatory measures had been taken against Cameroonian residents in Chad after this broadcast. In April 2002 the HCC once again banned all political programs on the radio stations before the legislative elections, thus confirming that "it has become an instrument of the government for controlling information."[33]

Professional Institutions and Associations: Public vs. Private

Since the media sector was liberalized, professional groups have multiplied. The Union des Journalistes Tchadiens (UJT) was very active during the years immediately following its creation, in 1989. It drew up a professional standards charter in 1994. It was joined that year by the Syndicat des Professionnels de la Communication (SPC), which had about a hundred members (mainly staff of the minister of communications, who automatically become members when they begin to work at the ministry). This structure remained lethargic for a long time, because it had been infiltrated by people close to the government. The Association des Editeurs de la Presse Privée Tchadienne (AEPT), composed of the ten or so editors in the country, was formed in 1995. The Union des Radios Privées du Tchad (URPT) and a self-regulatory body, the Observatoire de la Déontologie et de l'Ethique des Médias du Tchad (ODEMET), were founded more recently.

There is a real division between the public and private media, but no splits within the privately owned press, as seen in many neighboring countries. The privately owned press has on several occasions shown genuine professional solidarity. In 2002 the press organized a week without newspapers to protest the questioning of a trainee journalist from Le Temps. Three private radio stations supported this movement and stopped transmitting for two days.

And yet, despite this solidarity, the professional associations are not very dynamic. If some people point to "the fragmentation of the Chadian press, subject to waves of divergent interests and in which numerous idiosyncrasies manifested themselves,"[34] it should be stressed that all media outlets face daily difficulties; their managers are more preoccupied with the survival of their companies (most are obliged to find moneymaking activities outside journalism), than with union activities.

Conclusion

The Chadian privately owned media play an essential role in giving a voice to those who do not have access to the state media, whether they are rebels or NGOs that have written reports about human rights violations perpetrated throughout the country, reports that the government would prefer to leave in silence.[35] In a context of multiple antagonisms, the privately owned media have steadfastly continued to show their opposition to the nondemocratic nature of the Chadian regime.

The privately owned media have not called for ethnic or intercommunal conflict or the use of violence against the government. Although they lack the means to cover this immense country, they do not focus merely on town-based debates. They raise issues about important internal dissensions between the north and the south, Christians and Muslims, farmers and herdsmen, and their various spin-offs. In contrast to the government, which exploits these tensions to guarantee itself a political base, the privately owned press mainly plays a denunciatory role and takes the side of the victims. However, the most virulent journalists from the privately owned press are often from the same regions as the victims, which gives the regime, and occasionally the public media, an opening to discredit their work as being motivated by ethnic, regional, and political biases.

Notes

I thank Nadjikimo Benoudjita, president of the AEPT, for his scrupulous proofreading and comments.

1. Reporters sans Frontières, *Rapport annuel, 2002* (Paris), p. 1.

2. Its former publishing director, Mahamat Hissène, is a member of parliament for Idriss Déby's party, the MPS.

3. R. Buijtenhuijs, "Tchad: l'année des élections," in *L'Afrique Politique, 1997* (Paris: Karthala, 1998), p. 149. Often cited is the case of Saleh Kebzabo, former director of *N'Djaména Hebdo* and well-known opposition leader of the UNDR party. He joined Déby between the two rounds of the presidential election in 1996.

4. A. Sougnabe Misset, "La presse tchadienne reste figée sur ses étiquettes," in Institut Panos Paris and COTA (eds.), *Briser les silences: paroles d'Afrique centrale* (Paris: Karthala, 2003), p. 143.

5. *N'Djaména Hebdo,* June 13, 1996, cited in Buijtenhuijs, "Tchad," p. 142.

6. Cited by the Committee to Protect Journalists, *Attacks Against the Press, 2002,* p. 1.

7. F. Minery Lemoine, *L'état des médias au Tchad* (Paris: GRET, April 2001), p. 3.

8. C. Arditi, "Les violences ordinaires ont une histoire: le cas du Tchad," *Politique Africaine* no. 91 (October 2003), p. 51.

9. Ibid., p. 52. The schools have become strategic places for upward social mobility. Because people from the north since the colonial period refused schooling, power was handed over to an educated elite from the south at independence, which reversed the traditional hierarchies between the communities. The wish of the "northerners" to make up for their backwardness in instruction, in order to claim positions of responsibility, has led to the emergence of corrupt practices in higher education (where the teachers are still mainly "southerners"), which has become rife with interregional conflicts.

10. Cited in Arditi, "Les violences ordinaires ont une histoire," p. 58.

11. Sougnabe Misset, "La presse tchadienne reste figée sur ses étiquettes," p. 145.

12. B. Moussa, Pan-African Press Agency.

13. *Notre Temps,* August 2003.

14. *N'Djaména Hebdo,* May 29, 1997, and *Notre Temps,* November 11, 2002, cited in Arditi, "Les violences ordinaires ont une histoire," p. 61.

15. Moussa, Pan-African Press Agency.

16. There is a debate concerning the use of the word "slavery" by the press to describe the situation. See C. Arditi, "Les 'enfants bouviers' du Sud du Tchad, nouveaux esclaves ou apprentis éleveurs?" *Cahiers d'Etudes Africaines* 45, nos. 3–4 (2005), pp. 713–729.

17. Institut Panos Paris, *Africentr@lemédias* no. 10 (April 2003), p. 6.

18. Committee to Protect Journalists, *Chad, 2000: Country Report,* p. 1.

19. Ibid., p. 5.

20. Institut Panos Paris, *Afrique centrale: des mots pour la démocratie,* p. 197.

21. See L. Gondje, "Difficultés de la presse publique: par quel bout commencer?" *Tchad et Culture* no. 227 (May 2004).

22. Committee to Protect Journalists, *Chad, 2000,* p. 1.

23. US Department of State, *Country Report on Human Rights Practices, 1996,* p. 4.

24. Interview with Youssouf Djambaye of the SPC, Kinshasa, December 5, 2004.

25. Institut Panos Paris, *Africentr@lemédias* no. 4 (October 2002).

26. Institut Panos Paris, *Africentr@lemédias* no. 26, (September 2004).

27. Minery Lemoine, "L'état des médias au Tchad," p. 10.

28. Institut Panos Paris, *Africentr@lemédias* no. 12 (June 2003), p. 7.

29. G. Maoundonodji, "Chronique des tentatives de bâillonnement d'une radio iconoclaste," in Institut Panos Paris, *Briser les silences,* p. 142.

30. Institut Panos Paris, *Africentr@lemédias* no. 10 (April 2003).

31. Committee to Protect Journalists, *Attacks Against the Press, 2001,* p. 2.

32. See Maoundonodji, "Chronique des tentatives de bâillonnement," p. 141.

33. Committee to Protect Journalists, *Attacks Against the Press, 2002,* p. 1.

34. Institut Panos Paris, *Afrique centrale*, p. 186.

35. For example, the press behaved impeccably in the case of Hissène Habré. The former dictator was prosecuted for crimes against humanity by some of the families of the 40,000 victims of his bloody regime. The papers took care to give the points of view of both the victims and some of the people responsible for the massacres, without forcibly uniting the victims against the perpetrators; rather, the press insisted on the necessity of judging the former head of state, so that the truth could be told and families could grieve and move on with their lives.

8

CAMEROON

The Media Between
Protest and Submission

IS IT RIGHT to speak of a "conflict" in Cameroon? Though not experiencing war, the country is in the grip of a series of internal and external tensions that give rise to sporadic outbreaks of violence. At the beginning of the 1990s, violent clashes occurred between the government and opposition, and the newly emerging private press contributed fully to the debates. A decade and a half later, the political system has become more stable. It has gradually eliminated, divided, and discredited its opponents. The media landscape has also taken a beating. After many years of great popularity, newspapers are now experiencing economic difficulties coupled with the desertion of their readers.

Fading Written Press and Temporary Radio Stations

The written press, liberalized more than a decade ago, has since concentrated on politics. But it has never really tried to deepen the many potential schisms in Cameroonian society (historical-linguistic, identity, regional, community, economic, and territorial), except in a few cases, discussed below. Moreover, according to some, it has developed a marked penchant for sensationalism and provocation.[1]

The written press today mainly consists of one progovernment, bilingual state newspaper, the *Cameroon Tribune,* and several private newspapers, the most important of which are the dailies *Le Messager,*[2] *La Nouvelle Expression,* and *Mutations* (all have appeared three times a week for a lengthy period) and the biweekly *Dikalo.* Two English-language publications, the *Cameroon Post* and *The Herald,* have had some success, despite their limited circulations. In recent years, online newspapers (such as

171

CAMEROON

Size	475,440 sq. km.
Population	16.3 million
Capital	Yaoundé
Ethnic groups	240 (Ewondo, Bulu, Peulh, Bamileke, Douala, etc.)
Official languages	French, English
Human Development Index ranking (2005)	148 (out of 177 countries)
Life expectancy	48 years
Literacy rate	67.9 percent

Chronology

1885: German colony.

1916: The territory is placed under British and French control, and then under a League of Nations mandate implemented by France and Great Britain.

1960: French Cameroon, the only case in the French Union experiencing an anticolonialist armed movement, becomes independent. Amadou Ahidjo becomes president.

1961: British Cameroon opts to join the federal state of Cameroon by referendum.

1966: Ahidjo establishes a single party, the Union Nationale Camerounaise (UNC)/Cameroon National Union (CNU).

1972: Cameroon becomes a unitary bilingual republic. Some English-speakers fear that their cultural heritage might be lost.

1982: Ahidjo resigns as president for health reasons, in favor of his prime minister, Paul Biya.

1984: Biya is elected president.

1985: The Rassemblement Démocratique du Peuple Camerounais (RDPC)/Cameroon People's Democratic Movement (CPDM) replaces the UNC/CNU as the single party.

1988: Biya is reelected president.

1990: Facing rising opposition, Biya allows multipartyism.

1991: "Ghost town" campaigns are organized regularly to show popular discontent.

1992: The political opposition, mainly gathered around the Social Democratic Front (SFD), led by Anglophone John Fru Ndi, radicalizes its demands.

(continues)

1992: Biya is reelected president, facing a widely divided opposition.
1993: An armed conflict arises between Cameroon and Nigeria about
    the Bakassi Peninsula.
1997: Biya is reelected president.
2002: The RDPC/CPDM wins the legislative election.
2004: Biya is reelected president.

Cameroun Actualité, Cameroon Online, and *Cameroon-info*) have also emerged. In 2000, 1,300 newspapers were officially registered, though barely 30 actually appeared, and fewer than 20 appeared regularly.[3] This figure fell to 15 in 2004.

The privately owned press in Cameroon is one of the oldest in French-speaking Africa. It probably had the largest combined circulation at the start of the 1990s. Several private newspapers appeared well before political liberalization. *Le Messager* has been in existence since 1979. *L'Effort Camerounais,* the paper of the national Episcopal conference of Cameroon, was created in 1955; after two decades it vanished in early 1975 and then reappeared in 1995. The *Cameroon Post* dates from 1969; *Le Patriote* was established in 1984.

The liberalization of radio and television, however, provided for by act the December 1990 law on freedom of social communication, has been slow to materialize. The monopoly of Cameroon Radio and Television (CRTV) lasted more than ten years after pluralism was officially authorized. Broadcasting pluralism became effective only on April 3, 2000, when a decree was signed that laid out operating conditions for private audiovisual communication companies.

Nonetheless, a few private radio stations, essentially denominational in nature, had already started to broadcast. The first was Radio Reine in 1997 (created by a Catholic priest of the Yaoundé archdiocese), followed in 1999 by Radio Lumière (linked to a private college), Radio Soleil, Radio Bonne Nouvelle, Radio Vénus, and Radio Siantou. Also in 1999, the minister of communications stated on CRTV that stations without an operating license were broadcasting "at their own risk."[4]

While the Ministry of Communication has not yet issued any licenses, it does issue temporary authorizations. The numbers of local stations in the interior of the country, however, have grown rapidly. There are concerns that these stations could interfere in local disputes, which the written press in Douala and Yaoundé ignore.[5] About ten private radio stations and a few television channels now compete with the state-run broadcasters. "While radio stations sometimes show a degree of independence and criticism, the television channels content themselves with relaying official information and only address uncontroversial subjects."[6]

As for the state-run media, they have not really gained any independence. They are supervised by two quasi-state bodies: the Société de Presse et d'Edition du Cameroun (SOPECAM)/Cameroon News and Publishing Corporation, which publishes the daily *Cameroon Tribune;* and the CRTV, which oversees national radio and television. The CRTV is the heir to Radio Douala, created in 1941 by the French colonizers and transferred in 1963 to the Cameroonian government, and also to Cameroon Television (CTV), established in 1985.[7] The CRTV controls regional radio stations. Four other local radio stations were established in the provinces in the 1990s with the support of the ACCT/AIF.

Many private carriers exist, which means there are a considerable number of foreign channels available. As the CRTV devotes more than 60 percent of its airtime to foreign productions, there is a growing outward-looking perspective that leads to "a dramatic acculturation initiated by cable and satellite broadcasters that are flooding our homes with other people's dreams,"[8] according to Michel Tjade Eone.

The Media and Sociopolitical Tension

The Press in the Turmoil of Political Pluralism

Since the privately owned press appeared well before the multiparty system, it preceded political opposition in terms of government criticism and protest. In December 1990, *Le Messager* published an open letter to Paul Biya from Célestin Monga, an economist and newspaper contributor, who denounced "this country where every day, the most fundamental human rights are ridiculed and where the majority of people do not have enough to live on, while a small handful of opportunists share the country's riches with impunity."[9]

After Monga and the newspaper's editor, Pius Njawe, were summoned to appear in court, there was an extraordinary outpouring of popular support. Monga and Njawe became true heroes in the name of the private press. From then on, their paper, along with other privately owned papers, including *La Nouvelle Expression* and *Challenge Hebdo,* played a fundamental role in lifting the veil of mysticism from government authority. They established a forum where authority could be criticized, and exposed the racketeering of local elites.

Faced with these antiestablishment newspapers, the government could still claim the *Cameroon Tribune, L'Action* (the weekly newspaper of the ruling party, the Rassemblement Démocratique du Peuple Camerounais [RDPC]/ Cameroon People's Democratic Movement), and some privately owned papers, such as *Le Patriote* and *Le Témoin,* which remained loyal to the government. Thus, in 1991, *Le Patriote* condemned Operation Ghost Town as the product of a "diabolical plan" and described the National Conference, which the opposition was attempting to establish, as "a mirage and a sham."[10]

A virtual state of war existed among the newspapers.[11] Relying on sensationalism, aggression, and provocation, they all focused on politics. As Fabien Eboussi Boulaga, professor of philosophy at the Catholic University of Yaoundé noted several years later, the Cameroonian media "did little to educate the public in terms of criticism, compromise or negotiation, nor in terms of accuracy of information and respect for opponents."[12] As Francis Beng Nyamnjoh says, this private press tried to "confront an indecent government with indecent language," using libel and blackmail, exacerbating the fragmentation of civil society, and heightening ethnic tensions.[13]

In 1992, a presidential election was held and the results were strongly contested. The announcement of Paul Biya's victory triggered a wave of violence in English-speaking provinces, which had voted overwhelmingly for John Fru Ndi, leader of the Social Democratic Front (SDF). Indeed, "the polls noted a massive division along ethno-regional lines,"[14] and the regional issue became a central theme in political discussion. The newspaper *Galaxie* emphasized, "As the single party has been replaced by a multi-party system without democracy, our disabused compatriots have decided to gather together by ethnic groups and form inter-tribal alliances as in the pre-colonial era."[15]

Fully engaged in political debate, and often not hesitating to criticize opposition and government alike, the newspapers follow the reorientation of the political parties, which crystallize around region or ethnic groups. The political landscape is increasingly marked by a split between the west (Bamiléké and Anglophones) and the south-center (Béti). Political parties follow clear regional contours. The RDPC is established in the greater south and the center, the SDF in the west, and the Union Nationale pour la Démocratie et le Progrès (UNDP)/National Union for Democracy and Progress in the north. "Ethnicity and region have become the cardinal identifiers influencing social relations either formally or implicitly."[16] Therefore, each election proves that Cameroonians are inclined to vote along ethnic and regional lines, "endorsing national leaders primarily through their ethnic and regional elites."[17]

Paul Biya's regime, strongly tainted by proprietary interests, allocated many positions of authority to members of its ethnic group, the Bulu/Béti.

This was done in such a way as to make the Béti an overwhelming majority in the upper ranks of the army, and disproportionately represented (compared to the other 250 communities in Cameroon) in the administration, state-owned companies, the ruling party, and successive governments.

The current regime has gradually weakened the opposition and reinforced its own political base. The written press, losing momentum, is now suffering from a double burden: the weariness of the people, who have seen that polemics have not led to the hoped-for changes; and the economic crises, which force people to "make do" in order to survive. Obsolete equipment is not replaced, journalists are underpaid and therefore open to corruption, and costs are high. Circulation has fallen spectacularly. *Le Messager,* which had a circulation of over 70,000 at the start of the 1990s, today scarcely manages to sell 5,000 copies. Though circulation figures for the opposition and private press are declining, during election times, when tensions rise, the media step up their activity and the government counters with increased repression of journalists. Concurrently, the party in power creates new publications that are loyal to it. The 2004 presidential election demonstrated this yet again.

The Privately Owned Press
"in the Service of the Bamiléké"?

"The Bamiléké think that all of Cameroon is theirs, which explains their rampant search for space and land, which is worrying many indigenous peoples," *L'Aurore Plus* protests. "Unable to gain power by legal means, they have created themselves a divine pathway to achieve it—the privately owned press. This is their main weapon."[18]

Very often, the main players of the written Cameroonian press, principally *Le Messager, La Nouvelle Expression, Challenge Hebdo* (no longer published), and *Mutations,* have been accused by those close to the government of being instruments in the service of the Bamiléké cause, seeking to seize power at any price and remove the Béti from government. It is noteworthy that the publishing directors of these newspapers all have family ties with Bamiléké communities. *Le Messager, La Nouvelle Expression,* and *Challenge Hebdo* were even nicknamed "The Holy Trinity" (the Father, Son, and Holy Spirit), thereby mocking the omniscience on which the Bamiléké are accused of priding themselves.[19]

"Is being Béti becoming a sin?" asked *L'Eveil du Cameroun* at the start of the political liberalization process. The newspaper continued, "Isn't the multi-party system that Cameroonians so persistently demanded ultimately, for a good many of them, an unspoken and rather elegant way to bring about, without appearing to be inveterate tribalists, the departure of the Béti from power?"[20]

Another progovernment newspaper, *Le Temps,* went further: "The Bamiléké have realized that the Béti are the last and only obstacle standing in the way of their achieving domination over the country." The Bamiléké are viewed as ambitious and greedy for power and money. "A Bamiléké is a resentful person, characterized by a never-ending rumination on imagined harm and misfortune, blended with hatred and jealousy, all of which involves a narcissistic overinvestment in himself and the rejection of others. . . . The Bami are the cause of the economic crisis. If money is missing, it is because the Bamiléké have emptied the banks and are circulating the money between themselves with their tontines."[21]

The short-lived newspaper *Elimbi* was to call openly for the extermination of the Bamiléké, giving rise to the mobilization of organizations for the defense of human rights and freedom of the press.[22] As one expert notes, "many [newspapers] received all manner of support to arouse this hatred of the Bamiléké."[23] Through dint of impassioned editorials, reports of dubious quality, and debatable statistics, some newspapers stoked intercommunal tension.

In contrast, certain antiestablishment newspapers have not held back from pointing the finger at the entire Béti population. The Béti are alleged to be "thieves," "incurably stupid," "congenitally inept," lazy, and tribalist.[24] Nonetheless, according to a recent rigorous analysis, it appears that none of the "Holy Trinity" newspapers has ever concerned itself with "vindicating or defending Bamiléké interests." Consequently, the accusations of tribalism aimed at these newspapers would appear to be primarily a strategy of the government to justify its vaguely repressive impulses.[25]

Whatever the actual degree of "ethnicization" of the written media in Cameroon, the press is participating in a process of identity consolidation, which has other facets than crystallization around ethnic identities. The disintegration of the state, the progression of the informal economy, the growth of corruption, political repression, and divisions within the opposition, which leave no credible alternatives to the current government, combine to create a sense of insecurity that pushes people toward other kinds of solidarity networks ("ethnic," but also regional or religious).

The concept of "ethnic group" (which can represent fluid communities in Cameroon who form groups according to common interests) is manipulated by political opportunists who play on questions of identity. This strategy, which is not recent but deeply rooted in national politics,[26] has led to the instigation of a quota policy in the school system and in administrative offices, provoking a real sense of injustice within Bamiléké communities.

The press's political affinities rather than the ethnic origin of the publishing director are more important in determining their viewpoint on these issues.

Last, the written press in Cameroon is essentially one of protest and struggle. It aims to defend causes and make neglected voices heard. Some judge that this struggle has not always been directed at the defense of legitimate or neglected causes: "The press has been something of a handicap to democratic debate by practising trench-warfare journalism, with tribal-political trenches, tribal-economic trenches and tribal-religious trenches."[27] One Cameroonian journalist even states: "This press . . . is founded on tribal arrogance with an editorial policy which is limited to the resolution of quarrels (often caused by land disputes) and to revenge, via the written word for wrongs inflicted on its irreproachable ethnic group by the enemy tribe or ethnic group."[28] However, other analysts judge that accusations of tribalism, at least those leveled at the major privately owned publications, are often idle accusations and are not based on actual fact or known professional misdeeds.[29]

Besides these newspapers, which reach only a very limited number of individuals (literate, urban, and affluent), the radio stations, and more precisely the official regional stations that broadcast in national languages,[30] have incited hatred against the Bamiléké and English-speakers mainly in the south.[31] In 1994, the national radio station, broadcasting in Ewondo (the language of the group in power), called on the population "to beware of the Bamiléké." Radio Centre,[32] in Yaoundé, and Radio Ngaoundéré, were subsequently considered to be stirring up ethnic hatred. Today, the selective granting of temporary authorizations to new private stations, which betrays a strong desire to deny certain individuals access to the airwaves, could lead to deeply unbalanced presentations of information and, more specifically, to unbalances in relations between different communities.[33]

The Language Problem in the Media: English vs. French

Paul Biya's main opponent, John Fru Ndi, speaks English. Significantly, the opposition's slogan during huge demonstrations at the start of the 1990s was shouted in English: "Biya must go." Consequently, newspapers close to the government did not hesitate to point the finger at this anglophone community, accusing it of wanting to seize power, while the anglophone press made radical statements tinged with separatist sentiments. Though they are more moderate today, newspapers such as *The Herald* and *Cameroon Post* are accused of having fueled hatred in the English-speaking area. The "English threat" is connected to that of the Bamiléké through a myth about an "Anglo-Bami" conspiracy. Based on the Bamiléké's support for John Fru

Ndi's SDF, the importance attached to this threat caused violent incidents among members of both groups during the 1992 elections.

From 1992 to 1995, the English-speaking independence movement became more radical. While John Fru Ndi's party had always proclaimed its choice of nonviolent methods of political struggle and sought to decentralize power within a federation rather than through radical independence, separatist protest movements, including the Southern Cameroon National Council (SCNC), continued to exist.

What is the press's attitude in face of these tensions? There is an editorial split between the anglophone and francophone presses, even though the former does not necessarily reject the arguments of the latter, which broadly supports the secessionist designs of the SCNC. In 2002, on the national holiday celebrating the unification of English-speaking and French-speaking Cameroon, *The Post,* an English-language paper, ran the headline, "Thirty years of frustration for English speakers." The editor in chief maintained that "the survival of Cameroon can only come about by a return to federalism." On the eve of the June 2002 elections, the front page of *Star Headlines* declared, "If the ballot box fails, bullets will liberate English speakers."

Along with the newspaper *Postwatch Magazine,* published in Bamenda, Radio Buéa is one of the media outlets allowing the SCNC to express itself on the air, though not always of the station's free will. For instance, armed groups of English-speakers occupied the station in December 1999 and remained for three hours, broadcasting a statement proclaiming the independence of the two English-speaking provinces. In February 2000, three journalists from the station were arrested after a broadcast aired the views of English-speaking Cameroonians exiled in Europe who criticized how Paul Biya's government had marginalized their community.

On the contrary, the French-language press is hostile to any idea of splitting the country. Progovernment newspapers tend to ignore or give minimal space to the English-speaking communities. Therefore, the French-speakers are often surprised by the seemingly rapid radicalization of opinions and events in the English-speaking communities. It is as though their demands suddenly emerge full-blown onto the national scene, though they have been developing for some time.

It is true that journalists investigating tensions and claims emanating from the English-speaking area, whether they work in French or in English, are vulnerable to government reprisals. In October 2001 the editor in chief of *La Nouvelle Expression* was arrested for publishing confidential correspondence from the Ministry of Defense that authorized the police in English-speaking provinces to use force to break up antigovernment demonstrations. In November 2003 the police and high-ranking customs officials seized an entire edition of the English-language *Insight Magazine,* which had published an assessment of the government's breaches of commitments to integrate English-speakers made at the time the country was reunified.[34]

New Claims of the North

Northern areas are traditionally considered to fall within the "moderate or collaborator opposition." The Peulh community, although Muslim, has always been seen as an ally of President Biya's government. However, in September 2002 the press published a "Greater Northern Memorandum," which significantly mobilized locals over, among other things, the religious issue. In fact, people in the northern provinces are now drawing up claims on the basis that they have been neglected and marginalized by the "southern Christians" who run the country. Once again, Cameroonian newspapers, most of which are in French and located in the south, gave little coverage to these new regional dynamics, while progovernment media ignored them completely.

Local press initiatives, such as *La Tribune d'Adama* (linked to the group that publishes *Ouest Echos* in Bafoussam), which are more sensitive to these claims, are starting to develop in the north, but they face an enormous difficulty: a dispersed and illiterate public with little purchasing power.[35] Consequently, little news is reported about the northern regions. During the killings in the far north between Choa Arabs and Kotoko in 1993, only southern newspapers reported on and analyzed this conflict. Southern media have provided little coverage of conflicts between Muslim Peulhs and animist or Christian Kirdi, between herdsmen and farmers, or between landowners and serfs.

People from the north find even less to relate to in the southern-based media, since some of these media show an obvious bent for Catholic proselytizing. This is seen with the CRTV, which, under the leadership of its former director-general, Gervais Mendo Ze, who became a minister in December 2004, devoted significant airtime to Christian programs, a blatant contradiction of the public media's secular mission.

External Conflict with Nigeria

Cameroon and Nigeria have had a long dispute over control of the Bakassi Peninsula and its significant offshore oil reserves. The International Court of Justice in The Hague ultimately decided the dispute on October 10, 2002, in favor of Cameroon, but it didn't put an end to Nigeria's ambitions. The dispute, which flared into armed confrontation between December 1993 and

February 1994, provoked nationalist surges within the Cameroonian media, though they were still divided on this issue. Confronted with an outside enemy, journalists forgot their disagreements and were carried away by patriotic excesses.

The state did not hesitate to "call on the press to back up its arguments against Nigeria, while continuing to harass and detain journalists. Some saw this encouragement to cover the border dispute as a way of diverting the media's attention from other urgent internal issues, such as the on-going secessionist campaign in English-speaking provinces or the numerous human rights violations in the country."[36]

On the other hand, journalists who tried to carry out investigations in the Bakassi region risked encountering resistance. For instance, in July 2004, two BBC journalists who were reporting on the peninsula were arrested and accused of spying. They had been trying to verify whether Nigeria, which had been ordered to withdraw from the peninsula before September 15, 2004, was respecting this ruling.

Once again, the French-language and English-language media analyzed the situation differently. While the French-language press was unanimous in demonstrating full patriotic fervor, the English-language press tried to link the thorny issue of ownership of the peninsula with the broader English-language dispute within Cameroon.

The Media Environment

The positioning of the Cameroonian media in face of diverse national issues is influenced by several factors, ranging from the situation of state-run media to the legal framework and attacks on the freedom of the press.

Control of the State Media

The absence of any real reform in the public media has probably contributed to the radicalization of the privately owned press, now an outlet for those excluded by the state media. However, at the start of the liberalization process, there had been some hope for change. In June 1990, when six people were killed by government forces at a demonstration demanding the legalization of the SDF, the CTV (the predecessor of the CRTV) merely said that the victims had been "trampled by the crowd" (this gave rise to a new ironic expression: "trampled to death by bullets"). Some weeks later, two journalists working in the state sector sent an open letter to the Ministry of Communications, pointing out that "the official press also have the right to inform."

This letter, which highlighted the constraints under which the public media operated, was not entirely devoid of ambiguity. After arousing some passing excitement, it was quickly forgotten.

Despite pressures from the opposition, some journalists, and members of the public, the CRTV remained strictly progovernment, became increasingly corrupted, and was nicknamed "Centre de Rétablissement Total des Voleurs" (Center for the Total Recovery of Thieves), or "Confused Radio Television."[37] A special unit was created inside the public broadcaster to monitor private media that were criticizing the government. The CRTV's management progressively succeeded in silencing the internal discontent by transferring the journalists (mainly from the anglophone team) who were too critical.[38]

The CRTV remains the government's mouthpiece, though it had to create a weekly program on which all political parties in the National Assembly can speak. It has not hesitated, however, to censor or cut programs in which truly representative opposition parties, such as the SDF, are taking part. An opinion poll carried out in 1994 showed that 67 percent of respondents judged Cameroonian television to be "biased," 73 percent thought that television news was not "politically neutral," and 57 percent said that television had failed to promote democracy in the country.[39]

Legal and Regulatory Framework

The 1996 constitution recognizes and proclaims "freedom of communication, freedom of expression, freedom of the press, freedom to meet, freedom of association . . . under conditions determined by the law." The specific legislation is found in Law 90/052, of December 19, 1990, relating to "freedom of social communication." More liberal than the one previously in force, this law replaced prior authorization with a simple declaration. But it required lodging proof with the Ministry of Territorial Administration, which could lead to "partial or total censorship for breaching public order and accepted standards of behaviour" (Article 14). In January 1996, following the Communication Convention, this measure was abolished, allowing full and entire liberalization of the written press. The law nevertheless provides very severe sanctions against any violation liable to adversely affect state authorities.

The audiovisual sector, de facto liberalized by certain private proactive initiatives, has been governed since 2000 by Decree 2000/158. This decree imposes a set of limitations intended to protect the national airwaves from the influence of foreign capital, and to avoid any effects of concentration. It stipulates, among other things, that "the owner of a press publication cannot acquire shares in more than one private audiovisual communication company" (Article 20). According to an analyst, this is to avoid "the power that the audiovisual communication sector confers being concentrated solely in the hands of the aristocracies of money, built exclusively on the primary solidarity of blood and tribe. Such a tendency is already noticeable in the written privately owned press. Its consequences in radio and television would be immeasurable."[40]

One regulatory body has been established, the Conseil National de la Communication (CNC)/National Communication Council, in 1991. A "consultative body placed under the Prime Minister, the head of the government" (Article 1), it has limited powers and restricts itself to giving its opinion when consulted on "the general policy of social communication" (Article 4). It is not involved in granting licenses and frequencies to private audiovisual companies. Its recommendations have no legal force, and the government is not obliged to follow them. With no budget, staff, or infrastructure, the CNC struggles to meet twice a year, as stipulated, and its impact on the development of the Cameroonian media landscape is very limited.[41]

Finally, the state intervenes in the media sector through aid to the privately owned press. In February 2001 the minister of communications, as part of the policy of "communication renewal," announced exemption from VAT for more than 200 products intended for media-related activity (newspaper paper, ink, information technology, telephone equipment, etc.), but this measure has yet to be applied. Direct aid to the privately owned press was also administered through an initial grant of 100 million CFA francs (US$202,234) intended to "support" the privately owned press "in their coverage of the 2002 general and town council elections," which was soon followed by a second grant of 150 million CFA francs (US$303,351). *Le Messager* refused to accept its share for ethical reasons.

Obstacles to Freedom of the Press

Cameroonian journalists have been subjected to a multitude of abuses, which in the long term gives rise to fear and encourages self-censorship. These range from arrests and arbitrary sentencing, to direct and indirect intimidation (pressure on family members, publishers, and small-scale news vendors), to targeted harassment by the tax authorities, to even physical violence and disappearances. Seizures, suspensions, prohibitions, ransacking of editorial offices, beatings, tax harassment, and bullying were all noted by a researcher who listed over a thousand occurrences from 1990 to 2004.[42]

The most famous case is probably that involving Pius Njawe, iconic editor of *Le Messager,* who was sentenced to twelve months in prison in

1998 after his newspaper published an article suggesting that President Paul Biya appeared to be ill (not "was," but "appeared to be") while watching a football match. A recent study reveals that the number of prison sentences handed out to Cameroonian journalists between 1990 and 2003 exceeded 100, meaning almost eight imprisonments every year.[43]

The many trials of Cameroonian journalists (more than 400 between 1990 and 2003)[44] essentially involve revelations about certain political and business activities that are deemed defamatory, libelous, or insulting to a member of the government or a civil servant.[45] This is not surprising for a press that aims to expose and reveal abuses perpetrated by the judiciary, police, government, and the business community. Very often, the pressure exerted on the journalist is intended to make him reveal his sources, in spite of the profession's rule providing for protection of sources. Based on a very wide interpretation of the law and the penal code, a journalist and his newspaper can be prosecuted for biased reporting, removal of administrative documents,[46] destruction of documents, and spreading false information. This happens frequently, in spite of the absence of any tangible proof.

Relations between the state and the privately owned press are strained. "It is no longer open warfare, but a permanent guerrilla war."[47] The withholding of information is the prevailing norm, which forces journalists to rely on rumor and supposition. There are no official spokesmen, ministers rarely grant requests for interviews, and the president always turns them down. Accreditations for parliament and for official events are delivered sparingly. Certain subjects are taboo, such as land disputes involving key state figures, cases of corruption, and troubles in the provinces where the English-speaking separatist movement is active. While prior censorship was abolished for newspapers in 1996, seizures still occur.[48]

Radio stations often lose the right to broadcast. Correspondents from foreign media, often accused of being too close to the opposition, are not spared.

Weak and Divided Professional Associations

Professional associations, though numerous (about thirty), are weak and divided. In addition to political divisions, there is a lack of solidarity between journalists from the state-run and the privately owned presses, between salaried staff and freelancers, and between management and employees. The Union des Journalistes du Cameroun (UJC)/Union of Cameroon Journalists, which should play a unifying role, has long been paralyzed by the strong representation of public sector journalists at the management level.[49] As one observer states, "except for the surge of activity caused by the Monga-Njawe case in December 1990 to January 1991, almost all attempts to unify and become a unit on a national scale have failed."[50] In 1997, when Pius

Njawe was sentenced to a year in prison, *La Nouvelle Expression* and *Mutations* delayed taking up his defense. Only the growing mobilization of well-known international associations induced them to finally break their silence.

The lack of professional cohesion means that press enterprises and media professionals are alone and unsupported in face of their economic problems. Their isolation often leads to journalists being monopolized by local lobby groups, which is especially dangerous for the new private local radio stations. The profession lacks an identity and is blighted by unethical practices. There is corruption and racketeering, and disguised advertorials are frequent. "Gumbo" (small payments pocketed by journalists in exchange for writing on a particular subject) is common practice.

Growing Public Disaffection

The privately owned press is also suffering from growing public disaffection. Newspapers are expensive, at 300 CFA francs (US$.60) but distrust of journalists and their work has also led the public to increasingly turn its back on newspapers. This distrust is probably related to the increase in trials for defamation, libel, and spreading false information that have, sometimes rightly, been instigated against the press, tarnishing its credibility. One observer notes "the exasperation of many readers who see 'gumbo' behind every article in the Cameroonian press these days."[51] The decision by major newspapers (*Mutations, Le Messager,* and *La Nouvelle Expression*) to publish daily instead of three times a week has led to additional expense and thinner newspapers for regular readers, given the difficulties generated by this new frequency of production.

The public is therefore shunning local written media and is opting for international audiovisual media, some of which are available via FM radio or satellite television. An opinion poll conducted in 2004 by the Centre de Recherches et d'Étude en Économie et Sondage (CRETES) revealed that 80 percent of respondents prefered radio and television to the written press, which interested scarcely 10 percent of the population.[52] Many professional journalists are experiencing the same weariness, and are also distancing themselves, adding to the already long list of Cameroonian journalists in exile.

Conclusion

An assessment of the Cameroonian press leads to contradictory observations. For some outside observers, it does not seem to have fulfilled its mediatory functions during the period of tension. "In this powder keg context, one could have hoped that the press would play its informative role, exposing the multiple manipulations and ethnic analyses of the social and economic crisis. It could have played its role as a leader of social debate to calm the situation down. In contrast, it too often allowed itself to be trapped into political-ethnic discussions, passing on simplistic and racist messages."[53] Clearly, "it becomes difficult to argue that it has made a positive contribution to democratisation in Cameroon."[54]

However, for other Cameroonian journalists, the privately owned press, despite its imperfections and difficulties, "has done more for democratization and the struggle against society's ills" than any other player in the public domain.[55] And if it is accused of destabilization, this is similar to "certain traditions [where] he who announces the death of the king is held responsible for the death of the king and is punished as such."[56]

The problem for journalism in Cameroon is not that it pours oil on the flames in times of crisis, but rather its indifference to the concerns of various social groups whom the media, especially the public sector media, are neglecting. This discrepancy with the daily realities of life for a fringe population can only lead to surprise when all the warning signs of frustration have been ignored and then explode with violence, leading to ethnic and regional tensions. In a way, the private media are reinforcing the strategy of government media that promote the RDPC and deny the opposition forces access to public broadcasting. "Tribalism, nepotism, inequalities do not exist, only national unity, balanced regional development and the equitable distribution of national cake."[57]

In such a context, the long-awaited liberalization of the radio sector, which has led to the emergence of provincial radio stations, could lead to a "regionalization of the airwaves" and a crystallization of local opposition communities. Both possibilities are much riskier than any that could arise from the activities of the written press.

Notes

I thank Célestin Lingo, president of the UJC, for his critical proofreading.

1. M. Tjade Eone, *Démonopolisation, libéralisation et liberté de communication au Cameroun: avancées et reculades* (Paris: L'Harmattan, 2001), p. 65.

2. The press company Le Messager used to publish a satirical paper, *Le Messager Popoli,* twice a week, which allowed it to effectively be available every day. In 2002, *Le Messager Popoli* left the company to become independent.

3. Institut Panos Paris (ed.), *Afrique centrale: des médias pour la démocratie* (Paris: Karthala, 2000), p. 66.

4. US Department of State, *Country Report on Human Rights Practices, 1999,* p. 16.

5. UNESCO is implementing a program (in connection with the World Bank) aimed at developing fifteen community radio stations and multimedia centers in fifteen small towns all around the country.

6. Reporters sans Frontières, *Rapport annuel, 2003*, p. 1.

7. F. B. Nyamnjoh, *Africa's Media: Democracy and the Politics of Belonging* (London: Zed, 2005), pp. 126–155.

8. Tjade Eone, *Démonopolisation, libéralisation et liberté de communication*, p. 26.

9. *Le Messager,* December 27, 1990.

10. *Le Patriote,* August 8, 1991, p. 7, cited in M. E. Owona Nguini, "Conflits et démocratisation au Cameroun (1990–2003)," unpublished, p. 9.

11. As Nyamnjoh notes, the few papers (*Dikalo, La Détente, L'Effort Camerounais*) that tried to stay in the "middle ground," between progovernment and harsh opposition, were rare, and their journalists were treated with suspicion by both sides. Nyamnjoh, *Africa's Media,* p. 235.

12. F. Eboussi Boulaga, *La démocratie de transit au Cameroun* (Paris: L'Harmattan, 1997), p. 440.

13. Nyamnjoh, *Africa's Media,* pp. 189–192.

14. P. B. Logo and H. L. Menthong, "Crise de légitimité et évidence de la continuité politique," *Politique Africaine* no. 62 (June 1996), p. 19.

15. *Galaxie,* December 4, 1991, cited in F. Chindji-Kouleu, "Ethnies, médias et processus démocratique au Cameroun: analyse de contenu de quelques journaux," in D. Zognong and I. Mouiche (eds.), *Démocratisation et rivalités ethniques au Cameroun* (Yaoundé: CIREPE, 1997), p. 63.

16. L. Sindjoun, "Le champ social camerounais: désordre inventif, mythes simplificateurs et stabilité hégémonique de l'état," *Politique Africaine* no. 62 (June 1996), p. 61.

17. Nyamnjoh, *Africa's Media,* p. 114.

18. *Aurore Plus,* August 26, 1992, cited in Chindji-Kouleu, "Ethnies, médias et processus démocratique au Cameroun," p. 10.

19. T. Atenga, "Contrôle de la parole et conservation du pouvoir: analyse de la répression de la presse écrite au Cameroun et au Gabon depuis 1990." PhD thesis, Paris, Sorbonne, 2004, p. 70.

20. *L'Eveil du Cameroun,* February 28, 1991, cited in Chindji-Kouleu, "Ethnies, médias et processus démocratique au Cameroun," p. 10.

21. *Le Temps,* August 31, 1992, cited in Chindji-Kouleu, "Ethnies, médias et processus démocratique au Cameroun," p. 11.

22. The newspaper claimed to be defending the "native Sawa minority" against the "incomer Bamiléké majority" during a period of tension in urban planning in the town of Douala.

23. Atenga, "Contrôle de la parole et conservation du pouvoir," p. 171.

24. This emerged from an analysis conducted on the newspaper *Challenge Hebdo* by Valentin Nga Ndongo, in *Les médias au Cameroun: mythes et délires d'une société en crise* (Paris: L'Harmattan, 1993), pp. 130–135.

25. Atenga, "Contrôle de la parole et conservation du pouvoir," p. 176.

26. Nyamnjoh, *Africa's Media,* p. 245.

27. E. Paquot and S. C. Abega, *L'état des médias au Cameroun* (Paris: GRET, November 2000), p. 8.

28. H. Boh, *L'état de la presse au Cameroun* (Yaoundé: Friedrich Ebert Foundation, 1998), p. 41.

29. Atenga, "Contrôle de la parole et conservation du pouvoir," p. 176.

30. Given the multiplicity of local languages in Cameroon (over 260), CRTV television does not broadcast in vernacular languages, in order to avoid favoring one community over others. CRTV radio broadcasts in local languages according to the station's region.

31. US Department of State, *Country Report on Human Rights Practices, 1999*, p. 28.

32. Because Radio Centre was very aggressive toward the "Anglo-Bami," it was nicknamed "Radio Sept Collines," referring to the seven hills surrounding Yaoundé and Rwanda's RTLM.

33. In June 2004 the US nongovernmental organization Open Society Justice Initiative lodged a request with the African Commission on Human and Peoples' Rights to plead in favor of Freedom FM, a radio station of the Le Messager Group; Freedom FM's office had been banned and sealed off in May 2003 by the Cameroonian government, which maintained that the station had no license to broadcast.

34. Committee to Protect Journalists, *Attacks Against the Press, 2003*, p. 14.

35. At the start of the 1990s, a first attempt at a regional newspaper, *L'Harmattan*, came into being, but was short-lived.

36. Committee to Protect Journalists, *Attacks Against the Press, 2002*, p. 1.

37. Nyamnjoh, *Africa's Media*, p. 139.

38. As Nyamnjoh writes: "The anglophone journalists in the official media have, in general, tended to distance themselves from the sort of pro-establishment journalism defined by government and largely taken for granted by their francophone colleagues. The history of turbulence in the official media is principally the history of government's attempt to muzzle anglophone journalists." Nyamnjoh, *Africa's Media*, p. 144.

39. Article 19 (international human rights organization that defends and promotes freedom of expression), *Cameroon: A Transition in Crisis* (October 1997), p. 12.

40. Tjade Eone, *Démonopolisation, libéralisation et liberté de communication*, p. 124.

41. Institut Panos Paris, *Afrique centrale*, p. 75.

42. Atenga, "Contrôle de la parole et conservation du pouvoir," p. 2.

43. Ibid.

44. Ibid.

45. See T. Atenga, "Cameroun: presse privée/pouvoir, quinze ans de cohabitation houleuse," *Politique Africaine* no. 97 (March 2005).

46. In Cameroon, the law stipulates that "anyone who removes, takes or destroys any document entrusted to public authorities shall be punished by one to five years imprisonment and a fine of from 10,000 to 200,000 francs"; "anyone not qualified or authorized to do so who takes a copy of a document belonging to a government department shall be punished by imprisonment from one month to one year."

47. Paquot and Abega, *L'état des médias au Cameroun*, p. 7.

48. *Le Messager* has experienced 527 censorships and seizures since its creation; *La Nouvelle Expression*, 243. Atenga, "Contrôle de la parole et conservation du pouvoir," p. 396.

49. The UJC lost further credibility when its president, Amadou Valmouké, became a member of the central committee of the RDPC. He is now the general director of CRTV.

50. Atenga, "Contrôle de la parole et conservation du pouvoir," p. 121.

51. Ibid., p. 149.

52. The survey involved a sample of 1,200 people living in five towns: Yaoundé, Douala, Bafoussam, Garoua, and Bamenda.

53. Paquot and Abega, *L'état des médias au Cameroun,* pp. 3–4.

54. Nyamnjoh, *Africa's Media,* p. 249.

55. Interview with Célestin Lingo, president of the UJC, Kinshasa, December 5, 2004.

56. Ibid.

57. Nyamnjoh, *Africa's Media,* p. 154.

9

GABON

The Press Facing
the Bongo "System"

A VAST AND underpopulated country, Gabon is not experiencing war. It benefits from relative stability thanks in particular to an economic boom linked to the exploitation of its mineral and oil resources and to the state's authoritarian control, which is often challenged by opposition parties. Nevertheless, some structural factors could lead to instability, and the current equilibrium remains fragile. Democratic governance is not ensured and the lack of respect for human rights and freedom of the press might lead to tensions. The economic crisis is also growing and wealth is very unequally distributed. The significant number of immigrants is being increasingly perceived as a threat to national unity in a country where the population faces growing resource problems.

Pluralism Gradually Subdued

With the acceptance of a multiparty system in 1990, a pluralist written press became a reality for the first time in the history of Gabon. More than 200 newspapers were registered in the space of a few months,[1] though only about thirty appear regularly. After years of a state monopoly on public statements, criticism was finally possible. "The head of state can now be attacked other than by vicious and clandestine pamphlets."[2]

Most of the newspapers that appeared in 1990 were linked to political parties. The Mouvement de Redressement National (MORENA), probably the largest opposition party, first published *La Clé,* a newspaper devoted to exposing disproportionate wealth, preferential treatment, and corruption of members of the government.[3] In September

191

GABON

Size	267,667 sq. km.
Population	1.4 million
Capital	Libreville
Ethnic groups	60 (Fang, Pounou, Téké, Myéné, Echira, Adouma, Kota, etc.)
Official language	French
Human Development Index ranking (2005)	123 (out of 177 countries)
Life expectancy	53 years
Literacy rate	71.0 percent

Chronology

1910–1960: French colony (French Equatorial Africa).

1960: Independence. Léon M'Ba becomes president.

1967: M'Ba dies. The vice president, Albert-Bernard Bongo, becomes president.

1968: Bongo bans political parties and imposes a single party, the Parti Démocratique Gabonais (PDG).

1973: Bongo converts to Islam and becomes Omar Bongo.

1974: Gabon becomes a member of the Organization of Petroleum-Exporting Countries (OPEC) (until 1995).

1990: Under international pressure and growing local unrest, the regime organizes a national conference and allows multipartyism.

1991: A new constitution is adopted.

1993: Bongo wins a very controversial presidential election. Demonstrations and civil unrest multiply.

1994: Agreements are signed in Paris between the government and the main opposition parties.

July 1995: The Paris agreements are approved by referendum. A government of national union is formed.

1998: Bongo is reelected president for seven years. His challenger, Paul Mba Abessole, from the Rassemblement National des Bûcherons (RNB), leads the opposition, which remains very divided.

2003: The National Assembly ratifies a constitutional amendment that removes the limit on the number of terms a president can serve.

2005: Bongo is reelected president.

1990, after MORENA split into various groups, including the Rassemblement National des Bûcherons (RNB), the weekly *Le Bûcheron* was founded. With a circulation of some 7,000 copies, it clearly met with great success. In addition, there were the newspapers of other political parties: *La Voix du Peuple* of the Parti pour l'Unité du Peuple (PUP), *Le Progressiste* of the Parti Gabonais du Progrès (PGP), *La Passion de l'Unité* of the Union Socialiste Gabonaise (USG), and *L'Effort Gabonais* of the Parti Social Démocrate (PSD).

Among this crop, two newspapers profoundly marked the liberalized media landscape in Gabon: *La Griffe,* a satirical newspaper that appeared in August 1990, and *Misamu,* which appeared in October 1990. The first, funded by a former minister in Omar Bongo's government,[4] was initially quite moderate vis-à-vis the government, but became increasingly impertinent and even irreverent. The paper was very popular, with a circulation at 10,000 copies, but its license was suspended on numerous occasions and it ultimately folded in 2001. The second, initially linked to MORENA, became independent in 1992 under the leadership of Abbot Noël Ngwa Nguema. *Misamu* was for a long time in the shadow of *La Griffe,* which was clearly more popular, but *Misamu* became well known when its competitor was suspended and its circulation grew to 5,000 copies. Very critical of Bongo's government, its staff soon became subject to constant pressure and threats. In May 2003 it was suspended indefinitely.[5]

Alongside these two, *La Cigale Enchantée, Esprit d'Afrique, L'Insolite,* and *La Transparence* were also part of the first generation of private newspapers. With recurring suspensions of *La Griffe,* journalists from the satirical paper produced a series of other publications, such as *Le Temps, Le Nganga,* and *Le Scribouillard.* Often appearing only sporadically, they criticized government decisions and the behavior of political leaders from all parties and of the president himself. But in a context marked by financial constraints and numerous suspensions ordered by the authorities, their appearance was unpredictable. Most were printed in Cameroon,[6] where costs were nearly three times less than in Libreville, because the Gabon printing sector was dominated by the company Multipresse, which had a monopoly on newsprint.[7] The papers were distributed by the distribution company Sogapresse, which retained 40 percent of the sales revenue.

The precarious situation of the privately owned press contrasts strongly with the relatively comfortable operating conditions for the only daily newspaper in Gabon, the state-run *L'Union,* which first appeared in 1974. Although essentially a vassal of the government, it sometimes criticizes the state without actually attacking the president or those close to him. Its journalists are often asked to take institutional or political posts. The supremacy of *L'Union,* which has many institutional readers, has been harmful to the development of the Agence Gabonaise de Presse (AGP), which was created in 1966. For a long time the AGP published a bulletin of dispatches, but today it is hardly functional.

In the written sector, the most widely distributed publications in Gabon remain largely foreign in origin, as 75 percent of all newspapers on sale come from abroad.[8] As one Gabonese journalist observes, "These newspapers strengthen the plurality of the existing press. That they exist at all is a good thing; they are, however, reserved for a small elite."[9] The foreign press is not always shielded from the influence of President Bongo or his entourage. In November 1991, *La Griffe* revealed several cases in which major French and African newspapers (*Le Monde, Le Quotidien de Paris, Jeune Afrique Economie*) were given considerable sums to produce special features on Gabon.[10] President Bongo's regime makes a great effort to woo the foreign press.

In the audiovisual sector, the state has two radio stations, which cover the entire country, plus two television channels, Radiodiffusion Télévision Gabonaise 1 (RTG1) and Radiodiffusion Télévision Gabonaise 2 (RTG2). Public audiovisual media are essentially devoted to coverage of official events, but a more critical tone is occasionally adopted when commenting on certain government decisions or ministerial actions.

The first experiment with privately owned radio stations was shortlived: Radio Liberté, linked to the RNB, was destroyed in February 1994 in a raid by the presidential guard that was allegedly carried out "with the help of a dozen French and South African military advisors."[11] While this information has never been confirmed, the army's presence has.

More than ten private radio stations currently operate in Gabon, though the number fluctuates as they appear and disappear, generally for economic reasons: Radio Nostalgie, Radio Génération Nouvelle, Radio Unité (close to the government), Radio Mandarine, Radio Notre Dame du Gabon (denominational), Radio Emergence (schools), and Radio Soleil (licensed in 1995 and affiliated to the RNB). Most of these stations do not offer news programs, except for Radio Soleil, which was very critical of President Bongo. It was suspended five times and then ceased broadcasting in June 2002, a victim of managerial issues and internal political dissensions. Considered "by the government and by some public opinion as a station of hatred and incitation to violence,"[12] it was deprived of any access to advertising revenue. As Marguerite Makaga Virginius, former manager of Radio Soleil, said in 1999, "For four years, no company has accepted working in partnership with Radio Soleil; the causes seem to be linked to Radio Soleil's lack of subservience to the government whose power is intimately linked to business in Gabon."[13]

The pan-African radio station based in Libreville, Africa No. 1, is also noteworthy. Its shareholders are essentially French and Gabonese. It broadcasts on shortwave and has FM relay stations in most of the large cities of francophone Africa. While recognized for its professionalism when dealing with news items in most African countries, the station shows much more subservience when covering events in Gabon or in countries where President Bongo is involved in his diplomatic conflict-resolution activities.[14] Other international radio stations also broadcast on FM in Libreville: Radio France Internationale since 1998 and the BBC since 2003. Three privately owned television stations exist, all of them apolitical.

Shrinking Criticism

In Gabon, "conflict" mainly refers to the fits and starts of the political struggle between the government and the opposition for access to the nation's resources. This conflict, evident from the start of the 1990s, has gradually declined, as the most virulent opponents, weakened by internal divisions, have either rejoined the system or tired with fighting. The written press remains the prime vector of protest against an increasingly restrictive system of government, although the most critical voices have been forced into silence.

Internal weaknesses have made private media companies particularly vulnerable to attack from the government. It has always been easy to accuse them of excessive politicization, ethnic bias, or lack of professionalism.

Politicization Rooted in Instability

The Gabon media are developing in an unfavorable economic context. Admittedly, Gabon has a certain economic dynamism, but it benefits only a very limited fringe of the ruling class who takes care not to maintain relations—in terms of advertising contracts—with the media that are unfavorable to President Bongo. The president himself seems aware of the problem. In June 2000 he stated that he was going to "make a statement to inform advertisers that there will be no reprisals if they choose to advertise in the privately-owned press."[15]

Consequently, newspapers are mainly funded thanks to their affinities with politicians, "and can become pawns on the political chessboard of the struggle for power."[16] High printing costs and low sales figures make it difficult for private newspapers to remain independent. "The Gabonese press is highly politicized and most newspapers serve up party propaganda."[17] The "gumbo" system, which enables journalists to pad their low and irregular salaries, is widespread in Gabon.

Their excessive closeness to political parties and politicians undermines the Gabon private media. For example, when opposition politician Paul Mba Abessole (of the RNB) joined the government as senior minister, Radio Soleil lost a sponsor who no longer wanted to support a station that was too critical of the authorities.[18] Faced with inextricable financial problems and with staff claiming six months of back salary, Radio Soleil closed in June 2002. Its equipment was reclaimed by its promoter, who launched a new station, Ogoué FM, in September 2003, which was to be better attuned to the new political views of Mba Abessole.

The Gabon press is criticized for excessive politicization, which the press itself willingly acknowledges. "We cannot deny the accusation that we are involved in politics or that we grant too much importance to political news," explains the editor in chief of *La Griffe*. "How can it be otherwise in a country like Gabon where the president is involved in everything to the extent that he even chooses the uniform for the hostesses of the national airline? Everything is political here. The overexposure of politics in our newspapers is a measure of the over-politicization of our society." And a journalist from *Misamu* adds: "Whatever subject you are dealing with, you always come across politics and politicians in spite of yourself. . . . Politics are everywhere in Gabon. Everything is political. It is in the nature of our regime, which likes it that way. The press, like a thermometer, just shows the temperature."[19]

However, this politicization of the press, which is sometimes linked to survival, has led to a certain disaffection by the public, who has become less willing to buy newspapers, which has led to a fall in sales in recent years. Conversely, the commercial media, based on entertainment, are successful, as shown by the experience of the BO Communication group, a private conglomerate of diversified initiatives (TV+ Gabon, Radio Nostalgie,[20] the poster company Médiaffiche, the corporation Africa Networks).[21]

The current regime is aware of the importance of the economy in harnessing the media. In November 2000 the government gave 250 million CFA francs (US$505,584) to the media, but it was allocated according to criteria that did not entirely satisfy the profession, provoking rifts within the privately owned press. In May 2003 the minister of communications, Mehdi Teale, announced the government would give direct aid amounting to 500 million CFA francs (US$1,011,168), but he specified that this grant would be for newspapers that showed "professionalism,"[22] thereby clearly revealing the nature of the strategy underlying this generous gesture.

Stirring Ethnic Feelings

There has never been serious antagonism among local communities in Gabon, which has about sixty separate ethnic populations. However, in April 2003, Prime Minister Jean-François Ntoutoume Emane denounced some of his compatriots, who "in a blaze of media messages are stirring ethnic feelings to satisfy their personal ambitions to the detriment of national unity."[23] This declaration was part of a critical debate on the question of "geopolitics," or power based on regional origins. The subject is effectively taboo. When *Misamu* published an organizational chart for the Ministry of Finance showing clearly that all the strategic posts were held by individuals who were "regionally" close to President Bongo, the Conseil National de la Communication (CNC) intervened to call the journalist to order, underlining the danger of a tribalist approach.

The newspapers deny the accusations, throwing them back at the government, and maintain that they are just doing their job. The editor in chief of *La Griffe* explained, "We confine ourselves to reporting the tribalism which blights our nations and our societies, tribalism that is set up as a management technique by the nepotistic regimes that have governed us for three decades as in Gabon. The newspapers did not invent the notions of regional balance, quotas, self-centred development and the methods and ideologies which have bolstered tribalism in our countries."[24] In 2003, *La Sagaie* was suspended, accused of not having regularly registered and of "inciting tribal division" for an article that suggested that members of the president's ethnic group were overrepresented in government and in the army. Tribal divisiveness, or a simple observation?

No newspaper openly defends one community or another in Gabon, even if some are suspected of contacts with ethnoregionally based political parties, including those in the hands of the Fangs. The creation in June 2004 of the newspaper *Le Citoyen,* by a Gabonese with Pygmy roots who is also the founder of an NGO for the defense of Pygmy culture, might have led people to think that the first ethnic press initiative had been born.[25] However, *Le Citoyen* rapidly positioned itself as a general newspaper and not as a community-based stronghold.

Repression of Criticism

Whatever accusations are leveled by the government against the privately owned press, the latter has undeniably played a role in removing the mystique surrounding those in power, relentlessly exposing the regime's failings, including misappropriation and confiscation of national resources by President Bongo and those close to him. "A caste of *nouveaux riches* has the easy life," reported an infuriated *Le Temps*. "Salaries and other perks to take your breath away, top-notch fleets of cars and villas worthy of Western dynasties. Basically, a Gabon with two categories of Gabonese—the 'haves' who grab everything, to the great displeasure of the 'have-nots' who still must live from hand to mouth."[26]

During the July 2003 review of the constitution, the bimonthly *La Sagaie* commented that "making Bongo president for life will permanently put Gabon in the category of a republican monarchy." The newspaper also reminded readers that "since the return to a multi-party state in 1990, Bongo has altered the Constitution five times."[27]

Resistant to the perpetual criticism leveled as much at President Bongo as at those around him and the workings of his "system," the current regime has used an array of repressive tools to silence antiestablishment journalists.

A Repressive Legal and Institutional Framework

The 1991 constitution guaranteed freedom of expression and of the press. But in 1995 the National Assembly adopted a communication code that has the power of law and explicitly notes journalists' rights and duties. It leaves the way open for lengthy prison sentences and colossal fines to punish offenses by the press. In December 2001 a new communication code was promulgated that strengthens the repressive nature of the previous code by expanding the definition of libel, with the aim of protecting the "dignity of the individual."

The CNC, created in 1992, is an independent institution with the status of a state constitutional body. Its aim is to promote freedom of the press and monitor journalistic quality. However, since 1998 it has had a repressive role, ordering the suspension of numerous newspapers. At a meeting at a press club after the suspension of two publications, *Misamu* and *Gabaon* in 2002, professionals from the private media noted, "The

National Communication Council, the body that regulates the national press, has retreated into an irrational destruction of democracy's major assets."[28] The RNB used the occasion to reiterate that the CNC "is a council and not an inquisitors' court." It "cannot act as a substitute for a court, punishing without trial anything that it considers to be an offence."[29] In September 2004, President Bongo promised to abolish custodial sentences for press offenses, although this has not yet happened.

Repression of the Privately Owned Press

In 1991, President Bongo warned journalists of the limits that he was prepared to tolerate. "I think that the time has come for this to stop and for journalists to report what is worth being heard and worth being understood. Insults, attacks and provocation must stop. We will not turn our democracy into a makeshift democracy."[30]

Since then, mechanisms for repression of the press have been gradually put in place, based mainly on the withdrawal of publishing licenses and on trials, generally for defamation. According to an expert, almost 250 press trials have taken place in Gabon since 1990. More than thirty have resulted in custodial sentences for journalists.[31]

The first newspaper to pay the price was *Le Bûcheron,* the RNB's weekly newspaper, which had its license suspended by the Ministry of Communications in 1995, by the Ministry of Interior in 1997, and then twice by the CNC. Most of these suspensions followed the publication of caricatures or articles that were critical of President Bongo and those around him. In 1998, Pierre-André Kombila, editor of *Le Bûcheron,* was fined US$1,800 for accusing Bongo of practicing witchcraft.

In March 1995 national printers received direct orders from the Ministry of Interior to stop printing *Le Bûcheron* and *La Griffe.* The CNC then reversed the decision. At the same time, *La Griffe* unveiled an "infiltrator" in its staff, an informer from the presidential guard.[32]

Beginning in 1998, the CNC played an active role in repression of the written press by means of suspensions, which multiplied on the eve of the tension-filled presidential election. *La Cigale Enchantée* observed at the time, "Bongo is thus importing a pattern current in the region, particularly in Cameroon. This involves using the judiciary to wipe out the opposition on the eve of important elections."[33]

But the pressure did not ease after the disputed reelection of President Bongo. On the contrary, a strategy to systematically eradicate dissenting voices was put in place. *La Griffe* was the first victim. The newspaper was suspended from August 1998 to February 1999. Its publishing director, Michel Ongoundou Loundah, was found guilty of defamation for publishing an article on Air Gabon's general director, who used the company to smuggle ivory. Sentenced along with one of his journalists to eight months in prison, he left the country. The following year, President Bongo granted him an "amnesty." The newspaper reappeared in February 1999, but was once again suspended, from March to August 1999, for publishing unsigned editorials (the law stipulates that all published articles state the writer's name), and because its publishing director was living abroad. In February 2001, *La Griffe* had to halt publication again, apparently because it had been less than respectful about a book recently published by Bongo, *Blanc comme nègre*. This time, the CNC banned the editor, Loundah, and the editor in chief, Raphaël Ntoutoume Nkoghe, from practicing journalism in Gabon,[34] on the pretext that their articles had systematically attacked the integrity of President Bongo and his family, an act that is alleged to be "anticonstitutional."

Each time that *La Griffe* disappeared from the newsstands, *Misamu*, in turn, was harassed. In May 1999 its management was fined 10 million CFA francs (US$20,223.40) for defamation following an article on corruption in the government's road development program, a fact discovered in an audit carried out by the African Bank for Development (ABD). In September 2002, *Misamu* was suspended, along with *Gabaon*, for exposing misappropriation of exchequer funds.[35] *Misamu* reappeared on December 13, 2002, only to be once again banned in May 2003, under the pretext of a dispute between the publishing director and a senator who both claimed ownership of the newspaper.[36]

Misamu has denounced "the delaying tactics intended to muzzle the written press implemented by the government" many times over. The government's response has been to describe the press as "irresponsible in dealing with information."[37] Very often, during legal proceedings brought against newspapers for defamation, the court's concern is less with verifying the truth of the facts than with finding out how journalists gained access to confidential information and documents. The satirical newspaper *La Griffe* and *Misamu* have together, since their creation, been the subject of more than 150 repressive measures (seizures, suspensions, and bans), mainly affecting *La Griffe*. They have suffered many times from hostile reactions from the judiciary (twenty trials for *La Griffe*, three for *Misamu*) and the police (fifteen people taken in for questioning, and seven raids of *La Griffe*'s editorial offices).[38]

In 2003, relations between the written press and the government became particularly strained when the National Assembly adopted a constitutional amendment allowing Bongo to stand for the presidency an unlimited number of times. The opposition press reacted violently to this amendment, which threatened the survival of the political opposition as well as its own. Four periodicals—*Le Temps, La Sagaie, L'Autre Journal*,[39] and *L'Espoir*—were suspended for various reasons, mostly after exposing certain corrupt practices. The former director of *Misamu*, Noël Ngwa Nguema,[40] created *Sub-Version*, after the permanent suspension of *Misamu* in May. But *Sub-Version* was short-lived—its third edition was seized for having "attacked the dignity of the president, his family and the institutions of the republic," by suggesting that the president's wife was too involved in politics. Bongo summoned Noël Ngwa Nguema and personally lectured him.

Pressure exerted on the radio sector has sometimes been much more violent. On February 22, 1994, Gabonese army tanks destroyed the premises of Radio Liberté, considered to be an opposition propaganda tool. President Bongo's response was, "Radio Liberté? It was Radio Devil. . . . The army and security services . . . have destroyed their premises. And now normal democratic service has been resumed."[41]

Radio Soleil, created in 1995, then became the government's number one target. In December 1998, during a delay in announcing results of the presidential election, the station's broadcasts were jammed and the telephone lines cut. In February 1999 the CNC suspended *Feedback*, an extremely popular open-mike program, on the grounds that a listener who insulted President Bongo had been allowed to speak.

Last, even Africa No. 1, the private pan-African radio station in which the Gabonese state and French investors have large holdings, is under state control. In 2002, one of its presenters, Edgard-Oumar Nziembi-Doukaga, was sacked for mispronouncing on the air the name of Congolese president Denis Sassou-Nguesso, whose daughter is Bongo's wife.

Such measures have led to wider self-censorship, and not only by the journalists. A journalist for Radio Soleil explained the difficulty of finding guests who will take part in radio discussions, to the point that an hour-long talk show had to be canceled: "The specialists we invited to explain certain socio-political topics to the public said they preferred to talk off the air."[42]

Control of the State Media

In 1986, Vincent Mavoungou said of the state media, "They organize the exchange of information between the governing and the governed by political propaganda intending to legitimize their power. This communication is marked by the personalization of the power of the man who is both head of state and head of the only party."[43] Has the situation really changed with the emergence of the multiparty system? During celebrations for World Press Freedom Day on May 3, 2002, the minister of communications, André-Dieudonné Berre, said, "The state media must continue to play their role of relay station for government actions, driven by the head of state."[44]

The appearance of the privately owned press probably helped the public media negotiate a certain amount of space to maneuver. However, a genuine opening to pluralism and criticism is still problematical. Hence in August 1998, Charles Moussavou Mabika, an RTG journalist, was fined and sentenced to one month in prison with no right of appeal, for attributing the misappropriation of US$3.5 million to the minister of communications.

In February 2003 the only two-sided debate program on public radio station RTG1, *Agora,* was suspended by the station's management. The program presenter was criticized for being unable to control a guest who had placed responsibility for the low election turnout on President Bongo's running of the country,[45] and had also accused him of starving the army.[46]

L'Union, which has a near advertising monopoly, nonetheless allows itself a certain leeway relative to the government. In 2001 the newspaper deplored the obvious "desire of the government to muzzle the national press in any way possible."[47] It, too, was subjected to sanctions. In 2001 the CNC ordered the temporary suspension of the popular "Makaya" column, which was changing into a forum for settling scores between government dignitaries. After a few weeks, the column, which had revealed mutual accusations by ministers of corruption and practices leading to illicit personal enrichment in Gabonese society, was reinstated. But personal attacks were no longer permitted.[48]

Public media as a whole remain very submissive to the government. "Even in cases where we receive no instructions, we do tend to side with the government," acknowledged a journalist for *L'Union.*[49] While journalists in the public sector regularly strike (as was the case in 2000, 2001, and 2004), it is not for greater editorial freedom but to demand the payment of back salaries and better working conditions.

Conclusion

The media are undeniably a central element in President Omar Bongo's strategy of controlling, harnessing, and undermining the credibility of public statements, by force if necessary. A man of peace outside Gabon and a media-friendly mediator, Bongo benefits from most press and broadcasting companies close to the government, which enhance the prestige of his foreign diplomatic activities. However, within his country, Bongo has not chosen the path of dialogue and pluralism. The image that the regime would like to project is one of a peaceful, consensual country, a nation united around its leader. But the privately owned press continues to reiterate, sometimes bluntly and arrogantly, the major questions that hang over the country's future: the many foreigners, who are becoming less and less welcome; widespread corruption and the deep inequality that this engenders; the exhaustibility of an oil supply perceived as inexhaustible; and the succession disputes that will surface if the Bongo system ever finds itself leaderless. None of these criticisms are welcome by a government that is extremely anxious about how it is perceived abroad.

While the fragility of the Gabonese press in terms of professionalism and economic capacity are genuine and should be of deep concern, the government manages to exploit it to achieve its policy of subservience. Moreover, the regime benefits, as often happens when the press is highly politicized, from the lack of solidarity within the profession. During a meeting of editors held in September 2002, after the suspension of several newspapers, participants rejected a proposal to show solidarity by striking for a few days. Those who refused to strike did not hide their satisfaction about their resulting dominance of the market.[50] While there are a wide range of professional organizations, mostly bogus, this plurality is a weakness rather than an asset, because the government does not have to face an organized front.[51]

Notes

I thank Norbert Ngoua Mezui, editor of *Nku'u Le Messager* and president of APPEL, for his critical proofreading and comments. I also thank Thomas Irénée Atenga for sharing his documentation and information.

1. T. H. Atenga, "Contrôle de la parole et conservation du pouvoir: analyse de la répression de la presse écrite au Cameroun et au Gabon depuis 1990," PhD thesis, Paris, Sorbonne, 2004, p. 1.

2. F. Gaulme, "Le Gabon à la recherche d'un nouvel ethos politique et social," *Politique Africaine* no. 43 (October 1991), p. 60.

3. Ibid., p. 57.

4. The founder, Jérôme Okinda, then returned to the corridors of power—which led to an editorial rift with the newspaper's staff, particularly with Michel Ongoundou Loundah, who was also his nephew—and became publishing director.

5. Cited in Reporters sans Frontières, *Rapport annuel, 2004*, p. 1.

6. The Macacos religious printing works in Cameroon was printing, in September 2002, almost a dozen Gabonese newspapers: *Misamu, Le Scribouillard, Le Nganga, La Nation, Le Temps, Le Journal, La Lowe, Elite Afrique Magazine, Nku'u Le Messager, Gabaon,* and *Le Peuple.*

7. Multipresse is affiliated with a company based in Monaco. It has close ties to the Gabonese government, having benefited from funding granted by UNESCO to *L'Union* to modernize its equipment. See Institut Panos Paris (ed.), *Afrique centrale: des médias pour la démocratie* (Paris: Karthala, 2000), pp. 145–146.

8. Sogapresse distribution being a monopoly, it distributes both local and foreign press and has reliable distribution statistics.

9. Interview with Norbert Ngoua Mezui in RAP21, *Newsletter* no. 49.

10. Atenga, "Contrôle de la parole et conservation du pouvoir," p. 462.

11. A. Maja-Pearce (ed.), *Annuaire de la presse africaine* (Brussels: FIJ, 1996), p. 126.

12. B. Ndinga, "Radio Soleil: une libéralisation des ondes très contrôlée," in Institut Panos Paris and COTA (eds.), *Briser les silences: paroles d'Afrique centrale* (Paris: Karthala, 2003), p. 81.

13. Institut Panos Paris, *Afrique centrale*, p. 148.

14. President Bongo has lent his services as a peacemaker in Chad, Congo, Burundi, the DRC, Angola, Côte d'Ivoire, and São Tomé and Principe, among other countries.

15. Atenga, "Contrôle de la parole et conservation du pouvoir," p. 417.

16. Committee to Protect Journalists, *Attacks Against the Press, 2003,* p. 24.

17. Reporters sans Frontières, *Rapport annuel, 2002*, p. 1.

18. Institut Panos Paris, *Africentr@lemédias* no. 1 (July 2002).

19. Cited in Atenga, "Contrôle de la parole et conservation du pouvoir," p. 229.

20. The first two stations belong to a minister, André Mba Obame.

21. Institut Panos Paris, *Africentr@lemédias* no. 22 (May 2004).

22. Cited in Reporters sans Frontières, *Rapport annuel, 2004*, p. 1.

23. Panapresse dispatch, April 7, 2004.

24. Raphaël Ntoutoume Nkoghe, editor in chief of *La Griffe,* cited in Atenga, "Contrôle de la parole et conservation du pouvoir," p. 177.

25. Institut Panos Paris, *Africentr@lemédias* no. 23 (June 2004).

26. *Le Temps,* September 12, 2002, cited in Atenga, "Contrôle de la parole et conservation du pouvoir," p. 51.

27. Cited in Reporters sans Frontières, *Rapport annuel, 2004*, p. 1.

28. Club de la Presse statement, September 7, 2002.

29. Cited in Institut Panos Paris, *Africentr@lemédias* no. 3 (September 2002).

30. Extract from a speech by Omar Bongo, published in *La Griffe,* May 17, 1991, cited in Atenga, "Contrôle de la parole et conservation du pouvoir," p. 189.

31. Atenga, "Contrôle de la parole et conservation du pouvoir," pp. 2, 360.

32. *La Griffe,* June 23. 1995.

33. *La Cigale Enchantée,* September 16, 1998.

34. Michel Ongoundou Loundah then moved to Paris, where he launched *Gri Gri International,* a pan-African satirical paper. Published irregularly, it published its sixtieth edition in October 2006 after several interruptions. It has been banned from distribution in Gabon since October 2001.

35. The deputy editor in chief of *Misamu* was then sentenced to twenty-one days in prison, which he did not serve.

36. Senator Nzoghe Nguema, who registered *Misamu* with the administration before it became independent in 1992, and its publishing director, Noël Ngwa Nguema, who headed and managed the paper after its independence, both claimed ownership. The dispute arose when the Gabonese government decided to grant aid of 500 million CFA francs (US$1,011,168) to all of the privately owned press, with *Misamu*'s share to be released only when ownership had been clearly established.

37. Cited in Reporters sans Frontières, *Rapport annuel, 2002,* p. 1.

38. Atenga, "Contrôle de la parole et conservation du pouvoir," pp. 403, 407.

39. A few days after his newspaper was suspended, the editor in chief died under mysterious circumstances; some thought he may have been poisoned.

40. Years after *Misamu* disappeared, its former staff was still subject to harassment. In October 2006, in the midst of a new media saga pitting Norbert Ngoua and *Nku'u Le Messager* against progovernment journalists, Ngoua was jailed for nineteen days for a sentence handed down in 2003 for "defamation via the press" after publishing an article in *Misamu* stating that Equatorial Guinea was paying the salaries of officials from Gabon.

41. O. Bongo, *Blanc comme nègre,* cited in Côme Damien Georges Awoumou, *Gabon: un émirat stable mais plein de doute* (Yaoundé: Fondation Paul Ango Ela, 2003), p. 7.

42. Ndinga, "Radio Soleil," p. 82.

43. V. Mavoungou, "Institutions et publics de la radio-télévision au Gabon: essai sur la personnalisation du pouvoir à travers la communication politique par les médias," PhD thesis, University of Paris, 1986, p. 47.

44. Cited in Reporters sans Frontières, *Rapport annuel, 2003,* p. 1.

45. Ibid.

46. Institut Panos Paris, *Africentr@lemédias* no. 9 (March 2003).

47. Cited in Reporters sans Frontières, *Rapport annuel, 2002,* p. 1.

48. Atenga, "Contrôle de la parole et conservation du pouvoir," p. 405.

49. Ibid., p. 451.

50. Ibid., p. 120.

51. Professional organizations include SYPROCOM, for employees of various newspapers, especially public papers; AJGA; APPEL; AEPLI; the Club de la Presse; and SAPPAP.

10

EQUATORIAL GUINEA

A Media Sector
Under Lock and Key

EQUATORIAL GUINEA, AN authoritarian and neopatrimonial state, is organized for the benefit of a single family who monopolizes the state's resources and functions.[1] The country is not experiencing war, but an analysis of the sociopolitical and economic situation highlights huge seeds of tension: bad governance and constant violation of human rights might someday lead to a violent explosion. In such a context, the "fourth estate" of the media is obviously in a stranglehold. While in theory the constitution guarantees freedom of expression, in reality journalists have extremely limited room for maneuver. The written press is almost nonexistent, and the few independent journalists are constantly harassed by the government, accused of working to destabilize the state or urging the population to revolt. The media are far from playing the role of the troublemakers they are accused of being, because there is no opportunity to play this role.

An Atrophied and Ossified Media Sector

The media sector in Equatorial Guinea is extremely limited. There are a few publications, but they have connections to the state or members of the government and appear infrequently. The most regular are the monthly *La Gaceta* and the bimonthly *El Correo Guineo Ecuatoriano* (both published by the company SOGEDISA, a group close to the government), the bimonthly *Ebano,* and occasionally *Poto Poto,* a state newspaper in the hands of the Ministry of Information, Tourism, and Culture. Two opposition bulletins, *La Opinion* (founded in 1998) and *El Tiempo* (2000), which received official authorization to publish in 1999 and

207

EQUATORIAL GUINEA

Size	28,050 sq. km.
Population	0.5 million
Capital	Malabo
Ethnic groups	Fang, Bubi, Annobonnais
Official languages	Spanish, French
Human Development	
Index ranking (2005)	121 (out of 177 countries)
Life expectancy	43.5
Literacy rate	84.2 percent

Chronology
1778–1968: Spanish colony.
1968: Independence. Francisco Macias Nguema is elected president.
1970: Equatorial Guinea becomes a one-party state.
1972: Nguema proclaims himself "president for life."
1979: Lieutenant Colonel Teodoro Obiang Nguema Mbasogo, the president's nephew, seizes power by a military coup.
1985: Equatorial Guinea joins the CFA franc zone.
1987: The military dictatorship gives birth to a single political party, the Partido Democrático de Guinea Ecuatorial (PDGE).
1989: Teodoro Obiang Nguema is elected president.
1991: Under pressure from the international community, the constitution is amended and multipartyism is accepted.
1993: The first multiparty legislative elections are organized, but the opposition decides not to take part because of the restrictions imposed by the government.
1995: Equatorial Guinea develops its capacity for oil production, quickly becoming the third such state in the region (after Congo and Gabon).
1996: Nguema is reelected president. The election is flawed by massive vote rigging.
2002: Nguema is reelected president.
2004: The presidential party overwhelmingly wins the legislative elections.

belong to the same owner, appear every two or three weeks. *Ayo,* published by a student group, and *El Patio,* published by the Guineo-Hispanic cultural center, have a cultural emphasis.

Last, two party newspapers, *La Voz del Pueblo* (from the presidential party, the Partido Democrático de Guinea Ecuatorial [PDGE]) and

La Verdad (from the main opposition party, the Convergencia para la Democracia Social [CPDS]), appear once or twice a year.[2] The independent weekly *El Sol,* created in 1993 by three journalists from *Ebano,* disappeared in 1996.

The creation of newspapers is still subject to a regime of prior authorization, which the government does not hesitate to misuse. *La Verdad* (The Truth), though mentioned in the statutes of the CPDS, which were authorized in 1993, has not been formally authorized by the state, which regularly describes it as "clandestine."[3] A few other nonauthorized news sheets circulate illicitly from time to time.

Radio broadcasting is under a strict state monopoly and is essentially restricted to Radio Nacional de Guinea Ecuatorial (RNGE). Its premises are in Malabo and Bata. While the first private radio station, Radio Asonga (which broadcasts on FM in Malabo), was licensed in 1998, it belongs to the president's son, who is also minister of forestry, environment, and fishing. Radio France Internationale has also been allowed to broadcast on FM in Malabo since 1995. Other requests for authorization have been on hold for years.

Television is limited to a single public channel, Radio Television Guinea Ecuatorial (RTVGE), which only broadcasts for a few hours each day. Television Asonga, owned by President Teodoro Obiang Nguema Mbasogo and managed by his son Teodorino, broadcasts only in Bata, by cable. Foreign channels, including the Cable News Network (CNN), can be received by satellite, but the significant cost is a limiting factor.

Numerous subjects are taboo in Equatorial Guinea. The president, his entourage, the management of oil resources, and the security forces are all absolutely untouchable. The public audiovisual media essentially broadcast institutional information about government activities, attacking all "enemies of the homeland," meaning all those who do not have the same opinions as the current regime.[4] The occasional repression of the Bubi minority, and the border disputes that may arise, are equally taboo. In May 2003, Manuel Nzé Nzogo Angué, owner of *La Opinion,* was summoned by the head of state for reporting a statement by Gabonese president Omar Bongo claiming the island of Mbana.[5]

All journalists must be registered with the Ministry of Information. In 2003, eighteen listed professionals belonged to the private sector and about forty others were employed by state media. Foreign correspondents may only travel in the country if accompanied by a guide supplied by the Ministry of Information, but some cleverly avoid this constraint. In May 2002, a few months before the presidential election, the deputy minister of press, radio, and television, Alfonso Nsue Mokuy,[6] adopted a measure obliging all foreign media correspondents to register with the ministry, and prior accreditation was compulsory for all travel by a foreign journalist within the country. Any media company that wanted to cover the election had to apply for prior approval by sending a dossier to the Ministry of Information, which was anxious to avoid "people without experience or perhaps with the intention of causing harm arriving and disrupting the smooth running of the process."[7]

International media, especially Radio Exterior de España (REE), Spain's international shortwave station, play an important role, because they are alone in broadcasting objective information about what is happening in the country. They also provide an outlet for representatives of the political opposition to speak from abroad. In 1991 the Spanish station decided, in addition, to devote a daily one-hour program to Equatorial Guinea, "letting those who can give clear information on reality under Nguema speak."[8] The government of Equatorial Guinea soon protested.

In December 1992 the head of state declared in a speech broadcast by Radio Malabo that "the current campaign of indoctrination and defamation being conducted by certain foreign radio stations—who call themselves defenders of human rights—against the people and government of Equatorial Guinea, is palpable proof of the tendency of these countries to seriously interfere with internal affairs."[9] In 1998 the government made it known to Spain that the programs broadcast by Radio Exterior de España "could cause problems."[10]

On the other hand, the search for external legitimacy is inducing the Obiang regime to buy, at great expense, space in those pan-African and international newspapers that are prepared to print advertorials favorable to the government, and paint an almost golden image of the country.

The Media Environment

These constraints weigh heavily on Equatorial Guinea, making it extremely difficult for the privately owned press to emerge, develop, and become professional. A range of factors prevent dissident voices from being heard. While the government, in order to justify its control over the sector, claims that the media could potentially destabilize the country, it is difficult to imagine that journalists could contribute to the appearance of any dissent, given the coercive measures taken against them for the slightest wrong move.

Legal and Regulatory Framework

The law relating to the press that is currently in force was adopted in 1992 (Law 13/1992) and is heavily based on legislation in force in Spain under General Francisco Franco. It imposes prior authorization and prima facie control on all publications. In reality, the Ministry of Information does not always require prior submission of all publications before printing, since self-censorship is so strong that few excesses filter through.

Conversely, the prior authorization rule is zealously respected, such that it has become the first obstacle to the development of a free press. In spite of very clear provisions contained in the 1997 law (Law 06/1997) on the conditions that must be met to carry out prior authorization requests, many projects are never examined. The files lodged by *El Tiempo* in July 1996 and *La Opinion* in March 1998 were ignored until September 1999, and were only acknowledged following pressure from the United Nations. The excuses put forward to justify refusals are revealing. In 2001, a request lodged by journalist Pedro Nolasco Ndong, president of the local journalists' association, the Asociación de la Prensa de Guinea Ecuatorial (ASOPGE), to launch a new paper, *Liberacion,* was rejected because the name of the newspaper supposedly evoked communist ideology and suggested a lack of respect for democratic principles.[11]

The judiciary is often used as a weapon to silence newspapers. In 1992, journalists from *La Verdad* were charged with "insulting the head of state and subversive propaganda." Then the newspaper was banned in 1993 for "publishing false news and information prejudicial to public spirit and morale."[12] Such accusations are common from the Equato-Guinean authorities.

The law also stipulates strict control of foreign publications, which mostly come from Spain. The presence of any articles unfavorable to the government immediately results in confiscation of the newspapers. In 1993, threats were leveled against airlines and shipping companies that had allowed passengers carrying foreign newspapers and magazines to disembark.[13] The government informed the companies that this required "the prior permission of the Secretary of State responsible for the press, radio and television."[14] The companies were requested to warn their customers that newspapers and magazines (including the in-flight magazine of the airline, Iberia) must remain on board. In November 1998, four members of the CPDS who wanted to bring sixty copies of a book published in Spain, *La Encrucijada de Guinea Ecuatorial,* into the country from Gabon, were arrested and imprisoned in Bata's police station.[15]

The only way to get foreign publications into Equatorial Guinea is through ordinary travelers. There is no organized and authorized import procedure for the press, and the only bookshop in Malabo where foreign newspapers are available sells copies surreptitiously retrieved from arriving flights. The Guineo-Hispanic cultural center no longer offers Spanish titles.[16] In 2002 the minister of information told a special representative of the UN Human Rights Commission that passengers carrying foreign newspapers as they left an airplane were no longer being harassed. But, the minister added, "We cannot say since when nor until when."[17]

Simple possession of documents critical of the regime can lead to severe punishment. In 1992, two women were caught reading *La Verdad* and were arrested near a cinema in Malabo. One spent more than six months in prison on a charge of "reading material counter to state security."[18] In 1995, some twenty people were arrested for the same reason.[19] While selling newspapers on the streets of Malabo has gradually been permitted, or rather is no longer hindered by bans and open pressure, that particular newspaper is still blacklisted. "From short periods in police custody to simple oral threats," via provocation by the regime's "Antorchas" militia, "all methods are used to dissuade Equato-Guineans from reading *La Verdad*."[20]

In December 1999, Mariano Oyono Ndong, a member of an underground opposition party, was sentenced to three years in prison for "possession of documents of doubtful origin" when the police found a copy of *La Verdad* and an old Amnesty International report in his house. The same year, two other people were detained in prison and sentenced for possessing a photocopy of an article from the Spanish press.[21]

Hijack of the State Media

There is no freedom of expression emerging within state media, which are used exclusively to reinforce and legitimize the government. Opposition parties do not have access to state media, and public sector journalists refer negatively to the opposition, describing them as the "radical opposition." On the eve of the 2002 presidential election, the national radio station presented the CPDS candidate, Celestino Bacale, as a foreign "satellite" having sympathies for "terrorist" elements.[22]

Journalists in public media work under a perpetual fear of sanction. "A misplaced comma could lead to a salary suspension for a journalist in the official press."[23] In 1997, a journalist from the national radio and television company, though a supporter of the presidential party and a member of the regime's political police, was arrested and imprisoned for a month for mentioning a teachers' strike.[24]

The public media virulently attack outsiders who criticize the current regime, such as Swiss historian Max Liniger-Goumaz, one of the few specialists in the country. The former UN special representative for Equatorial Guinea, Gustavo Gallon, came under fire when his report, made public in 2001, was criticized by the newspaper *Ebano* for ignoring "completely the real human rights situation" in the country.[25]

In January 2002, *Ebano* and the national radio and television company allowed themselves to make a few criticisms of the government. The first raised questions about the lack of social housing, the other about the breaking of a promise to increase civil servants' salaries. The minister of information, Lucas Nguema Osono, reacted immediately, reminding management in the public press of their duty to maintain a strict editorial line.

The managers complied zealously. In July 2003, Radio Malabo fearlessly broadcast a program describing President Obiang as "the god of Equatorial Guinea," with total power over life and death. The program explicitly specified that the president could "decide to kill someone without anyone asking him for an explanation and without going to hell."[26]

Permanent, Direct Pressure

Journalists suffer from constant psychological pressure to say nothing of the physical aggression that vendors distributing opposition newspapers are subjected to. In 1992, while *La Verdad* was still blacklisted, its editor in chief, Placido Mico Abogo, was detained for a month and tortured so that he would reveal the names of the newspaper's staff.[27] He and his main partner, Celestino Bacale, were arrested, beaten, and imprisoned on countless occasions. Journalists from the weekly *El Sol* were also regularly harassed and beaten, and some editions were banned from sale, until the newspaper finally disappeared.[28] Today, journalists for *La Opinion* and *El Tiempo* frequently experience obstacles in accessing certain institutions, confiscation of identity documents, and death threats.

Some journalists have suffered from unrelenting harassment. In May 2000, Pedro Nolasco Ndong, a former journalist with the national radio and television station who was dismissed in 1992 for excessive liberty of tone and who later became publishing director of *La Opinion* and president of the ASOPGE, was arrested at Malabo airport on his return from a UNESCO meeting in Windhoek. Police confiscated documents he was carrying, including a report that described the limits on press freedom in Equatorial Guinea since 1991. The police extorted a hundred dollars from him.[29]

In December 2000, the Equato-Guinean administrative council suspended Nolasco Ndong from the newspaper for "management errors." Harassed many times for his numerous foreign contacts (he was local correspondent for Reporters sans Frontières), among other things, Nolasco Ndong launched *La Nacion* at the start of 2002, but then had to flee the country. He took refuge in Spain in July of the same year. At the time, the state media described him as "a second-rate journalist who publishes twisted, baseless information."[30]

Choosing exile is significant and weakens the Equatorial Guinea privately owned press. "Practically the entire intelligentsia is now outside the country."[31] The Spanish newspaper *Diaro 16* reported that "30–40 percent of the Equatorial Guinea population lives outside the country and 85 percent of intellectuals and executives are in exile."[32]

Local correspondents from foreign media do not escape this treatment. In May 2002, Rodriguo Angue Nguema, an AFP and BBC correspondent, came under great pressure while the regime was organizing the trials of the leaders of a supposed attempted coup in 2001. In 2003, after reporting on this event, he was once again arrested, and detained for more than eight days at police headquarters.

Suspensions and seizures are common. In 2000, the governor of the district of Mongomo ordered the seizure of *La Opinion* and *El Tiempo*, which were accused of spreading negative information about the country's leaders. Readers and vendors were harassed and fined 10,000–20,000 CFA francs (US$20–40).

In the same year, General Antonio Mba Nguema, head of the security forces and President Obiang's brother, suspended the Asonga radio and television stations, owned by his nephew, after the station broadcast a press release from its owner criticizing certain recent government appointments. A week later, after family discussions, the radio and television stations started to broadcast again. Even disputes within the government (practically family quarrels) do not generate dissonant voices, condemning the last hope of internal pluralism.

Unstable, Arduous Working Conditions

Private newspapers are developing in a state of total destitution. As a report from Reporters sans Frontières emphasized in 2002, "No newspaper has managed to produce more than half a dozen editions over the year, for lack of resources. There is no printing works in the country and newspapers are published as photocopies. Paper, imported from Cameroon, is expensive."[33] The state press also suffers from this shortage. Dependent for years on the support of Spanish cooperation, *Ebano* (in Malabo) and *Poto Poto* (in Bata) were forced to stop publishing at the start of the 1990s when this aid was suspended.

In 1997, recurrent power cuts, once for five months, contributed to the closure of the private weekly *El Sol,* whose printer had been declared "persona non grata" in the country and forced into exile.[34] Lack of electricity also led to the suspension of *La Voz del Pueblo,* the paper of the presidential party. The blackout was then deliberately extended for many months to leave the premises of the opposition party, the CPDS, without electricity, long after power had been restored to the rest of the town. As a result, *La Verdad* appeared only three times in 1997.[35]

Journalists' work is also hampered by a permanent withholding of information. "Very few civil servants or government officials grant interviews to private publications. Independent journalists are still viewed as opponents."[36]

Last, the privately owned press suffers from a chronic instability in staffing, because of the many journalists who go into exile or leave the profession, and also because of recurrent internal dissension. At *La Opinion,* there have been more than ten firings and resignations of management in the space of a few years. One manager who left the newspaper in October 2002 openly criticized the authoritarianism of owner Manuel Nze Nzogo, and complained of a lack of editorial independence and censorship. He also criticized the owner's lack of financial transparency, and even his "connivance with the government."[37]

Eviction of the Foreign Press

The government of Equatorial Guinea has managed to gradually remove all the foreign media formerly in the country. Visa applications by correspondents from the major Spanish newspapers (*El Mundo, El País, Diaro 16,* etc.) are regularly rejected. Those who manage to get into Equatorial Guinea are frequently harassed or even deported. In September 1992, a journalist from *Diaro 16* was imprisoned for "terrorism" and "espionage" because he took photos around Black Beach prison. He was freed only after intervention by Spain's minister for foreign affairs, Javier Solana.[38] The following year, an *El Mundo* correspondent was expelled barely three days after he had arrived in Malabo. In May 1998, eight journalists sent by Spanish newspapers and Public Spanish Television to cover the trial in the war council of 113 members of the opposition (accused of an attempted coup) were deported for "biased" coverage.[39]

In November 1994 the Spanish press agency Efe decided to permanently close its Malabo office and cover Equatorial Guinea events from Libreville. This closure followed nonstop government pressure and the departure into exile in Gabon of the agency's main correspondent. For months, Equatorial Guinea's minister of foreign affairs criticized "the campaign of denigration and indoctrination against this country's government, orchestrated by certain internal and external agents."[40] After the departure of the AFP correspondent in 1990, who also headed for Libreville, the closure of the Efe office reinforced Equatorial Guinea's insularity.

This isolation is accentuated still further by the threats leveled at anyone who maintains contact with Radio Exterior de España. In May 1995 the government of Equatorial Guinea forbade its officials and any public sector employees "from granting any interview whatsoever with REE."[41] The government emphasized that any Equato-Guinean saying anything over the airwaves of the REE would be arrested once he or she returned to Guinea. The authorities even went so far as to state that "any individual listening to REE is liable to imprisonment."[42] In February 1996 the police began to seize the radios of people accused of listening to the REE.[43] Despite such operations, the government has not managed to squash the success of the Spanish station.

Finally, media assistance initiatives by the Spanish Agencia Española de Cooperación Internacional, Equatorial Guinea's main foreign partner, have also been progressively interrupted. *Africa Dos Mil,* a quarterly cultural magazine produced by the Spanish foreign aid department, has ceased publication. The cultural radio station of the same name, also funded and managed by the Spanish foreign aid department, was suddenly closed in December 1993; the journalists were given barely an hour to leave the station.[44]

Weak and Manipulated Professional Institutions and Associations

The network of media associations is obviously very weak in a country where there is no freedom of any form, preventing the emergence of civil society organizations. The ASOPGE, created in 1997, is legally recognized and supposedly independent. But in April 1999 the government ordered the suspension of the association's president, Manuel Nzé Nzogo, owner of the weekly *La Opinion.* Though he had been democratically elected, the government judged that he was "not qualified to hold this position."[45] In February 2000 the association was suspended by the mayor of Malabo, Gabriel Mba Bela, following its criticism of the town's public transport.

In 2002, after a long period of lethargy, the ASOPGE tried to organize, along with *La Opinion,* professional demonstrations to celebrate World Press Freedom Day on May 3. But these were banned by Deputy Minister Mokuy, who accused the association of being illegal and not conforming to the ministry's requirements. *La Opinion* was then given notice that "given the current unusual circumstances, the Ministry of Information, Tourism and Culture is taking over the patronage of these festivities and, as a result, does not accede to the proposed activities planned by *La Opinion.*"[46]

Following the departure into exile of the ASOPGE's new president, Nolasco Ndong, in July 2002, a temporary board was appointed by the minister of information, Lucas Nguema Esono, to manage the association. The board was composed exclusively of people close to the government, including the director of *El Correo,* a weekly associated with the regime, the director of the national radio station, the director-general of the written press, and a presidential adviser responsible for information. "None of the founders or former management of the association were warned of this decision."[47] During the official ceremony to appoint the new board, the minister reminded journalists that "defending the dignity of the state must prevail over the profession."[48]

Despite this "infiltration," internal rifts soon appeared. In November 2003, following the arrest of local AFP and RFI correspondent Rodrigo Angue Nguema, the director of *El Correo* sent a letter of protest to the authorities. The secretary-general of the ASOPGE, Roberto Martin Prieto, a Spanish businessman and director of *La Gaceta* who was also seen as the minister of information's "henchman," then suddenly announced his resignation, openly dissociating himself from the ASOPGE's letter of protest.

Indifferent, Ambiguous Foreign Partners

Foreign partners are not rushing to support the Equato-Guinean press. Any intervention in the country depends on collaboration with government organizations, which, not surprisingly, are completely hypocritical. For instance, a large conference on the importance of the independent press in African democracies was organized in August 1997. All local journalists, including the staff of *La Verdad,* were invited. In July 2002 the Ministry of Information, in partnership with UNESCO, held a three-day seminar on "freedom of the press and the rule of law," offering Prime Minister Candido Muatetema Rivas an opportunity to remind journalists to "respect the ethics of the profession so as not to violate the rights of others."[49] The recommendations of this seminar involved adoption of a professional code of ethics, regulation of the issuance of press cards, and establishment of clear and organized media regulation mechanisms. None of these potential initiatives has been followed up with any material progress.

Most foreign countries are happy to close their eyes to what is happening in Equatorial Guinea, a small, oil-producing country that has become the domain of Washington and US oil companies. In 2002, a journalist from *El País* observed that "Equatorial Guinea is an exemplary case of how Western governments avert their gaze from the most despicable violations of democratic standards going on in a place, where, in addition a highly sought-after resource is available."[50]

Conclusion

The media landscape in Equatorial Guinea is in a state of total devastation. Apart from *La Gaceta,* no newspaper, whether government-supporting, party-based, or privately owned, appears regularly. Repression is combined with constant electrical cuts to hinder media functioning. Since the eviction of the foreign press and the threats leveled against those who would be its customers, the national authoritarian policy has been played out in total isolation. Even apart from journalists, any citizen who attempts to obtain more balanced information by listening to foreign radio stations, reading foreign newspapers, or even reading one of the few papers close to the opposition, risks reprisals. In such a situation, most journalists either leave the profession or take the path to exile.

Notes

1. The all-powerful national security forces are headed by the brother of President Obiang, two of his sons hold strategic ministerial posts (one in Infrastructures and Forests, the other in Mines and Hydrocarbons), and his sister-in-law is secretary of state for foreign affairs.

2. At the beginning of the 1992 process that opened the way to a multiparty system, various opposition parties announced the creation of newspapers, but

none of these papers managed to appear regularly: *De El Ocho, Cambio 93, Tu Guia,* and *La Luz.* A. Maja-Pearce (ed.), *Annuaire de la presse africaine* (Brussels: FIJ, 1996), p. 155.

3. Amnesty International, *Equatorial Guinea: No Free Flow of Information* (London, June 2000), p. 5.

4. J. L. Ewangue, "Guinée Equatoriale: des cris de détresse sous l'odeur du pétrole," unpublished (2003), p. 6.

5. Reporters sans Frontières, *Rapport annuel, 2004.*

6. Former director of state television and presenter of television news, he was dismissed in 1990 for "journalistic conspiracy." In 1992, his political party, the Convención Liberal Democrática, was made legal and joined the president's political sphere.

7. Cited in Institut Panos Paris and COTA (eds.), *Briser les silences: paroles d'Afrique centrale* (Paris: Karthala, 2003), p. 87.

8. M. Liniger-Goumaz, *Who's Who de la dictature de Guinée Equatoriale* (Geneva: Editions du Temps, 1993), p. 147.

9. Reporters sans Frontières, *Rapport annuel, 1993,* p. 175.

10. US Department of State, *Country Report on Human Rights Practices, 2000.*

11. G. Gallon, *Report on the Human Rights Situation in Equatorial Guinea* (Geneva: UN Human Rights Commission, 2002), p. 19.

12. Maja-Pearce, *Annuaire de la presse africaine,* p. 156.

13. Liniger-Goumaz, *Who's Who de la dictature de Guinée Equatoriale,* p. 145. The involved airlines are Spain's Iberia Airlines, Cameroon's Camair, and Nigerian Airways.

14. Maja-Pearce, *Annuaire de la presse africaine,* p. 156.

15. A. Artucio, *Report on the Human Rights Situation in Equatorial Guinea* (Geneva: UN Human Rights Commission, 1999), p. 7.

16. Reporters sans Frontières, *Rapport annuel, 1994,* p. 213.

17. Gallon, *Report on the Human Rights Situation in Equatorial Guinea,* p. 19.

18. This was Maria Pilar Manana Obono. Reporters sans Frontières, *Rapport annuel, 1993,* p. 174.

19. Amnesty International, *Equatorial Guinea,* p. 6.

20. Reporters sans Frontières, *Rapport annuel, 1996,* p. 71.

21. Juan Obiang Latte and Teodoro Abeso Nguema were arrested in November 1999, and held in prison for two months, for possession of an article from the daily *El Mundo,* available on the Internet, that reported on the president's possible ill health. They were sentenced for "insults and slander against the head of state and reproduction of a newspaper of doubtful origin." Amnesty International, *Equatorial Guinea,* p. 8.

22. M. Liniger-Goumaz, *A l'aune de la Guinée Equatoriale* (Geneva: Les Editions du Temps, 2003), p. 211.

23. Reporters sans Frontières, *Rapport annuel, 2002.*

24. Reporters sans Frontières, *Rapport annuel, 1998,* p. 44.

25. Cited in Reporters sans Frontières, *Rapport annuel, 2002.*

26. Reporters sans Frontières, *Rapport annuel, 2004.*

27. Maja-Pearce, *Annuaire de la presse africaine,* p. 155.

28. In 1994, two of its founders were obliged to leave *El Sol* and forced to join, given their civil servant status, *La Voz del Pueblo,* after being accused of "a lack of professional ethics and national spirit." Reporters sans Frontières, *Rapport annuel, 1995,* pp. 184–185.

29. Reporters sans Frontières, *Rapport annuel, 2002.*

30. Committee to Protect Journalists, *Attacks Against the Press, 2002,* p. 1.

31. M. Liniger-Goumaz, *La démocrature: dictature camouflée, démocratie truquée* (Paris: L'Harmattan, 1992), p. 27. In 1992, a quarter of the population was effectively living in exile.

32. Cited in Liniger-Goumaz, *Who's Who de la dictature de Guinée Equatoriale,* p. 150.

33. Reporters sans Frontières, *Rapport annuel, 2002.*

34. Reporters sans Frontières, *Rapport annuel, 1998,* p. 44.

35. Institut Panos Paris, *Afrique centrale,* p. 159.

36. Reporters sans Frontières, *Rapport annuel, 2002.*

37. Institut Panos Paris, *Africentr@lemédias* no. 4 (October 2002).

38. Reporters sans Frontières, *Rapport annuel, 1993,* p. 175.

39. Reporters sans Frontières, *Rapport annuel, 1999,* p. 43.

40. Reporters sans Frontières, *Rapport annuel, 1995,* p. 185.

41. Reporters sans Frontières, *Rapport annuel, 1996,* p. 72.

42. Ibid.

43. Reporters sans Frontières, *Rapport annuel, 1997,* p. 72.

44. Reporters sans Frontières, *Rapport annuel, 1994,* p. 212.

45. US Department of State, *Country Report on Human Rights Practices, 1999,* p. 5.

46. Letter from Alfonso Nsue Mokuy, deputy minister for radio, press, and television, cited in Institut Panos Paris and COTA, *Briser les silences,* p. 87.

47. Reporters sans Frontières, *Rapport annuel, 2003.*

48. Cited in Institut Panos Paris, *Africentr@lemédias* no. 5 (November 2002).

49. Committee to Protect Journalists, *Attacks Against the Press, 2002,* p. 2.

50. Cited in Liniger-Goumaz, *A l'aune de la Guinée Equatoriale,* p. 312.

11

African Conflicts in the Global Media

Jean-Paul Marthoz

SINCE THE FIASCO of the US intervention in Somalia at the beginning of the 1990s and the Rwandan genocide in 1994, "African news," or to be more exact, the version of African reality provided by the major Western media organizations, has proceeded from the war of the Great Lakes to the implosion of Côte d'Ivoire, from the confrontations in Liberia to the conflict in Darfur, moving through compassion, cynicism, and despair.

In 1995, after five years of reporting as the African correspondent for the *Washington Post,* US journalist Keith Richburg wrote a tragic and brutal epitaph:

> I watched the dead float down a river in Tanzania. I have covered the famine and civil war in Somalia; I've seen a cholera epidemic in Zaire; I've interviewed evil "warlords," I've encountered machete-wielding Hutu mass murderers; I've talked to a guy in a wig and a shower cap, smoking a joint and holding an AK-47, on a bridge just outside Monrovia. I've seen some cities in rubble because they had been bombed, and some cities in rubble because corrupt leaders had let them rot and decay. I've seen monumental greed and corruption, brutality, tyranny and evil.
>
> I've also seen heroism, honor and dignity in Africa, particularly in the stories of small people, anonymous people—Africans battling insurmountable odds to publish an independent newspaper, to organize a political party, usually just to survive.
>
> Somewhere, sometime, maybe 400 years ago, an ancestor of mine whose name I'll never know was shackled in leg irons, kept in a dark pit, possibly at Gorée Island off the coast of Senegal, and then put with thousands of other Africans into the crowded, filthy cargo hold of a ship for the long and treacherous journey across the Atlantic. Many of them died along the way, of disease, of hunger. But my ancestor

survived. . . . Then one of his descendants somehow made it up to South Carolina, and one of those descendants, my father, made it to Detroit during the Second World War, and there I was born, 36 years ago. And if that original ancestor hadn't been forced to make that horrific voyage, I would not have been standing there that day on the Rusumo Falls bridge, a journalist—a mere spectator—watching the bodies glide past me like river logs. No, I might have instead been one of them—or have met some similarly anonymous fate in any one of the countless ongoing civil wars or tribal clashes on this brutal continent. And so I thank God my ancestor made that voyage.

I empathize with Africa's pain. I recoil in horror at the mindless waste of human life, and human potential. I salute the gallantry and dignity and sheer perseverance of the Africans. But most of all, I feel secretly glad that my ancestor made it out—because, now, I am not one of them.[1]

Is Africa then the "desperate continent" that British weekly magazine *The Economist* wrote about in May 2000? From time to time, newspapers have tried to give "another image," less one-sided and therefore closer to the reality of Africa, by promoting the economic achievements of Botswana or Ghana, the calm electoral processes in Senegal or Benin, the rural development initiatives, or the courage of human rights defenders. But this journalistic effort that aims to illustrate the complexities and specificities of the continent remains the exception. The media machine sticks to its methods and its habits.

Thus in 2000, a study by the TransAfrica Forum on African coverage in two of the most influential US daily newspapers, the *New York Times* and the *Washington Post,* demonstrated that of eighty-nine articles published between March and August of that year, sixty-three covered war, military uprising, and civil rebellions, and twelve covered the AIDS epidemic.[2] Four articles broached economic development issues, but only from the angle of international aid or the relationship with the United States.

Africa Is Not the Exception

The indifference of the international press with regard to African dramas, or the accent placed on "negative events," is regularly condemned by analysts from the South who point a finger at the latent racism that allegedly pervades Western news desks. A comparison between the coverage given to the war in the Balkans during the 1990s and the insipid media reaction when faced with the genocide in Rwanda or the war in the DRC, does indeed give the impression that there is a double standard in the world of international information.

The coverage of the crisis in Zimbabwe is another example. "Zimbabwean journalists filing for Western news organizations learned that in their country's ongoing crisis the story for the Western media was the plight of the 4,000 dispossessed white farmers, while the African journalist might have sought to highlight the plight of the hundreds of thousands of displaced farm workers as well," noted Geoffrey Nyarota, the former editor in chief of the *Daily News* and winner of the UNESCO prize for freedom of the press. He added, "When three journalists from the *Daily News* and a foreign correspondent were arrested I received calls from foreign news organizations outside of Africa. They asked me for the details of the arrest and welfare only of the foreign correspondent."[3]

These failings are not limited to Africa, however. They have also been rife in other countries, such as in Peru's highlands in the 1980s, during the Shining Path guerrilla campaign, or in Indonesia during the anticommunist massacres in 1965. Although journalists defend themselves, sometimes very sincerely, a sort of color bar nevertheless exists within the majority of the Western media, and it separates the whites from all the others: black, brown, or yellow. "All these major news organizations are run by whites, generally Anglo-Saxon, predominantly male . . . and they see the world through that prism," observes Bill Kovach, former editor of the *New York Times* and of the *Atlanta Constitution*.[4] This state of affairs is aggravated by the "law of kilometric death": a death on the doorstep is worth ten deaths in a neighboring country and tens of thousands of deaths in Africa.

What is described by its critics as the specificity of the media coverage of Africa also reflects conventional journalistic practices when dealing with countries that do not constitute a major geopolitical or economic stake, or that have not been designated as such by the major Western capitals. "By tradition and experience, the press is a follower, not a leader," wrote two observers with experience of US media.[5] Decisions regarding international information tend to reflect the priorities of the White House. In the 1980s, when civil wars and repression were rife in Central America, the nature of the international coverage was barely any different. Only coups and earthquakes, torturers and guerrillas. When the civil wars petered out, the press deserted the Managua Intercontinental and the Camino Real in San Salvador. Since then, Central America has not had an image problem, because there are no images of it.

Throughout the world, from Sri Lanka to Chechnya, from Iraq to Algeria, the "interminable conflicts" and the "dirty wars" have provoked the same simplistic attention. Today, a study of the conflicts that devastate Colombia would give, in all evidence, quite similar results. At the "stock exchange" of international journalism, clashes among paramilitaries, drug traffickers, and the military take precedence over any other type of information: art, the legal economy, literature, music. Who even knows that Gabriel García Márquez is Colombian? And that in this country destroyed by a hundred years of solitude, its citizens resist, create, construct, and love?

"Good Bye World!"

The coverage of Africa reflects a fairly generalized tendency within the Northern media, a withdrawal when faced with the tumults of the world. In this context, a study of the US press is particularly important, not only because it dictates part of the global media agenda, but also because, by turns, it forges and relays the policies of the United States regarding the continent.

Yet since the end of the 1980s, the space reserved for international issues has been constantly shrinking in the majority of the US media. Localized journalism—that is, short-sighted journalism—has imposed itself as the norm for healthy editorial management. "Good Bye World!" exclaimed former CNN star reporter Peter Arnett in 1998 at the end of an inquiry into the treatment of international news by the US press.[6] In 2000 the major regional dailies of the United States gave only 3 percent of their news space to international questions. On the major television channels—such as ABC, CBS, and NBC—serious news, and particularly international news, has been ever-diminishing and is being replaced by scandals, shock items, and "lite news." In 2001, a study by the Aspen Institute, covering 10,000 subjects of international news on the national and local US television channels, concluded that they proposed "little which could reasonably help citizens understand global issues."[7]

Already in 1991, Sanford Ungar and David Gergen had observed that if one excluded information regarding South Africa, Ethiopia, and Libya, the whole of Africa had less airtime than whales stuck in the Arctic ice or the doping scandal of a US athlete. They concluded that "there is far more public interest in Africa's wildlife than its poverty. So that endangered elephants are more likely than endangered people to appear on the cover of a major U.S. newsmagazine."[8]

The September 11, 2001, terrorist attacks and the wars in Afghanistan and Iraq have resulted in more space for international news, but the nature of the coverage has barely changed. While a number of the more deadly attacks by the Islamic networks have been perpetrated in Kenya or Tanzania, and the plundering of African resources (gold, diamonds, coltan) finances Al-Qaida, Africa has once again lost its importance thanks to a stereotypical analysis of the terrorist threat, localized in an Arab-Muslim world that is barely understood. And this is plain wrong, warned two US experts who, in January 2004 in a long article in the journal *Foreign Affairs,* described a dangerous negligence by the United States of the terrorist threats in Africa.[9]

In fact, a large part of the information on Africa is now produced by NGOs that specialize in the study and analysis of conflicts (Human Rights Watch, International Crisis Group, etc.), acting as "news wholesalers," like the international news agencies. Barely reported by the major commercial media (with the exception of the quality press), their reports and news articles circulate mainly in the world of think tanks, charity networks, and diplomatic circles.[10]

Journalism by Stereotype

The coverage of Africa is particularly influenced by the classic reflexes of the US press, which needs a story line—a label—"ethnic war," "ancestral traditions"—onto which the individual or complex elements can be grafted; it also needs to simplify the issues, to designate the good guys and the bad guys, and to find a local angle via a US aid worker, priest, or soldier.[11] The struggle against apartheid in South Africa offered a positive version of this formatting of news, such as finding some link with the United States (the struggle for civil rights in the US Deep South), a moral fable (freedom vs. oppression), or a personalization of the conflict around Nelson Mandela or, to an even greater degree, around Bishop Desmond Tutu, the Martin Luther King of South Africa.[12] The negative version was seen in the coverage of the humanitarian crises of the 1990s: the US press generally arrived too late, caricatured the issues at stake, made clichés of the main participants, and ultimately created more confusion than clarity.[13]

This journalism by stereotype (ancestral hatreds, tribal warfare) is even more prevalent because the US media, with rare exceptions, never set foot in Africa unless there are particularly dramatic and significant events, and even then they send "parachutists"—all-purpose journalists who have no particular knowledge or understanding of the continent and who therefore present the most conventional interpretations of events.

Certain elements of the US media have escaped this trend and attempt to provide their readers with a more comprehensive and complex perspective, "a multifaceted journalism" that is keen to reflect the diversity of communities. The major dailies, such as the *New York Times, Washington Post, Los Angeles Times,* or even the *Christian Science Monitor,* cover the Great Lakes and Sudan with care and in detail; the alternative publications (*The Progressive, Atlantic Monthly, Mother Jones, The Nation*) regularly return to forgotten conflicts; National Public Radio covered the crisis in Darfur with tenacity. But African coverage suffers from two key handicaps: the low volume of economic exchanges between the United States and Africa, and the political weakness of the members of the African American community, which is dominated by the "Americans by birth," descendants of slavery who, because their relationship with Africa is more symbolic than real, are unable to make coverage of Africa a priority, as opposed to what the Jews, Mexicans, or Cubans have managed to do with their countries of reference. The ephemeral nature of North American publications that specialize on Africa is one illustration of this point.

All the same, the burgeoning presence of new African migrants (Nigerians, Senegalese, Ghanaians, etc.), the activism of the Evangelical churches in Africa, the emergence of South Africa as an international diplomatic force, and the growing importance of the continent in the geopolitical context of oil production, could change the equation and modify the conventional parameters of media coverage of the continent.[14] The press will inevitably reflect the interest and the attention of these communities and interest groups for a continent that until now has been largely forgotten.

The European media have not sunk as deeply into the shifting sands of localized journalism. Even though it has had some losses, international coverage is still given greater importance in the newsrooms. The principal media still have journalists who have the time, resources, and space to cover the continent. From Ramon Lobo (*El Pais*) to Stephen Smith (former–*Le Monde*), from Colette Braeckman (*Le Soir*) to Georges Alagiah (the BBC), some of the best-known names in European journalism are Africa specialists.

This coverage remains tainted, all the same, by colonial links and the practice of metropolitan journalism. The Belgian press mainly covers the DRC and Rwanda, the British journalists talk more about Nigeria and Kenya, Italy prefers Sudan and the Horn of Africa, France divides its attention among countries of former French Western Africa, French Equatorial Africa, and Central Africa. An exception to these divisions is coverage of the Great Lakes region and Sudan, where the continentwide stakes, the scale of the humanitarian tragedy and brutality, have drawn all European press.

In Europe as in the United States, however, Africa is not a priority. Permanent correspondents are rare and are mainly posted to South Africa, Kenya, and to a lesser extent, Dakar. Though they may have spent years traveling across the continent, too few Western journalists have bothered to learn any African languages, though some, such as Swahili in East Africa or Pulaar in West Africa, are spoken by tens of millions of people. This lapse means that journalists are cut off from sources of information, opinions, and perspectives other than those given by ministry spokesmen, the UN, or the NGOs. Who can imagine a Moscow correspondent who does not speak Russian? The use of local stringers is often only a stopgap measure.

Responsibilities

Articles in the major international newspapers and programs on the principal radio and television stations, such as Radio France Internationale or the BBC, have a "cross-border" influence that can affect the actions of the international community and the debate within the African countries, especially when the news is transmitted in local languages, which the BBC does in Haoussa, Swahili, or Kinyarwanda, or the Deutsche Welle in Amharic.

Africans frequently learn about themselves via the international press, not only because of government repression of the media, particularly on radio and television,[15] but also because African journalists do not have the financial resources to do their own reporting. After the humanitarian crisis of November 1996 in Zaire, columnist Adewale Maja-Pearce noted bitterly: "We were all here . . . the Western media . . . we watched the refugees return except that there was no representative of the African media amongst us to cover an event that one would have thought was above all an African subject. . . . There was someone from the *Philadelphia Enquirer* and another from the *Baltimore Sun,* but there was no-one from Africa."[16] This international media perception affects the image that the African people have of themselves. "One may wonder," wrote Swedish anthropologist Ulf Hannerz, "how much the street-level pessimism, by any name, is affected by foreign media coverage, in the same way as Western Orientalism is said to have provided an Orient with a self-image."[17]

Not only does the international press report the conflicts, but it is also one of the protagonists. It crystallizes the debates within diasporas and on the ground, to such an extent that, as Théophile Vittin wrote, the "political reality and the formation of public opinion is out of the control of the local channels and is located outside the African political system. African news is broken up according to the perceptions, the concepts, the preoccupations and the sensitivities of journalists in Paris or London, who do not necessarily bother themselves with analytical nuances."[18]

The international media also influence the choice of actors, "validate" official decisions, and cover up or expose situations. Frequently they are the intermediaries through which governments decide on their course of action—or inaction. "Take those black babies off the screen," US president Lyndon B. Johnson is said to have declared in 1968. Already entangled in the Vietnam War and under pressure from certain camps to intervene in the Biafra War, he was convinced that overinsistent media coverage would force him into a military and humanitarian intervention that he could not afford.

On a number of occasions, the media have shaped Western politics. The flow of humanitarian aid to Ethiopia in 1984 can be mainly attributed to a BBC report on the famine. Similarly, the US intervention in Somalia would perhaps not have taken place had the George H. W. Bush administration not been influenced by media dramatization of the situation. The passiveness of the international community when faced with the Rwandan genocide can also be explained by the failings of journalistic coverage of the events. A number of journalists had left for South Africa to cover the first postapartheid nonracial election, and also because of an interpretative framework that saw the killings as motivated by ancient ethnic hatreds, when, in fact, they constituted a coldly prepared and terribly modern genocide that could have been halted.[19]

Information Management

Globalization has also accelerated the "mirror effect" and the development of international information. Relayed by the Internet, decoded by diasporas, broadcast on the international radio stations, the articles and programs of the world's press are on a continuous loop, conditioning the actors at grassroots level. It is now essential for governments and rebel groups to control the international media coverage, to ban it or to shape it. Thus rebel groups are equipped with satellite connections to follow coverage of their activities on the Internet, and to immediately respond by e-mail or mobile phone to accusations or "disinformation."

In this battle of images and influence, the "messieurs Afrique" and public relations offices in Paris, London, and Washington are ubiquitous. Their role is to "sell" a positive image of their clients; they organize invitations of journalists who go along with them in hiding governmental abuses and excesses. South Africa under apartheid, Côte d'Ivoire during the years of Félix Houphouët-Boigny, and Joseph Désiré Mobutu's Zaire have been a few of their favored terrains. And as for corruption—Africa has become a continent crisscrossed at high speed by journalists cum "special guests" who are supervised by media-savvy communications directors.

Certain humanitarian organizations, whether nongovernmental or intergovernmental, have developed the same logic. While providing information on forgotten conflicts and access to forbidden areas, they also attract penniless journalists whom they expect will provide coverage that will at the very least be uncritical, and ideally be favorable. In this way, they, too, contribute to masking the reality and the complexity of the issues at stake. NGOs can offer another point of view, either because they have worked for a long time in regions neglected by the media, or because they are engaged in grassroots projects and are close to local populations and associations. But "because they provide the money and the equipment," notes Annalena Oeffner, "NGOs have considerable power over the 'frame of mind' and they can therefore, in certain cases, increase the production of Westernized images of the Third World, instead of compensating for the imbalances in the media coverage."[20]

The role of the Western countries, "mentor powers" in the continent's affairs, is no less important. The United States, France, the United Kingdom, and Belgium have constantly sought to control the flow of information about "their" areas of Africa. They accomplish this by co-opting journalists and courting and manipulating them during ministerial field missions. In 2002, Jean-François Dupaquier denounced the "exploitation of French journalists in the trucks of operation Turquoise" during the Rwandan genocide.[21] Similarly, the disinformation organized by the Bill Clinton administration and UN Security Council during the genocide in Rwanda will rival the lies of the George W. Bush administration on Iraq. Forbidding its diplomats to speak of genocide, the White House limited itself to evoking "acts of genocide." The UN spoke of a "humanitarian crisis."[22] "Why not rename the 'Crystal Night' the 'Crisis of Plate Glass Windows' and the systematic rape in Bosnia a 'Gynaecological Crisis,'"[23] said a scandalized Rony Brauman of Médecins sans Frontières.

The conformism of the majority of the US press during these events was just as astounding. During April 1994 the three big US television channels (ABC, NBC, and CBS) gave thirty-six minutes of airtime to the genocide. Some media, such as the *Washington Post* and the *Christian Science Monitor,* were desperately preaching in the desert. Eight hundred thousand deaths later, a section of the press—those who had the least to reproach—made their mea culpa. "It is the government which indicates the route to be followed by the media," noted Baffour Ankomah, editor in chief of *New African* (London). "Although it claims to be free, the Western press almost always follows the route indicated by its government."[24]

Without Heroes

"Americans need to see the world in terms of good guys and bad guys,"[25] wrote Susan Moeller, professor at the University of Maryland, in 1999. This remark also applies to a section of the European press. During the conflicts that have punctuated African independence, journalists could always fall back on their magic formulas. Amilcar Cabral, Patrice Lumumba, and Samora Machel were emblematic figures with whom a progressive public opinion could identify. Nelson Mandela, in many ways, was the last real hero of the continent. With the victory over apartheid, a cycle of history—and of journalism—came to an end.

During the "dirty little wars" that followed, certain journalists, despite everything, have confirmed their biases, covering or favoring leaders, keeping silent about corruption and despotism. As Mobutu had his sycophants and his flatterers within the European press, so Paul Kagamé and Laurent-Désiré Kabila benefited for a time from the favors of Western journalists converted to their cause or seduced by their rhetoric.

In common with the other continents, however, Africa no longer inspires the romantics and the revolutionaries. Kabila is not Che Guevara, and Charles Taylor is not Commandant Ahmed Shah Massoud. Yoweri Museveni and the other "new leaders" of Africa, so celebrated at the beginning of the 1990s, have deviated from the destiny of modernity that their international patrons (mainly Anglo-Saxon) had promised them. In Côte d'Ivoire, the protégé of the French socialists, Laurent Gbagbo, is playing with the fire of ethnicity. Today, in Africa as elsewhere, the international press no longer has models or grand designs to defend.

The Rise of Humanitarian Journalism

During the 1980s and 1990s, much of the press was content to practice humanitarian journalism. This development was magnified by the reporting policies of a number of media organizations. Confronted with the reticence and refusal of their editors in chief, brandishing the arguments of costs or lack of interest, a number of journalists became increasingly dependent on invitations from humanitarian organizations or national armies for their travels in Africa. In other words, the coverage of the continent was no longer in the hands of the journalists; it was being determined by NGOs and military headquarters.

Humanitarian journalism was sometimes exercised with decency, sometimes with shamelessness. The coverage of famines and massacres saved lives by forcing the international community to care for and feed the victims. But by only speaking of crises and wars, it also tarnished the image of the continent. This "humanitarian porn," as it has been called by Régis Debray, dominated a number of reports: "These nihilistic bodies, without roots or context, are not strewn across a battlefield, they are not milestones on an advance towards the front, they no longer punctuate a major speech. They have fallen there by chance, the abstract litter of pointless killings."[26]

With its excesses, "humanitarian" journalism seems to be telling us that, in a sense, there is an underclass of subhumans on the information planet, either because we do not mention them as individuals, or because we expose their misfortunes, their mutilated bodies, and their destroyed lives with less respect than for victims who are close to us. "The more distant and exotic the place, the more we feel able to see death and dying close-up," noted Susan Sontag in her essay "Regarding the Pain of Others." "The most frank representations of war and of corpses massacred by disaster are those where the photographic subject is a complete stranger, someone whom we have absolutely no chance of knowing."[27]

Taking the side of the victims can lead, whether voluntarily or unconsciously, to making choices that deform reality, as was seen after the genocide in Rwanda and the refugee camps of Goma, where many of the victims were in fact guilty. In reality, this victimology often reflects a refusal to think seriously about conflicts, a refusal to seek and to analyze their causes and their dynamics. "If the dominant ethics in television today is that there are no good causes left—only victims of bad causes—there is no guarantee that the medium will not succumb to the next moral fashion. There is even a danger that television's healthy cynicism towards causes will topple into a shallow kind of misanthropy," observed the Canadian philosopher Michael Ignatieff in his book *The Warrior's Honor*. "The TV spectacle of corpses encourages a retreat from the attempt to understand. Faced with the deep persuasiveness of ideologies of killing, the temptation to take refuge in moral disgust is strong indeed. Yet disgust is a poor substitute for thought."[28]

This emotional simplification inevitably leads to a simplification of analyses, as in "the return of barbarism," and also to a simplification of solutions. Talking about media silence on Sudan, Véronique Nahoum-Grappe and Pierre Bachet noted in *Esprit* that "one form of this relative indifference consists of disguising as a 'humanitarian' catastrophe (population movements, famine, difficulties in delivering aid) what is, in fact, a *political* disaster, constructed by a State which seeks, and often finds, international complicity."[29]

As with other countries—Chechnya, Bosnia—that are enmeshed in wars with no mercy or noble cause, Africa appears ravaged by conflicts so violent as to appear incomprehensible. Seen under the angle of massacres, rapes, mutilations, and destruction, these wars give rise to an atmosphere of powerlessness and despair that revolts public opinion—and that also encourages editors in chief to close their eyes to these red zones thousands of kilometers from Brussels or New York that implicate no Northern citizens. "I do not believe that if you have seen one mass grave, you've seen them all," wrote Scott Peterson in *Me Against My Brother.* "But how many synonyms can be found for the word 'killing,' how many degrees of fear and anger can be conveyed when even the thesaurus lets you down?"[30]

In this way, the media contribute to policy decisions made by international organizations. "One of the consequences of the 'new barbarist' paradigm," observed Philippa Atkinson regarding Liberia and Sierra Leone, "is to obscure the role of those countries involved in the modern war economies of West Africa and to mask their responsibility for the social damage that results. The images presented of African conflicts as primitive and backward reinforce existing prejudices and limit further examination of their causes and impact. Conclusions are drawn . . . that the West can play no positive role . . . , with disengagement seen as the only sensible strategy, and that perhaps humanitarian aid can be offered through the non-commital channel of the NGOs."[31]

Very quick to denounce local politicians and leaders of ethnic groups, the media often shy away from investigating the responsibilities of nations, companies, and the European, North American, and sometimes South African or Asian networks that have participated in plundering African resources, manipulating conflicts, and dealing in arms.

Invisibility

In the past few years, despite the media focus on deadly crises, many African wars have been invisible. In contrast to the Biafra War in 1968, which was one of the most emblematic moments of photojournalism and humanitarian reporting, the conflicts that have devastated a number of African countries since the 1990s have only attracted sporadic journalistic coverage.

In 1994 the genocide in Rwanda practically took place behind closed doors. Ten years later, in Darfur (western Sudan), the rebellion of "African" tribes and the repression led by the army of Khartoum, assisted by "Arab" militias (the Janjaweeds), have been (dis)covered at a distance. While rebel attacks started in March 2003 and the repression reached a peak between September and December 2003 (resulting in more than a million displaced persons and refugees, and causing many thousands of deaths), the first articles—in *Le Monde* and the *New York Times*—did not appear until January 2004.[32] The vast majority of the European and US media only woke up to the problem in April 2004, after a solemn warning issued by Kofi Annan at the commemoration of the Rwandan genocide. In 2004 the three major US television networks (ABC, NBC, and CBS) dedicated only twenty-six minutes of evening news programming to Darfur.[33] "The media does not cover genocides," said a human rights activist. "It covers the anniversaries of genocides."[34]

Dangers

The brutality of the wars that devastate a part of Africa is another reason for the relatively small space accorded to events on the continent. Risks for journalists have dangerously increased. An editor in chief once told me during a conference in London on the security of war correspondents that nothing is worth the death of a journalist.

If the level of violence has yet to reach that of Iraq, Africa during wartime remains one of the most dangerous destinations for the international press. The deaths of Kurt Schork and Miguel Gil in Sierra Leone in 2000, the arrest of journalists by the regime of Charles Taylor in Liberia in 2000, and the assassination of Jean Hélène and the disappearance of Guy-André Kieffer in Côte d'Ivoire in 2004 have dissuaded a number of newsrooms from covering Africa. The number of "no-go" zones has multiplied. Though journalists were still able to visit rebel-held areas during the conflict in Biafra in 1968, and during the wars of independence in Angola or Mozambique, this option is now practically impossible. The level of generalized insecurity, the cost of reporting and insurance, in addition to the desire of the armed groups to keep witnesses at a distance, all prohibit journalists from covering conflict in Africa. The fear of being hauled before the International Criminal Court in The

Hague for crimes against humanity leads increasingly to the exclusion of the media from the theater of war: "Hush please, we are killing!"

Alternatives

"Africa could be covered differently." This phrase has been bandied about for years by a profession that at regular intervals is affected by remorse and scruples. Africa has sometimes been covered with tenacity, even in the US media. That was the lesson given by Nicholas D. Kristof of the *New York Times,* Emily Wax of the *Washington Post,* and Christiane Amanpour of CNN, who very early on realized the scale of what was happening behind closed doors in Darfur and have obstinately followed an "unsellable" story. The US press has also covered stories in a less one-dimensional manner: instead of only speaking of killers and rapists, instead of fixing the camera on the powerless victims, the death, the decay, and the famine, some journalists have sought to present the positive actions of the continent: artists, doctors, community organizations, human rights activists. Others have focused on describing the extraordinary ingenuity of populations forced to survive in the midst of particularly difficult conditions. "From the toughest refugee camps in Sudan to the bustling streets of the Johannesburg townships," wrote Fergal Keane of the BBC, "I have been relentlessly overwhelmed by displays of humanity, of compassion and of generosity."[35]

However, above and beyond this legitimate desire to show "another Africa," one that is humane, united, generous, or inventive, certain media organizations quite simply apply to the African continent the rules that are the norm for quality journalism everywhere. In accordance with the celebrated Hutchins Commission of 1947—the reference point for public interest journalism—they seek to give "a representative vision of the news": a vision that is diversified and multifaceted.

"Tell the whole story," advised Ebere Onwudiwe, author of a book on Afropessimism. "For a every horrific political story in Africa, there is another story of courageous and creative political entreprise accomplished under circumstances that those who live and vote in developed democracies could not even begin to imagine."[36] Charles Onyango-Obbo, of the Nation Media Group in Nairobi, insists, "There should be no special type of journalism reserved for the coverage of Africa. The patronizing reporting we witness today is as bad as the condescending form of the past. What Africa needs is good journalism, one that tells stories as they are reported and observed."[37]

In this regard, the university presses can boast of some titles that are of a rare quality, titles that, like *Politique Africaine,* persist in thinking seriously about the future of the continent. The foreign policy journals—*Foreign Affairs* and the *World Policy Journal* (New York), *Le Monde Diplomatique* (Paris), *Critique Internationale* (of Paris's Centre d'Études et de Recherches Internationales), *Enjeux Internationaux* (Brussels), and others—propose illuminating essays and unconventional analyses of the continent. The development press—*The New Internationalist* (London), *MO* (Brussels)—and the missionary press—*Mundo Negro, Nigrizia*—illustrate both the dramas and the hopes of Africa, going against the tide of "commercial" journalism, which is hindered by its conventional mechanisms for the selection (most often silence) and treatment (most often sensationalist) of the news.

Comfortably installed in its "niche" as the round-up of the foreign-language press, the Paris-based *Courrier International* presents Africa via its own media, a strategy that highlights the existence of an African journalism that is audacious, original, and high-quality. News agencies such as Rome's Inter Press Service (IPS) and Syfia/Infosud (a network of correspondents in ten or so countries), and Internet sites such as allafrica.com or AfriK.com, cover subjects often dismissed by the major media and bring a real diversity to the market of African information.

Despite doubts that regularly surface concerning their preferences and their choices, the specialized magazines in Paris or London—*Jeune Afrique, Le Nouvel Afrique-Asie*—provide a wide range of information about the continent. The space that they give to arts, literature, the economy, and society, and their coverage of national situations, offer another angle on African realities.

The international radio stations—Radio France Internationale, the BBC, Deutsche Welle, Africa No. 1, Channel Africa, Voice of America—play an essential role in this alternative coverage of the continent. Their consistency, the diversity of their editorial staff, and the breadth of their network of correspondents make them key players in the African media universe, within which they bring an extra measure of professionalism and diversity. Television also has some channels, such as TV5 (the global francophone public service channel) and BBC World, that strive to cover the continent in a more complete and representative manner.

The battle of images and imaginations also takes place on the shelves of the bookstores. In the past few years, Africa has provided the material for a number of bestsellers that encompass the past and the present of the continent: the apocalyptic travel books of Robert Kaplan,[38] the disillusioned observations of Stephen Smith,[39] the reporting from the field by Polish journalist Ryszard Kapuscinski, the testimony of Frenchman Jean Hatzfeld, and the notes by roving Belgian writer Lieve Joris and Spaniard Javier Reverte have contributed to creating an image of the continent—and in doing so have demonstrated, above all, the desire of readers to find in these books the confirmation of their hopes, fantasies, and stereotypes.

The international coverage of Africa is also determined by the evolution of journalism in Africa itself. Since the beginning of the 1990s, in the midst of immense difficulties, the plague of the hate media, and frequent abuses and errors, a generation of professional journalists was born, keen to preserve their independence and determined to test the limits of freedom of expression.[40] Although the current media cacophony can increase the risk that outsiders will misread the situation and get it wrong, certain people consider this pool of talent to be one of the keys to another kind of coverage of the African continent. Not only because the international foreign correspondents can rely on the local media as a source of information, contacts, and analysis, but also because the use of more experienced local journalists can contribute to doing away with the stereotypes that afflict the Western media and help portray African realities in a more relevant manner.

One World

The study of international media coverage of Africa, like that earlier of Central America or of Afghanistan, brings to light the mechanisms of selection and treatment by the world's media, particularly their subservience to official priorities. It also reflects the temptation to consider Africa as a continent that has no effect on the world and that provokes only either revulsion when faced with the atrocities committed, or compassion when confronted with its poverty.

In a globalized world, however, the misfortunes and the hopes of Africa are part of the reality of us all. Faced with the African tumults, the "refuge" that television news appears to offer—"television is a window, it gives us a view on the world but also seems to offer a protective screen between the world and ourselves"[41]—is not a realistic option. The examples of interaction are multiple: the immigrants from sub-Saharan Africa constitute one of the most important European issues; the wars for resources in Central Africa reflect a globalization of the criminal economy that affects all societies, whether in the North or the

South; the struggle for protection of the African environment—by Kenyan Wangari Maathaï, winner of the 2004 Nobel Peace Prize, and millions of others—concerns the whole planet. The success of the multiracial society in South Africa and the challenge of justice and reconciliation in Rwanda are issues for the North as much as the South. There is, inextricably, only one world.

Notes

1. *International Herald Tribune,* March 27, 1995. This bitter observation provoked a lively reaction: "If an African correspondent went to the US and only covered the deprived areas of Chicago or the neo-nazi militias," replied Tina van der Heyden, "maybe he would be very pleased that his ancestors managed to stay on their continent."

2. TransAfrica Forum, *Press Coverage of Africa* (Washington, D.C.: December 2000).

3. G. Nyarota, "Africa Through the Eyes of African Reporters," *Nieman Reports* (Fall 2004), pp. 35–37.

4. In S. J. Ungar and D. Gergen, *Africa and the American Media,* Occasional Paper no. 9 (New York: Freedom Forum Media Studies Center, Columbia University, November 1991), p. 8.

5. Ibid., p. 5.

6. *American Journalism Review* (November 1998). Peter Arnett was the CNN correspondent in Baghdad during the Gulf War.

7. D. E. Admunson, L. S. Lichter, and R. S. Lichter, *The Myopic Neighbor: Local and National Network Television Coverage of the World* (Washington, D.C.: Frameworks Institute, 2001).

8. Ungar and Gergen, *Africa and the American Media,* p. 5.

9. N. Lymanp and J. S. Morrison, "The Terrorist Threat in Africa," *Foreign Affairs* (January–February 2004), pp. 75–86.

10. A. Oeffner, "Can NGOs Fill the Gap Left by the Media?" (May 2002), http://www.jmk.su.se/global102/annalena/essay.

11. S. Moeller, *Four Habits of International News Reporting* (Waltham, Mass.: Brandeis University, December 1999).

12. See J. Sanders, *South Africa and the International Media, 1972–1979: A Struggle for Representation* (London: Frank Cass, 2000).

13. See S. Moeller, *Compassion Fatigue: How the Media Sell Disease, Famine, War, and Death* (New York: Routledge, 1999).

14. See M. Clough, "Afrique: la stratégie américaine," *Enjeux Internationaux* (1st Quarter 2005).

15. See S. Kanuma, "No Easy Life for Journalists in Africa," *Nieman Reports* (Fall 2004), pp. 37–39. Also see the annual reports of Reporters sans Frontières and of the Committee to Protect Journalists.

16. A. Maja-Pearce, "On the Road Again," *Index on Censorship* (January 1997).

17. U. Hannerz, *Foreign News: Exploring the World of Foreign Correspondents* (Chicago: University of Chicago Press, 2004), p. 132.

18. T. Mattelart (ed.), *La mondialisation des médias contre la censure* (Brussels: INA–De Boeck, 2002), pp. 10–11.

19. A. des Forges, *Aucun témoin ne doit survivre* (Paris: Karthala, 1997).

20. Oeffner, "Can NGOs Fill the Gap?"

21. J. F. Dupaquier, "Informer sur l'Afrique: silence, les consommateurs d'informations ne sont pas intéressés ou ne sont pas solvables," *Mouvements* nos. 21–22 (May–August 2002), pp. 89–95.

22. For a critical analysis of this period, see S. Power, *"A Problem from Hell": America and the Age of Genocide* (New York: Basic, 2002), pp. 329–389. For an explanation by the US administration, see J. Shattuck (Bill Clinton's assistant secretary of state for democracy, human rights, and labor), *Freedom on Fire: Human Rights Wars & America's Response* (Cambridge: Harvard University Press, 2003), pp. 21–50.

23. R. Brauman, "Genocide in Rwanda: We Can't Say We Didn't Know," in J. François (ed.), *Populations in Danger* (Paris: Médecins sans Frontières, 1995), p. 89.

24. I. Seaga Shaw, "Entre les 'enfants chéris' et les 'salauds,'" *Média@ctions* no. 29 (January–March 2002), p. 18.

25. Moeller, *Four Habits of International News Reporting,* p. 1.

26. R. Debray, *L'œil naïf* (Paris: Le Seuil, 1994), pp. 155–161.

27. S. Sontag, *Devant la douleur des autres* (Paris: Christian Bourgeois, 2003).

28. M. Ignatieff, *The Warrior's Honor: Ethnic War and the Modern Conscience* (New York: Henry Holt, 1997).

29. V. Nahoum-Grappe and P. Pachet, "Silence sur le Soudan," *Esprit,* July 2002, p. 29.

30. S. Peterson, *Me Against My Brother: At War in Somalia, Sudan, and Rwanda* (New York: Routledge, 2000), p. 324.

31. P. Atkinson, "Mythologies of Ethnic War in Liberia," in T. Allens and J. Seaton (eds.), *The Media of Conflict* (London: Zed, 1999), p. 212.

32. K. H. Bacon, "Hiding Death in Darfur, Why the Press Was So Late," *Columbia Journalism Review* (September–October 2004), pp. 9–10.

33. S. Ricchiardi, "Déjà Vu," *American Journalism Review* (December–January 2005).

34. C. Bogert, "Another African Calamity: Will Media Slumber On?" *Houston Chronicle,* May 4, 2004.

35. F. Keane, "Trapped in a Time-Warped Narrative," *Nieman Reports* (Fall 2004).

36. E. Onwudiwe, "Africa's Other Story," *Current History* (May 2002), p. 228.

37. C. Onyango-Obbo, "Seeking Balance in a Continent Portrayed by Its Extremes," *Nieman Reports* (Fall 2004), pp. 6–8.

38. R. D. Kaplan, *The Ends of the Earth: A Journey at the Dawn of the 21st Century* (New York: Random House, 1996).

39. S. Smith, *Négrologie: pourquoi l'Afrique meurt* (Paris: Calmann-Lévy, 2003).

40. S. Ellis, "Reporting Africa," *Current History* (May 2000), pp. 221–226.

41. A. Aubrun and J. Grady, *A Window on the Storm: How TV Global News Promotes a Cognitive "Refuge Stance"* (Washington, D.C.: Frameworks Institute, October 2, 2002).

12

Conclusion

G IVEN THE COMPLEX situations and the diversity of media experiences presented in this book, drawing general conclusions about
the media's role in the multifarious situations of crisis and tension in
Central Africa since 1990 seems a little hazardous. In the majority of
the nine countries analyzed here, the media have for a long time been
under state monopoly regimes and it is only the political upheavals at
the beginning of the 1990s that have led to the appearance of political
pluralism along with the liberalization of the media. However, in at
least six of these nine countries, the euphoria of democracy has been
followed by an explosion of violent conflicts, internal and external (the
DRC, Rwanda, Burundi, the Central African Republic, and Congo-
Brazzaville), or the resurgence of old quarrels (Chad)—conflicts in
which the media have often found themselves involved due to the sheer
force of events, because the media always reflect on the societies in
which they work.

It is very difficult to know why, in certain countries, in a period of
crisis, the media descend into a maelstrom of hatred, violence, and
stigmatization of certain communities, while others try to calm the tensions. Recently, in Côte d'Ivoire, both the public and the private sector
media have sunk into practices much more likely to poison minds than
to restore dialogue. Meanwhile, some rare publications in the written
press have tried to maintain a degree of balance. These have then had
their offices ransacked and have had to cease publication on several
occasions.

This situation in Côte d'Ivoire has shaken some widely held con-
victions. For here is a country with many well-trained journalists, where
influential professional associations of the media are well-established,

241

where a press ethics council, established in 1995, is recognized for its remarkable work, and where collective agreements guarantee, in principle, acceptable working conditions for all journalists. It is also a country where the media benefit, thanks to a buoyant advertising market, from significant financing. Conditions are therefore much more favorable in Côte d'Ivoire than in many other countries on the continent for the blossoming of professional and responsible media. Nevertheless, the media in Côte d'Ivoire have been, since 2000, a major concern and, for most of that time, a real obstacle to peacebuilding.

Based on the nine Central African countries analyzed in this book, some factors can be underlined that influence how media players position themselves in times of conflict. These factors originate in three main areas: the internal organization of the media, the relationships between journalists and political players, and the professional environment. Of course, none of the factors identified here inevitably leads on its own to a positive or negative attitude on the part of the media in times of conflict. It is a combination of all the factors that can cause the progressive or brutal deterioration of professionalism. Besides, each country, each media sector, has its own logic and its own evolution.

The Internal Seeds for War-Mongering Media

Conflict is generally a time of widespread failure of the media to respect the rules of professional journalism, which may prove to have grave consequences for the population. The catalog of dangerous ethical violations includes stereotyped and radical analysis of a situation, with a strong identification with one of the belligerent parties (as in the written press in Burundi in 1993–1995). It also includes amalgamation of the political actors who are "representative" of the enemy community, with the actual members of this community, in the name of which a leader claims to speak and act, and deliberate distortion of certain facts for particular interests (e.g., to make a community believe that it is threatened and to lead it to react in the name of legitimate self-defense—one of the favorite practices of the RTLM in Rwanda). The media can also "sin" by proposing a debatable presentation of history (particularly the history of the conflicts in the country). In all countries at war or recovering from war, it is difficult to teach history, and historians still have not been able to agree on a common view of the past in Burundi (where history courses do not go further than 1970) or in Rwanda (where all history teachings were suspended after the genocide).

Media content also shows that journalists are inclined toward sensationalism and the dramatization of events (by publishing erroneous counts of victims, reports of inflammatory speeches of public figures, and the like). They sometimes do not hesitate to publish confidential information that risks jeopardizing peace negotiations, or they establish false comparisons between the situation in the country and other situations that are very different, in order to provoke fearful and violent reactions (e.g., the Burundian press of the "black years" [1993–1995] comparing the FRODEBU regime with the genocidal Hitler regime). The preponderance of commentary over information is widespread in almost all media (e.g., the Kinshasa written press and radio and television stations), as well as reiteration of the propaganda of the belligerents (e.g., the written press of Congo-Brazzaville before and during the war of 1998 is a clear illustration). Strict self-censorship leads to, for example, the systematic omission of positive points concerning "the other side."

In the field of radio, these distortions, lapses, and adoptions of partisan attitudes affect not only the news broadcasts but often the entire programming strategy. So, in Rwanda, hatred has essentially been communicated through songs broadcast as part of "light" entertainment. Conversely, Studio Ijambo in Burundi and Centre Lokole in the DRC have tried to engender better understanding between the communities by using a wide diversity of dramatic productions and entertainment.

Structurally, several factors inside the media encourage these drifts. The first is a generalized deficiency of training. In four of the six Central African countries that have been at war, there is no school of journalism worthy of the name. In the two countries that have a formerly well-known school (the IFASIC in Kinshasa and the Ecole Supérieure des Sciences et Techniques de l'Information et de le Communication in Yaoundé), the quality of teaching has not been maintained for the past decade, for financial and material reasons. However, the argument of lack of training, frequently given to explain some bad behavior of the press, is not entirely convincing. In countries that have experienced hate media, those in control were often professionals aware of what they were doing. The RTLM was not run by uneducated people, nor were the hate media in Serbia or Côte d'Ivoire.

Second is the fact that the first privately owned media in the region emerged at the beginning of the 1990s, alongside multiparty democracy—one could even say, emerged within the bosom of the new political parties. Several of these media are therefore more at the service of a political party or leader who, in a situation of conflict, may become a belligerent party or leader, than in the service of citizens and of honest and rigorous news. This was obvious, for instance, in Congo-Brazzaville in 1998, when the various newspapers that were close to the political players each had their headquarters in the zone controlled by their patron and his militia. The rare titles that tried to remain neutral, like *La Semaine Africaine,* found themselves without protection in the midst of the storm. In the DRC, on the eve of the presidential campaign, each of the four vice presidents had one or more "tame" television channels. In the second round of the presidential election, a real "media war" erupted between the channels close to Kabila and the ones belonging to Bemba. Media interests may also be held by businessmen who have a role in the conflict, which therefore restricts journalists' independence.

Third is the obvious question of financial resources. War often means higher costs for the media that want to report on it and cover the battles. Movement in the war zone is often difficult for the impoverished media, which scarcely have the capacity to leave the capital city. In Chad, it is practically impossible for journalists of the privately owned press in N'D-jamena to travel to the sites of confrontations between government forces and rebels, which are located in the north of the country, more than a thousand kilometers away. On two occasions, the government has organized transportation of journalists to sites that had suffered rebel attacks. However, journalists' conscientiousness in denouncing the violence committed in those places—by the army, against civilian populations considered sympathetic to the rebels—led to the end of such initiatives. The lack of materials and transportation also leads to concrete difficulties in collection, production, and distribution of news, and sometimes explains (but does not justify) the lack of balance in presentation of events.

Another finance-related problem is journalists' salaries. In many of the media sectors in the region, journalists are poorly paid, if at all. Whether in the private or the public sector, journalists are often confronted with survival problems, which makes them vulnerable to pecuniary gestures. Moreover, war often creates economic crisis for the media, whose provisioning of primary materials may suffer (this was the case for the Burundian media under the embargo, as well as for the DRC and CAR presses during the war). The media also see the pauperization of their public, and the disappearance of their advertisers. All this without counting the costs to replace pillaged media facilities.

However, despite these difficulties, there are media that manage to do their job in a rigorous and honest way, often, it must be recognized, thanks to support from foreign development agencies. In difficult contexts, they keep trying to inform their public, build confidence between communities, monitor the authorities and parties in conflict (playing a watchdog role), promote sources of identification other than ethnic ones, analyze and present the hidden reasons for the conflict, give a voice to all the protagonists, and promote peace efforts, all the while trying to remain "neutral." Some continue to publish clandestinely to ensure the circulation of news (and take great risks in doing so).

Given that support from foreign development agencies is precious, sometimes even indispensable (e.g., Radio Okapi in the DRC, Radio Ndeke Luka in Bangui), a crucial question remains: What happens when the external financial aid stops? For media whose working economies are often totally at odds with what the local market can provide, the question becomes one of survival.

The Media and Political Authorities

Aside from the elements internal to the media identified above, the behavior of the authorities is of course critical in causing the media to deviate far from their duty of rigor, balance, and honesty. A first aspect is the legal and judiciary framework. The media behave in a different way according to whether they are faced with a democratic or an authoritarian state, and according to the existence of an independent judiciary or whether it is manipulated by the executive. In numerous cases, it can be observed how impunity encourages violence not only for armed groups and militias who call for murder, attack civilians, and commit serious human rights violations, but also for journalists. In Rwanda, it is clear that impunity paved the road to genocide and the massacre of half of the journalists in the country.

In the majority of the countries of Central Africa, liberal legislations, recognizing pluralism in the media, were adopted at the beginning of the 1990s. But periods of conflict see a reestablishment of censorship and a resurgence of self-censorship, as well as sudden appointments to certain key positions in the sector (e.g., head of the Ministry of Communications or of the public media). All of this does not promote a pluralist news industry that gives voice to all parties. The dominant powers do not tolerate balanced information, and refuse to allow contesting voices to be heard. In Burundian radio, for example, the simple act of passing a microphone to representatives of the rebel forces had initially seemed intolerable to the regime in power. In the DRC, Radio Okapi was openly accused of giving "publicity to the belligerents" because it gave airtime to representatives of the rebel movements, which many Congolese doubted had real popular support.

Access to diversified sources of information is fundamental, but this is often hampered during a period of conflict. The state tries to keep a monopoly on what it calls "correct" information, and the privately owned media sometimes have difficulty in accessing other sources, which makes them "unbalanced." In a vast country like the DRC, the appearance of mobile telephones has been of paramount importance for coverage of the conflict. Satellite telephone technology has allowed journalists in Kinshasa to rapidly obtain news of events taking place in Bukavu or Kisangani, which was not possible, for example, during the first war, of 1996–1997. The Internet has also helped to change the working context, by allowing easier access to foreign sources, including the international media (even if these can also be partisan).

Seizure by the authorities of the public media is another determining factor for the emergence of a "neutral" press. When the state media are completely under the control of the authorities, the privately owned press tends to confuse "criticism of the government" and "independence." So, the more implicated and partial the public media are, the more radical and partisan some private media can become, and just as partial and excessive in their desire to oppose the grip of the state. All the critical media are therefore accused of being close to the opposition.

Aside from the government authorities, the whole of the political and military forces facing each other are liable to exercise pressure on the media and to directly threaten freedom of the press. There is more risk that journalists will be mistreated during conflict situations when the agents of repression increase in number (running government, opposition, army, militias, and the like). In the DRC, Journalistes en Danger bears witness to the fact that, since the beginning of the war, journalists have experienced numerous violations of their rights, including threats, kidnappings, assassinations, and assaults. In 1994 in Rwanda, they were among the first targets of the extermination. Often, as it has been pointed out for Congo-Brazzaville, journalists who are at the service of a belligerent faction are effectively better-protected. "Neutral" journalists are at greater threat, with "neutrality" being interpreted as treason or sympathy with the enemy.

As well, where the political context is affected by polarization and conflict, election periods (e.g., the end of the transition period in Rwanda in 2003, in the CAR and Burundi in 2005, in the DRC in 2006) are always moments of great tension. Journalists are subjected to heightened pressure and manipulation, increasing the complexity and risk of their profession.

The Media and the Professional Environment

Beyond the constraints internal to press enterprises, and the relationships between journalists and the authorities, the third set of determining factors that explain why the media may retain some degree of professionalism, or indulge in serious abuses, when faced with conflict, depend on the configuration of the professional environment.

The degree of structure and organization of the profession plays an essential role in allowing the media to continue to work in a rigorous and honest way during a period of crisis. In a country where the media are organized and united, it is easier to resist the pressures of the state or the belligerents. This is the case with the written press in Chad, for example, or the radio stations in Burundi. On the other hand, in contexts where there are unbridgeable enmities between owners and managers of the media, aligned with different political tendencies, a sense of unity becomes difficult and atomization weakens the profession. Again, during the war in Congo-Brazzaville, it was practically impossible to gather around the same table the publishers of the newspapers that supported the various belligerents. The professional structures and associations are often ineffectual during a conflict, as their internal working mechanisms are paralyzed by the divisions on the political scene. The existence of a code of professional conduct can be an aid to the structuring and cohesion of the profession during peacetime, but it often becomes a dead letter in time of war, when other priorities take precedence. Press ethics councils, whose functioning relies on a professional consensus, are paralyzed, the professional associations become lethargic, and media owners and journalists allow their professional identities to be overridden by other types of belongings. On the public side, the regulatory bodies of the communication sector often revert, during a crisis, to serving the government, taking on the role of censors rather than organizing the profession.

The economic environment, as already mentioned, suffers serious damage in a period of conflict, and often struggles to recover afterward. For example, repeated pillaging has resulted in the departure of the majority of the companies in Bangui, which constituted both advertising potential and a pool of buyers of the written press. Effectively, there are today in Bangui only sixteen large private companies left, whereas there were more than a hundred before the pillaging. The war is now over, but the press is today still badly affected by the economic depression. Consequently, the economic independence of the media is probably all the more difficult to ensure in time of war. Submission to the state or one or another of the belligerents often seems to be the only route to survival.

Wars also have heavy repercussions for the public, who generally become impoverished and distressed. It is often said that populations turn away from "neutral" media in a period of conflict. Some reckon that the public favor media that have a strong nationalistic tone, and that they reject balanced journalism. Not only does this theory remain unproven, but there are also numerous counterexamples: from Radio Ndeke Luka in Central Africa, to Radio Maendeleo in Kivu, positive results often accrue for those who try to guarantee neutrality, and try to present many points of view. Nevertheless, the poverty-stricken public, overwhelmed with other preoccupations, may turn away from the media. The audience or the readership, haunted by the fear of the "Other," may take refuge in discourses that promote solidarity with their own communities, or even self-defense against some "enemy aggressor."

Furthermore, the Northern media's reporting on African conflicts, which often produces local effects, can influence the behavior of the African media. In such cases, foreign coverage that emphasizes sensationalism, simplifies complex situations, or completely ignores certain African tragedies, can affect an internal situation by mobilizing the international community's attention (and that of the funding agencies), or by letting a genocide continue to be perpetrated in the shadows. In Chapter 11, Jean-Paul Marthoz has shown the constraints on the international media today when reporting on African conflicts, and how the current mechanism of information circulation at the global level is pushing the continent back into "the heart of darkness."

Finally, interventions by Northern financial partners in support of local media are also important in allowing local journalists to make a positive contribution, if not to the resolution of conflict, at least to the development of reconciliation initiatives or to the reconstruction of the social fabric, even if these interventions, which are frequently limited in nature, do not ensure the survival of a truly independent, balanced, and financially self-supporting media in the weakened economic context at the end of the conflict.

What Can Be Done?

The current conflicts in Central Africa pose a real challenge to methods of settling crises that are usually proposed by international organizations. Whether they are of high or low intensity, they can be seen as "new" conflicts that no longer involve professional and institutionalized armies but rely on a multiplicity of factions and ill-assorted militias, recruited on ethnic or regional bases, who are trying to gain control of the state and exploit a country's resources in a neoproprietary manner. The political liberalization at the start of 1990s, on the one hand, multiplied and whetted the appetites of those who could not, until then, carve out a piece of the "national cake" for themselves. On the other hand, the liberalization reinforced the desire of those in power to maintain their place in order to preserve their privileges, by ruse, by force, or by a cunning mix of the two.

Whether they like it or not, the Central African media are involved in this context of "criminalization" of methods of political action and control of power, of deployment of illegal networks, of struggle for the monopolization of resources. In such a context, where concern for the development and well-being of the population seems to take secondary importance, the media can provide the last arena in which the forgotten social players and silent civilian victims of the continent's wars can express themselves and be seen. The media can also provide a forum for alternative actions for managing collective existence.

If the Central African conflicts have pushed the mediators and peacebuilders to develop new proposals that are better suited to specific features on the ground, these conflicts also pose a considerable challenge to the local and international media, which must invent new methods of working, of solidarity, and of financing themselves, so that citizens of these countries can develop, continue, or reconstruct a dialogue among themselves and the rest of the world. This is also a challenge for donors and media partners.

Those who take up journalism during a period of open conflict are rare. There is, without doubt, great risk of seeing all one's efforts simply diverted or perverted, or of suffering recurrent losses. There are only a few "emergency" NGOs that intervene in the worst crises, but the majority of foreign donors prefer to wait for the "reconstruction" at the end of the conflict. The peculiar situation of the media during the conflict and postconflict periods in Central African countries has nevertheless brought new questions to NGOs that specialize in media support in Southern countries.

This support can aim either at reinforcing the media sector itself, or at providing news content through new outlets. Very seldomly will a donor or partner provide long-term structural support to a specific media outlet during conflict. Cases such as the DRC's Radio Maendeleo, which received help from a Belgian NGO partner throughout the war, or the RPA in Burundi that was supported by US foundations since its establishment, are rather rare. Indeed, the question of foreign support raises two main issues: why one specific medium should be selected (on which criteria), and how the donor can be sure that this particular medium will not "go to war" at some point, using its new capacities to serve one of the belligerents. Direct support can entail donation of material equipment (which can be a big financial risk in situations where the media are under constant threat of ransacking), provision of training (but without certainty that it will be used honestly, rather than being exploited to make better propaganda), or promotion of specific "peace-oriented" media content (but without certainty that the content will be used as intended, rather than being published or broadcast surrounded by other bias or propaganda features).

Since the neutrality of local media can never be guaranteed, some NGOs and donors prefer to establish new media outlets (e.g., Radio Okapi, Radio Ndeke Luka, Studio Ijambo) over which they have total control of content. The issue here is the integration of those new outlets into the local media landscape. These outlets often have financial means that far exceed those of local media: a journalist at Radio Okapi makes ten or twenty times the salary of a journalist working for a Congolese radio station. The United Nations studio in Bujumbura (Studio ONUB) also pays its employees, who are recruited from the best journalists in the private, local media, way above the average wage. If good wages and working conditions ensure that journalists will remain steadfast in face of political or economical pressures, other questions arise: What will such outlets become when the donors withdraw? Will the journalists accept work at a reduced "local" salary? Given a poor economic environment after years of conflict, will these outlets become dependent on funding from public authorities, which might soon try to control them? These media outlets play an important but punctual role. Meanwhile, they also create very artificial situations.

To avoid the difficulties inherent in direct support of media, some donors and partners prefer to help the "media environment": regulatory bodies, journalists associations and unions, press houses, schools of journalism. They may also provide equipment and training for capacity building, in the hope that these assets will be used in a collective way to help most of the local journalists and media. Nevertheless, such support only makes sense if the structure benefiting from it is very representative of the whole profession (and not of one "faction"), and if it is credible and legitimate, which might be a hazardous stance in a conflict situation.

Last but not least is the crucial question of what happens next. The end of an armed crisis often brings some relief for the media: certain material problems are lightened, the public regains an appetite for balanced news, self-censorship diminishes. The reaction of the state may vary; either it becomes more open and conciliatory, or it retains a distrust of the media that engenders a desire for greater control. New laws may be adopted, new media may see the light of day, and the interest of donors may revive. It can also fade away as some donors and NGOs, keen on peace-building initiatives and ready to act within UN peacekeeping missions in "fragile" or "crisis" states, can withdraw when the situation seems to stabilize, and to move to other war zones where their attention is requested. But rebuilding the confidence of the public, professionalism in the media, and a dynamic economic background is a path much longer than the one to war and destruction, or even to the signing of a peace agreement.

After a decade-long war in Burundi, thirty-six months of transition, and the establishment of a new elected government, donors and media partners are already starting to withdraw, causing great concern over the survivability of the country's radio stations. In the DRC, after the presidential and legislative election, most donors and partners are already claiming they will have decreasing support for the next three years, and are thinking about how to solve the Radio Okapi financial burden. But it will take more than three years to rebuild such war-torn countries and provide the media with sane and strong environments they can rely on to grow. Media support initiatives must continue in Central African countries, because real empowerment of local journalists is far from being achieved, and many traumatized populations, who have been silent for so long, still need to be convinced that they have the right to express themselves, and still need to be shown that their contribution to national debate is valuable. Media need adequate support until they become platforms of expression for full citizens who have a real capacity for leading their own lives, and act upon the decisions that their elected representatives make on their behalf.

Acronyms

ABD	African Bank for Development
ABJ	Association Burundaise des Journalistes (Burundian Journalists Association)
ABP	Agence Burundaise de Presse (Burundian Press Agency)
ACAP	Agence Centrafricaine de Presse (Central African Press Agency)
ACCT	Agence de Coopération Culturelle et Technique (Agency of Cultural and Technical Cooperation)
ACEPI	Association Centrafricaine des Editeurs de la Presse Indépendante (Central African Association of Independent Press Publishers)
ACI	Agence Congolaise d'Information (Congolese Information Agency)
ACP	Agence Congolaise de Presse (Congolese Press Agency)
AEJIK	Association Katangaise des Editeurs Indépendants (Katangan Association of Independent Publishers)
AEPLI	Association des Editeurs de la Presse Libre et Indépendante du Gabon (Association of Publishers of the Gabonese Free and Independent Press)
AEPT	Association des Editeurs de la Presse Privée Tchadienne (Association of Publishers of the Chadian Private Press)
AFDL	Alliance des Forces Démocratiques de Libération du Congo (Alliance of Democratic Forces for Liberation of Congo)
AFEM-SK	Association des Femmes des Médias du Sud Kivu (Association of Women in the Media in South Kivu)
AFEMEK	Association des Femmes des Médias du Katanga (Katangan Association of Women in the Media)

AFP	Agence France Presse (French Press Agency)
AGP	Agence Gabonaise de Presse (Gabonese Press Agency)
AIF	Agence Intergouvernementale de la Francophonie (Intergovernmental Agency of French-Speaking Countries)
AJGA	Association des Journalistes Gabonais (Association of Gabonese Journalists)
AJPR	Association des Journalistes Professionnels du Rwanda
AMI	African Media Institute (Democratic Republic of Congo)
AMJ	Association Mondiale des Journaux (World Association of Newspapers [WAN])
ANECA	Association Nationale des Etudiants Centrafricains (National Association of Central African Students)
ANR	Agence Nationale de Renseignements (National Intelligence Agency) (Democratic Republic of Congo)
APPEL	Association des Professionnels de la Presse Libre (Association of Free Press Professionals) (Gabon)
APPLE	Association pour la Promotion et la Protection de la Liberté d'Expression (Association for the Promotion and Protection of Freedom of Expression) (Burundi)
ARCO	Association des Radios Communautaires du Congo (Congolese Association of Community Radio)
ARCT	Agence de Régulation et de Contrôle des Télécommunications (Telecommunications Regulation and Control Agency) (Burundi)
ARFEM	Association Rwandaise des Femmes des Médias/Rwandan Association of Media Women
ARI	Agence Rwandaise d'Information/Rwandan News Agency
ARJ	Association Rwandaise des Journalistes/Rwanda Association of Journalists
ARP	Agence Rwandaise de Presse (Rwandan Press Agency)
ASOPGE	Asociación de la Prensa de Guinea Ecuatorial (Equato-Guinean Press Association)
ATP	Agence Tchadienne de Presse (Chadian Press Agency)
AZAP	Agence Zaïroise de Presse (Zairian Press Agency)
BBC	British Broadcasting Corporation
BONUCA	United Nations Observation Bureau in the Central African Republic
CAR	Central African Republic
CASPROM	Caisse de Solidarité des Professionnels des Médias (Solidarity Fund for Media Professionals) (Democratic Republic of Congo)

CATEL	Collectif des Agents de la Télévision (Television Staff Collective) (Chad)
CCIB FM	radio of the Chambre de Commerce et d'Industrie du Burundi (Burundian Chamber of Commerce and Industry)
CDR	Coalition pour la Défense de la République (Coalition for the Defense of the Republic) (Rwanda)
CENAP	Centre d'Alerte et de Prévention des Conflits (Center for Conflict Warning and Prevention) (Burundi)
CLADHO	Collective of Leagues and Associations for the Defense of Human Rights (Democratic Republic of Congo)
CLD	Convención Liberal Democrática (Liberal Democratic Convention) (Equatorial Guinea)
CMB	Channel Media Broadcasting (Democratic Republic of Congo)
CNC	Conseil National de la Communication (National Communication Council) (Burundi, Gabon)
CNDD	Conseil National pour la Défense de la Démocratie (National Council for the Defense of Democracy) (Burundi)
CNN	Cable News Network
CPDS	Convergencia para la Democracia Social (Convergence for Social Democracy) (Equatorial Guinea)
CRETES	Centre de Recherches et d'Étude en Économie et Sondage (Center for Research and Study on Economics and Surveys) (Cameroon)
CRP	Centre de Ressources pour la Presse (Center for Press Resources) (Republic of Congo)
CRTV	Cameroon Radio Television
CSAC	Conseil Supérieur de l'Audiovisuel et de la Communication (High Audiovisual and Communication Council) (RDC)
CSIC	Conseil Supérieur de l'Information et de la Communication (High Council for Information and Communication) (Republic of Congo)
CSLC	Conseil Supérieur de la Liberté de la Communication (High Council for Freedom of Communication) (Republic of Congo)
CTV	Cameroon Television
DEMIAP	Détection Militaire des Activités Anti-Patriotiques (Military Detection of Anti-Patriotic Activities) (Democratic Republic of Congo)

DIC	Dialogue Inter-Congolais (Inter-Congolese Dialogue)
DRC	Democratic Republic of Congo
DRTV	Digital Radio Télévision (Republic of Congo)
DSP	Division Spéciale Présidentielle (Special Presidential Division) (Democratic Republic of Congo)
EU	European Union
FARF	Forces Armées pour la République Fédérale (Armed Forces for the Federal Republic) (Chad)
FCK	Facultés Catholiques de Kinshasa (Catholic Faculties of Kinshasa)
FDD	Forces pour la Défense de la Démocratie (Forces for the Defense of Democracy) (armed wing of Burundi's CNDD)
FDP	Forces Démocratiques Patriotiques (Democratic and Patriotic Forces) (Republic of Congo)
FDU	Forces Démocratiques Unifiées (Unified Democratic Forces (Republic of Congo)
FNL	Front National de Libération (National Liberation Front) (Burundi)
FOPROMEDIA	Fédération des Organisations Professionelles des Médias (Federation of Media Professionals Organizations) (Democratic Republic of Congo)
FRODEBU	Front Démocratique du Burundi (Democratic Front of Burundi)
FROLINAT	Front de Libération National du Tchad (National Liberation Front of Chad)
FSTC	Fédération Syndicale des Travailleurs de la Communication (Federal Union of Communication Workers) (Central African Republic)
GEPPIC	Groupement des Editeurs de la Presse Privée Indépendante de Centrafrique (Group of Publishers of the Central African Independent Private Press)
GRET	Groupe de Recherche et d'Echanges Technologiques (Technological Research and Exchange Group)
HAM	Haute Autorité des Médias (High Media Authority) (Democratic Republic of Congo)
HCC	Haut Conseil de la Communication (High Council of Communication) (Central African Republic, Chad)
HCP	Haut Conseil de la Presse/High Council of the Press (Rwanda)
ICA	Institut Congolais de l'Audiovisuel (Congolese Audiovisual Institute)

ICTR	International Criminal Tribunal for Rwanda
IFASIC	Institut Facultaire des Sciences de l'Information et de la Communication (Institute for Information and Communication Sciences) (Democratic Republic of Congo)
IFEX	International Freedom of Expression Exchange
IPP	Institut Panos Paris (Panos Paris Institute)
IPS	Inter Press Service
JED	Journalistes en Danger (Journalists in Danger) (RDC)
LDGL	Ligue des Droits de la Personne dans les Grands Lacs/ League of Human Rights in the Great Lakes Region
LIPRODHOR	Ligue pour le Promotion des Droits de l'Homme au Rwanda/Rwandan League for the Promotion and Defence of Human Rights
MBC	Malebo Broadcast Channel (Democratic Republic of Congo)
MCDDI	Mouvement Congolais pour la Démocratie et le Développement Intégral (Congolese Movement for Democracy and Integral Development)
MDD	Mouvement pour la Démocratie et le Développement (Movement for Democracy and Development) (Chad)
MDJT	Mouvement pour la Démocratie et la Justice au Tchad (Chadian Movement for Democracy and Justice)
MDR	Mouvement Démocratique Républicain (Democratic Republican Movement) (Rwanda)
MINALOC	Ministère de l'Administration Locale, de l'Information et des Affaires Sociales/Ministry of Local Administration, Information, and Social Affairs (Rwanda)
MINURCA	United Nations Mission in the Central African Republic
MISAB	Mission Interafricaine de Surveillance des Accords de Bangui (Pan-African Mission for Monitoring the Bangui Accords)
MISNA	Missionary Service News Agency
MLC	Mouvement de Libération du Congo (Movement for Liberation of the Congo)
MLPC	Mouvement pour la Libération du Peuple Centrafricain (Movement for Liberation of the Central African People)
MONUC	United Nations Mission in the Democratic Republic of Congo

MORENA	Mouvement de Redressement National (Movement for National Recovery) (Gabon)
MPR	Mouvement Populaire de la Révolution (Popular Movement of the Revolution) (Democratic Republic of Congo)
MPS	Mouvement Patriotique du Salut (Patriotic Salvation Movement) (Chad)
MRND	Mouvement Révolutionnaire National pour le Développement (1975–1991), Mouvement Républicain National pour la Démocratie et le Développement (1991–) (National Revolutionary Movement for Development [1975–1991], National Republican Movement for Democracy and Development [1991–]) (Rwanda)
NGO	nongovernmental organization
NIZA	Nederlands Instituut voor Zuidelijk Afrika (Netherlands Institute for Southern Africa)
OBMA	Office des Biens Mal Acquis (Office of Illegally Aquired Property) (Democratic Republic of Congo)
OCM	Observatoire Congolais des Médias (Congolese Media Council)
ODEMET	Observatoire de la Déontologie et de l'Ethique des Médias du Tchad (Chadian Media Council for Ethics)
OLPCA	Observatoire de la Liberté de la Presse en Centrafrique (Council for Press Freedom in Central Africa)
OMEC	Observatoire des Médias Congolais (Congolese Media Council)
OPB	Observatoire de la Presse Burundaise (Burundian Press Council)
OPEC	Organization of Petroleum-Exporting Countries
ORINFOR	Office Rwandais de l'Information (Rwandan Office for Information)
ORTCA	Office de Radio Télévision de Centrafrique (Central African Radio and Television Office)
OZRT	Office Zaïrois de Radio Télévision (Zairian Radio and Television Office)
PALIPEHUTU	Parti pour la Libération du Peuple Hutu (Party for Liberation of Hutu People) (Burundi)
PARENA	Parti pour le Redressement National (Party for National Recovery) (Burundi)

PARMEHUTU	Parti du Mouvement de l'Emancipation Hutu (Party of the Hutu Emancipation Movement)
PCT	Parti Congolais du Travail (Congolese Labor Party)
PDG	Parti Democratique Gabonais (Gabonese Democratic Party)
PDGE	Partido Democrático de Guinea Ecuatorial (Equato-Guinean Democratic Party)
PDR	Parti Démocratique pour le Renouveau/Democratic Party for Renewal (Rwanda)
PGP	Parti Gabonais du Progrès (Gabonese Party for Progress)
PSD	Parti Social Démocrate (Social Democratic Party) (Gabon)
PUP	Parti pour l'Unité du Peuple (People's Unity Party) (Gabon)
RAF	Rwandan Armed Forces
RAP21	Réseau Africain pour la Presse au 21ème Siècle (African Press Network for the 21st Century)
RATECO	Réseau des Radios et Télévisions Communautaires de l'Est du Congo (Network of Community Radio and Television in the East of Congo)
RCD	Rassemblement Congolais pour la Démocratie (Congolese Rally for Democracy)
RDC	Rassemblement Démocratique Centrafricain (Democratic Central African Rally)
RDF	Rwandan Defense Forces
RDPC	Rassemblement Démocratique du Peuple Camerounais/Cameroon People's Democratic Movement
REE	Radio Exterior de España (Spanish Overseas Broadcasting)
RFI	Radio France Internationale (International French Radio)
RNB	Rassemblement National des Bûcherons (National Woodcutters Rally) (Gabon)
RNGE	Radio Nacional de Guinea Ecuatorial (Equato-Guinean National Radio)
RNT	Radiodiffusion Nationale Tchadienne (Chadian National Broadcasting)
RPA	Radio Publique Africaine (Public African Radio) (Burundi)

RPA	Rwandan Patriotic Army
RPF	Rwandan Patriotic Front
RTG	Radiodiffusion Télévision Gabonaise (Gabonese Radio and Television Broadcasting)
RTKM	Radio Télévision Kin-Malebo (Kin-Malebo Radio Television) (Democratic Republic of Congo)
RTLM	Radio Télévision Libre des Mille Collines (Free Radio Television of a Thousand Hills) (Rwanda)
RTNB	Radio Télévision Nationale du Burundi (Burundian National Radio and Television)
RTNC	Radiodiffusion et Télévision Nationale du Congo (National Radio and Television of Congo)
RTVGE	Radio Television Guinea Ecuatorial (Equato-Guinean National Television)
SAPPAP	Syndicat Autonome des Personnels de la Presse Audiovisuelle Privée (Trade Union of the Staff from the Broadcast Private Media) (Gabon)
SCNC	Southern Cameroon National Council
SDF	Social Democratic Front (Cameroon)
SFCG	Search for Common Ground
SOPECAM	Société de Presse et d'Edition du Cameroun/ Cameroon News and Publishing Corporation
SPC	Syndicat des Professionnels de la Communication (Union of Communication Professionals) (Chad)
SYPROCOM	Syndicat des Professionnels de la Communication (Union of Communication Professionals) (Gabon)
TVT	Télévision Nationale Tchadienne (Chadian National Television)
UCOFEM	Union Congolaise des Femmes des Médias (Congolese Union of Women in the Media)
UDPS	Union pour la Démocratie et le Progrès Social (Union for Democracy and Social Progress) (Democratic Republic of Congo)
UIJPLF	Union Internationale des Journalistes et de la Presse en Langue Française (International Union of Francophone Journalists and Press)
UJC	Union des Journalistes du Cameroun/Union of Cameroon Journalists
UJCA	Union des Journalistes Centrafricains (Central African Journalists Union)
UJR	Union des Journalistes Rwandais

UJT	Union des Journalistes Tchadiens (Union of Chadian Journalists)
UN	United Nations
UNAMIR	United Nations Assistance Mission for Rwanda
UNC	Union Nationale Camerounaise (Cameroonian National Union)
UNDP	Union Nationale pour la Démocratie et le Progrès (National Union for Democracy and Progress) (Cameroon)
UNDP	United Nations Development Programme
UNDR	Union Nationale pour le Développement et le Renouveau (National Union for Development and Renewal)
UNESCO	United Nations Educational, Scientific, and Cultural Organization
UNPC	Union Nationale de la Presse Congolaise (Congolese National Press Union)
UPADS	Union Panafricaine pour la Démocratie Sociale (Panafrican Union for Social Democracy)
UPC	Union de la Presse Congolaise (Congolese Press Union)
UPRONA	Union pour le Progrès National (Union for National Progress) (Burundi)
UPZA	Union de la Presse Zaïroise (Zairian Press Union)
URPT	Union des Radios Privées du Tchad (Chadian Private Radio Union)
USG	Union Socialiste Gabonaise (Gabonese Socialist Union)
VAT	value-added tax
VOA	Voice of America
WHO	World Health Organization

Bibliography

Admunson, D. E., L. S. Lichter, and R. S. Lichter. *The Myopic Neighbor: Local and National Network Television Coverage of the World.* Washington, D.C.: Frameworks Institute, 2001.

Allen, T., and J. Seaton (eds.). *The Media of Conflict: War Reporting and Representations of Ethnic Violence.* London: Zed, 1999.

APPLE. *Guide de la presse burundaise 1996.* Bujumbura: APPLE, 1996.

Arditi, C. "Les violences ordinaires ont une histoire: le cas du Tchad." *Politique Africaine* no. 91 (October 2003).

Atenga, T. "Cameroun: presse privée/pouvoir, quinze ans de cohabitation houleuse." *Politique Africaine* no. 97 (March 2005).

———. "Contrôle de la parole et conservation du pouvoir: analyse de la répression de la presse écrite au Cameroun et au Gabon depuis 1990." PhD thesis, Paris, Sorbonne, 2004.

Bailly, S. *Media résistance.* Paris: Karthala, 2000.

Barnabé, J. F. "Les médias assassins au Burundi." In R. de la Brosse and Reporters sans Frontières (eds.), *Les médias de la haine.* Paris: Editions La Découverte, 1995.

Barnes, J. "The Bongo Phenomenon: Power in Gabon." In Michael Reed and James Barnes, *Culture, Ecology, and Politics in Gabon's Rainforest.* Lewiston, N.Y.: Edwin Mellen, 2003.

Bayart, J. F. *L'état en Afrique: la politique du ventre.* Paris: Fayard, 1991.

Bayart, J. F., S. Ellis, and B. Hibou. "De l'état kleptocrate à l'état malfaiteur." In *La criminalisation de l'état en Afrique.* Brussels: Editions Complexe, 1997.

Bazenguissa-Ganga, R., and P. Yengo. "La popularisation de la violence politique au Congo." *Politique Africaine* no. 73 (March 1999).

Beauregard, C., and C. Saouter (eds.). *Conflits contemporains et médias.* Montreal: XYZ, 1997.

Ben Arous, M. (ed.). *Médias et conflits en Afrique.* Paris: Panos Afrique de l'Ouest-Karthala, 2001.

Berghezan, G., and F. Nkundabagenzi. *La guerre au Congo-Kinshassa: analyse d'un conflit et transferts d'armes vers l'Afrique centrale.* Brussels: GRIP, 1999.

263

Bizimana, J. D. *L'eglise et le génocide au Rwanda.* Paris: L'Harmattan, 2001.

Boh, H. *L'état de la presse au Cameroun.* Yaoundé: Friedrich Ebert Foundation, 1998.

Bouvier, P., and F. Bomboko. "Le dialogue intercongolais: anatomie d'une négociation à la lisière du chaos." *Cahiers Africains* nos. 63–64 (2004).

Braeckman, C. *Le dinosaure: le Zaïre de Mobutu.* Paris: Fayard, 1992.

———. *Les nouveaux prédateurs.* Paris: Fayard, 2003.

———. *Rwanda: histoire d'un génocide.* Paris: Fayard, 1994.

———. *Terreur africaine: Burundi, Rwanda, Zaïre—les racines de la violence.* Paris: Fayard, 1996.

Braeckman, C., M. F. Cros, G. de Villers, et al. *Kabila prend le pouvoir: les prémices d'une chute, la campagne victorieuse de l'AFDL, le Congo d'aujourd'hui.* Brussels: Editions Complexe, 1998.

Buijtenhuijs, R. "Tchad: l'année des élections." In *L'Afrique politique, 1997.* Paris: Karthala, 1998.

Chaliand, G. (ed.). *La persuasion de masse.* Paris: Robert Laffont, 1992.

Chindji-Kouleu, F. "Ethnies, médias et processus démocratique au Cameroun: analyse de contenu de quelques journaux." In D. Zognong and I. Mouiche (eds.), *Démocratisation et rivalités ethniques au Cameroun.* Yaoundé: Centre Interafricain de Recherches Pluridisciplinaires sur l'Ethnicité (Yaoundé: CIREPE, 1997).

Chrétien, J. P. *Le défi de l'ethnisme: Rwanda et Burundi, 1990–1996.* Karthala: Paris, 1997.

———. "Presse libre et propagande raciste au Rwanda." *Politique Africaine* no. 42 (June 1991).

——— (ed.). *Rwanda: les médias du génocide.* Paris: Karthala, 1995.

Chrétien, J. P., and M. Mukuri (eds.). *Burundi: la fracture identitaire—logiques de violence et certitudes "ethniques" (1993–1996).* Paris: Karthala, 2002.

Committee to Protect Journalists. *Attacks Against the Press.* New York, 2001–2003.

Coret, L., and F. X. Verschave (eds.). *L'horreur qui nous prend au visage: l'état français et le génocide au Rwanda.* Paris: Karthala, 2004.

Dallaire, R. *J'ai serré la main du diable: la faillite de l'humanité au Rwanda.* Quebec: Libre Expression, 2003.

de la Brosse, R., and Reporters San Frontières (eds.). *Les médias de la haine.* Paris: Editions La Découverte, 1995.

de Saint Exupery, P. *L'inavouable: la France au Rwanda.* Paris: Editions Les Arènes, 2004.

de Selys, G. (ed.). *Médiamensonges.* Brussels: Editions EPO, 1991.

de Villers, G. "Zaïre, années 90: faits et dits de la société d'après le regard de la presse." *Les Cahiers du CEDAF* nos. 1–2 (1992).

de Vulpian, L. *Rwanda: un génocide oublié? un procès pour mémoire.* Brussels: Editions Complexe, 2004.

Debray, R. *L'œil naïf.* Paris: Editions Le Seuil, 1994.

des Forges, A. *Aucun témoin ne doit survivre.* Paris: Karthala, 1999.

Destexhe, A. *Rwanda: essai sur le génocide.* Brussels: Editions Complexe, 1994.

Dorier Apprill, E. "Jeunesse et ethnicités citadines à Brazzaville." *Politique Africaine* no. 64 (December 1996).

Eboussi Boulaga, F. *La démocratie de transit au Cameroun.* Paris: L'Har-
mattan, 1997.
Ellis, S. "Reporting Africa." *Current History* (May 2000).
Frère, M. S. "Après les médias de la haine: la régulation en RDC, au Burundi
et au Rwanda." In F. Reyntjens and S. Marysse (eds.), *L'Afrique des
Grands Lacs, Annuaire 2005–2006.* Paris: L'Harmattan, 2006.
———. "RDC: les medias en transition." *Politique Africaine* no. 97 (March
2005).
———. *Presse et démocratie en Afrique francophone.* Paris: Karthala, 2000.
———. *Voyage dans la presse zaïroise.* Brussels: FIJ, 1996.
Gakosso, J. C. *La nouvelle presse congolaise: du goulag à l'agora.* Paris:
L'Harmattan, 1997.
Garreton, R. "Report on the Situation of Human Rights in the DRC." Geneva:
United Nations, 2001.
Gaulme, F. "Le Gabon à la recherche d'un nouvel ethos politique et social."
Politique Africaine no. 43 (October 1991).
Gauvrit, E. R. "Congo: l'épreuve des urnes." In *L'Afrique politique, 1997.*
Paris: Karthala, 1997.
Gouteux, J. P. *La nuit rwandaise: l'implication française dans le dernier
génocide du siècle.* Paris: L'Esprit Frappeur, 2002.
———. *Le Monde: un contre-pouvoir?* Paris: L'Esprit Frappeur, 1999.
———. *Un génocide secret d'état.* Paris: Editions Sociales, 1998.
Gruenais, M. E. "Congo: la fin d'une pseudo-démocratie." *Politique Africaine*
no. 68 (December 1997).
Guichaoua, A. (ed.). *Les crises politiques au Burundi et au Rwanda, 1993–
1994.* Lille: UST, 1995.
Hannerz, U. *Foreign News: Exploring the World of Foreign Correspondents.*
Chicago: University of Chicago Press, 2004.
Hatzfeld, J. *Dans le nu de la vie: récits des marais rwandais.* Paris: Seuil, 2000.
———. *Une saison de machettes.* Paris: Seuil, 2004.
Higiro, J. M. V. "Distorsions et omissions dans l'ouvrage *Rwanda: les médias
du génocide.*" *Dialogue* no. 190 (April–May 1996).
Howard, R. *Conflict Sensitive Journalism: A Handbook.* Copenhagen:
International Media Support and IMPACS, 2003.
Howard, R., H. van de Veen, and J. Verhoeven (eds.). *The Power of the Media:
A Handbook for Peacebuilders.* Utrecht: European Center for Conflict
Prevention, European Center for Common Ground, and Institute for Media,
Policy, and Civil Society, 2003.
Ignatieff, M. *The Warrior's Honor: Ethnic War and the Modern Conscience.*
New York: Henry Old, 1997.
Institut Panos Paris (ed.). *Afrique centrale: cadres juridiques et pratiques du
pluralisme radiophonique.* Paris: Karthala, 2005.
——— (ed.). *Afrique centrale: des médias pour la démocratie.* Paris: Karthala,
2000.
——— (ed.). *La situation des médias en République Démocratique du Congo.*
Paris: Karthala, 2004.
Institut Panos Paris and COTA (eds.). *Briser les silences: paroles d'Afrique
centrale.* Paris: Karthala, 2003.

Kabeya, P. E. M. M. (ed.). *Regards sur la presse congolaise: du Congo belge à celui de Kabila, sans oublier le Zaïre de Mobutu.* Palabres no. 10. Paris: L'Harmattan, 2004.

Kaburahe, A. *Burundi: la mémoire blessée.* Brussels and Paris: La Longue Vue, 2003.

Kaplan, R. D. *The Ends of the Earth: A Journey at the Dawn of the 21st Century.* New York: Random House, 1996.

Kasonga N. M., B. "La répression de la presse au Zaïre pendant la transition." *Cahiers Africains* nos. 9–11 (1994).

Konings, P. "Le 'problème anglophone' au Cameroun." *Politique Africaine* no. 62 (June 1996).

Koula, Y. *La démocratie congolaise brûlée au pétrole.* Paris: L'Harmattan, 1999.

Koyt, M., M. F. M'bringa Takama, and P. M. Decoudras. "République Centrafricaine: les vicissitudes du changement." In *L'Afrique politique, 1995.* Paris: Karthala, 1996.

Lanotte, O. *République Démocratique du Congo: guerres sans frontières.* Brussels: Editions Complexe, 2003.

Les Rencontres Internationales Média-Défense 1995. *Les manipulations de l'image et du son.* Paris: Hachette, 1996.

Liniger-Goumaz, M. *A l'aune de la Guinée Equatoriale.* Geneva: Les Editions du Temps, 2003.

———. *La démocrature: dictature camouflée, démocratie truquée.* Paris: L'Harmattan, 1992.

———. *Who's Who de la dictature de Guinée Equatoriale.* Geneva: Editions du Temps, 1993.

Logo, P. B., and H. L. Menthong. "Crise de légitimité et évidence de la continuité politique." *Politique Africaine* no. 62 (June 1996).

Lyman, P. N., and J. S. Morrison. "The Terrorist Threat in Africa." *Foreign Affairs* (January–February 2004).

Maja-Pearce, A. (ed.). *Annuaire de la presse africaine.* Brussels: Fédération Internationale des Journalistes, 1996.

Mathien, M. (ed.). *L'information dans les conflits armés: du Golfe au Kosovo.* Paris: L'Harmattan, 2001.

Mattelart, T. (ed.). *La mondialisation des médias contre la censure.* Brussels: INA–De Boeck, 2002.

Mavoungou, V. "Institutions et publics de la radio-télévision au Gabon: essai sur la personnalisation du pouvoir à travers la communication politique par les médias." PhD thesis, University of Paris, 1986.

Mbembe, A. *La naissance du maquis dans le Sud-Cameroun (1920–1960).* Paris: Karthala, 1996.

Moeller, S. *Compassion Fatigue: How the Media Sell Disease, Famine, War, and Death.* New York: Routledge, 1999.

Nga Ndongo, V. *Les médias au Cameroun: mythes et délires d'une société en crise.* Paris: L'Harmattan, 1993.

Nyamnjoh, F. B. *Africa's Media: Democracy and the Politics of Belonging.* London: Zed, 2005.

Okala, J. T. *Les télévisions africaines sous tutelle.* Paris: L'Harmattan, 1999.

Onwudiwe, E. "Africa's Other Story." *Current History* (May 2002).

Palmans, E. "La liberté de la presse au Rwanda et au Burundi." In *L'Afrique des Grands Lacs, Annuaire 2002–2003*. Paris: L'Harmattan, 2003.

Philippart, M. *L'état des médias au Burundi*. Paris: GRET-PARMA, October 2002.

Prunier, G. *Rwanda, 1959–1996: histoire d'un génocide*. Paris: Editions Dagorno, 1997.

Reporters sans Frontières (ed.). *Burundi: le venin de l'intolérance—etude sur les médias extrémistes*. Paris, July 1995.

———. *Rapport annuel*. Paris, 1992–2005.

Reporters sans Frontières and R. de la Brosse (eds.). *Les médias de la haine*. Paris: Editions La Découverte, 1995.

Reyntjens, F. *L'Afrique des Grands Lacs en crise: Rwanda, Burundi, 1988–1994*. Paris: Karthala, 1994.

———. "Rwanda, Ten Years On: From Genocide to Dictatorship." *African Affairs* no. 103 (2004).

Reyntjens, F., and S. Marysse (eds.). *L'Afrique des Grands Lacs, Annuaire 2002–2003, 2003–2004, 2005–2006*. Paris: L'Harmattan, 2003, 2004, 2006.

Richard, P. O. *Casques bleus, sang noir: Rwanda 1994– , Zaïre 1996—un génocide en spectacle*. Brussels: Editions EPO, 1997.

Semujanga, J. *Récits fondateurs du drame rwandais*. Paris: L'Harmattan, 1998.

Smith, S. *Négrologie: pourquoi l'Afrique meurt*. Paris: Calmann-Lévy, 2003.

Sontag, S. *Devant la douleur des autres*. Paris: Christian Bourgeois, 2003.

Tjade Eone, M. *Démonopolisation, libéralisation et liberté de communication au Cameroun: avancées et reculades*. Paris: L'Harmattan, 2001.

Ungar, S. J., and D. Gergen. "Africa and the American Media." Occasional Paper no. 9. New York: Freedom Forum Media Studies Center, Columbia University, November 1991.

United Nations Development Programme. *Global Report on Human Development, 2005*. Paris: Economica, 2005.

Uvin, P. *L'aide complice?* Paris: L'Harmattan, 1999.

Verschave, F. X. *Complicité de génocide? la politique de la France au Rwanda*. Paris: La Découverte, 1994.

Vidal, C. *Sociologie des passions: Côte d'Ivoire, Rwanda*. Paris: Karthala, 1991.

Willame, J. C. *Aux sources de l'hécatombe rwandaise*. Paris: L'Harmattan, 1995.

———. *L'odyssée Kabila: trajectoire pour un Congo nouveau?* Paris: Karthala, 1999.

———. *L'ONU au Rwanda (1993–1995)*. Brussels: Editions Labor, 1996.

Woodrow, A. *Information Manipulation*. Paris: Editions du Félin, 1991.

Index

Gallon, Gustavo, 213
García Márquez, Gabriel, 224
La Gardien, 122, 129
Garreton, Roberto, 57
Gasabo, 98
Gasana, Jean-Marie, 13
Gauhy, Médard, 129
Gbagbo, Laurent, 230
Gbossokoto, Maka Jean Rigobert, 142,
    143, 151, 154*n47*
genocide in Rwanda: Burundi as
    affected by, 23; Hutu's "final
    solution," 114*n36;* international
    media reaction to, 222, 228, 233;
    media after, 95–100; media scars
    from, 100–111; Operation Turquoise,
    87, 229; Radio Rwanda role in, 87;
    RTLM role in, 79, 87; US/UN
    disinformation on, 229; use of
    euphemisms for, 229
Gergen, David, 224
Gil, Miguel, 233
Le Globe, 138
Goumba, Abel, 149
Gouteux, Jean-Paul, 95
Grands Lacs Hebdo, 98
Great Lakes region. *See* Burundi;
    Rwanda; Congo, Democratic
    Republic of
Gri Gri International, 205*n34*
La Griffe, 193–194, 196–197, 199
Groupe de Recherche et d'Echanges
    Technologiques (GRET), 69
Groupement des Editeurs de la Presse
    Privée Indépendante de Centrafrique
    (GEPPIC), 143, 151
Gulf War, 6*n6*
gumbo, 185, 196

Habimana, Kantano, 91–92, 95,
    113*n25*
Habimana, Pasteur, 22
Habré, Hissène, 169
Habyarimana, Agathe, 83, 114*n43*
Habyarimana, Juvénal: anti-RPF radio
    broadcasts, 93; church-state rela-
    tions, 82; death of, 13, 86; discourse
    in rule of, 112*n17;* foreign media's
    denounciation of, 94
Hakizimana, Appolos, 103
Hakizimana, Joël, 118*n112*

Hannerz, Ulf, 227
hate media: in Burundi, 12–18; in
    Cameroon, 177–178, 186, 188*n32;* in
    Congo Republic, 125, 131; in DRC,
    48, 70; impunity for, 17–18; in
    Rwanda, 88–95; on trial at Arusha,
    110
Hatzfeld, Jean, 236
Haut Conseil de la Communication
    (HCC) (CAR), 147–148
Haut Conseil de la Communication
    (HCC) (Chad), 165
Haut Conseil de la Presse (HCP),
    97–99, 101, 106, 108, 116*n76*
Haute Autorité des Médias (HAM),
    establishment of, 41, 69
Havas, 110
Hélène, Jean, 233
Hema (people), 51
The Herald, 171, 178
Héritiers de la Justice, 75*n86*
Heyden, Tina van der, 237*n1*
Hieber, Loretta, 5
High Council of the Press (Rwanda),
    82
Higher Audiovisual Institute, 66
Higiro, Jean-Marie Vianney, 94,
    118*n109*
L'Hirondelle, 138, 140, 144–145
Hirondelle Foundation: CAR media
    supported by, 139, 142, 152; DRC
    media supported by, 69; Radio
    Agatashya, 73*n47;* Radio Okapi,
    53; reconstruction of Rwandan
    media, 109
Hissène, Mahamat, 167*n2*
historical revisionism, 88–89
history, 242–243
Holocaust, 17
Houphouët-Boigny, Félix, 229
Howard, Ross, 5
Human Rights Radio, 115
Human Rights Watch, 225
L'Humanitaire, 122
humanitarian journalism, 230–232; and
    "humanitarian porn," 231
Hutchins Commission (1947), 234
Hutu (people): DRC support for, 50;
    electoral victory of, 12; hate media
    of, 16–17; stereotyping of, 16, 36*n26*
Hutu power, 86, 112*n13,* 113*n26*

Thalassa, 122
El Tiempo, 207, 211, 213–214
Tjade Eone, Michel, 174
Togo, 140
Togoïmi, Youssouf, 161–162
Torment, the, 15–24
La Tortue Déchaînée, 135, 142
Trans World Radio, 38n56
TransAfrica Forum, 222
La Transparence, 193
"the transport," 64
tribalism. *See* ethnic groups/ethnicity
Le Tribun du Peuple, 95, 104, 117n88
La Tribune d'Adama, 180
Tropicana TV, 45, 68
Tshisekedi, Etienne, 44, 48, 52, 72n18
Tshivuadi, Tshivis, 58, 75n87
Tutsi (people): attemped coup (2001),
    20; extremism among, 12; feelings of
    victimization among, 13; hate media
    of, 16–17; persecution in DRC of,
    45, 50; stereotyping of, 16, 36n26
Tutu, Desmond, 225
TV Gabon, 196
TV5, 235
Twagiramungu, Faustin, 104

Ubumwe (Burundi), 9, 14
Ubumwe (Rwanda), 105
Uganda, 46, 85–86
Uhuru, 46
Ukuri, 98
Ukuri Gacaca, 96
Umoja, 44, 58
Umuco, 98
Umukundwa, Lucie, 104
Umuntu-Lumière, 14
Umunyamuryango Trafipro, 82
Umurava, 84
Umuravumba, 103
Umurwanashyaka, 84, 113n25
Umusemburo, 98
Umusemburo-Le Levain, 96
Umuseso, 98–99, 104–105, 108
Ungar, Sanford, 224
L'Union, 193–194, 202
L'Union, 204n7
Union de la Presse Congolaise (UPC),
    67–68, 76n103
Union de la Presse Zaïroise (UPZA), 67
Union des Journalistes Centrafricains
    (UJCA), 151, 154n47

Union des Journalistes du Cameroun
    (UJC), 184, 188n49
Union des Journalistes Tchadiens
    (UJT), 166
Union des Radios Privées du Tchad
    (URPT), 166
Union Internationale des Journalistes et
    de la Presse en Langue Française
    (UIJPLF), 130
Union Nationale de la Presse
    Congolaise (UNPC), 68
Union of Congolese Patriots (UPC), 64
Union pour le Progrès National
    (UPRONA), 11
United Kingdom, 229
United Nations Development Pro-
    gramme (UNDP), 109, 141
United Nations Educational, Scientific,
    and Cultural Organization (UNESCO):
    aid to Congo Republic professional as-
    sociations, 130; Burundian press center,
    40n98; CAR public media, 141; code of
    journalistic practice, 30–31; community
    radio development by, 187n5; education
    of journalists, 106; reconstruction of
    Rwandan media, 109; Rwandan press
    house, 96–97, 107, 117n103
United Nations Human Rights
    Commission, 212
United Nations International
    Commission on Burundi, 36n35
United Nations Mission in the
    Democratic Republic of Congo
    (MONUC), 46, 53
United Nations Observation Bureau in
    the Central African Republic
    (BONUCA), 141
United Nations Population Fund, 141
United States, 224–225, 229–230
University of Butare School of Journal-
    ism and Communication, 82, 106
University of Kinshasa Department of
    Communications, 65
University of Kisangani, 66
University of Lubumbashi, 48, 66,
    72n17
unstructured states, media role in, 3
Urumuli rwa Demokarasi, 84
Urumuri rwa Kristu, 98
Urunana, 98

Valmouke, Amadou, 188n49

About the Book

THIS IN-DEPTH investigation of the role that local news media play in Central African conflicts combines theoretical analysis with case studies from nine African countries: Burundi, Cameroon, the Central African Republic, Chad, the Democratic Republic of Congo, Equatorial Guinea, Gabon, the Republic of Congo, and Rwanda.

Each case study presents a comprehensive discussion of media influences during the various conflicts that have spread in the region and their impact on the peace process. Enriching the exploration, a chapter by Jean-Paul Marthoz (former director of information at Human Rights Watch) focuses on the ways in which the media in the global North cover crises on the African continent.

The book contributes greatly to a better understanding of the complex forces at play—and identifies ways that may contribute to strengthening the positive dynamics and mediating the negative ones.

Marie-Soleil Frère is research associate at Belgium's National Fund for Scientific Research and also professor of journalism, specializing in the African media, at the University of Brussels. She is an associate expert for the Institut Panos Paris, supporting media in Central Africa. Her recent publications include *Presse et démocratie en Afrique francophone.*

* * *

The Media and Conflicts in Central Africa is a project of the Institut Panos Paris, a nongovernmental organization established in 1986 to support the diversity of media and media content for a stronger civil society. The Institut's objectives are to support the emergence of a strong and independent media in the South (Central Africa, the Maghreb, and the Middle East); to encourage the visibility of media produced by and for communities of migrant origin; to support the production of information on critical issues (migration, peace, human rights, and good governance); to encourage the expression of diverse points of view; and to foster public dialogues and debates. The Institut Panos Paris is a member of the Panos Council, a network of eight independent institutes working on four continents.